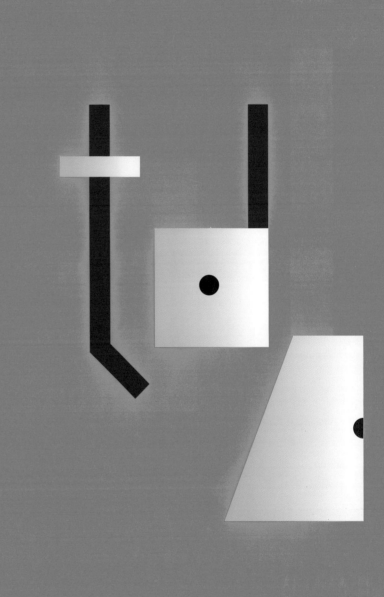

THE ANNUAL
OF THE
TYPE
DIRECTORS
CLUB

THE 68TH ANNUAL COMMUNICATION DESIGN COMPETITION

THE 25TH ANNUAL TYPEFACE DESIGN COMPETITION

First Edition published in 2022
by Verlag Hermann Schmidt
Gonsenheimer Str. 56
D-55126 Mainz
Phone +49 (0) 6131 / 50 60 0
Fax +49 (0) 6131 / 50 60 80
info@verlag-hermann-schmidt.de
www.typografie.de |
www.verlag-hermann-schmidt.de
🅕 Verlag Hermann Schmidt
🅧 VerlagHSchmidt

verlag hermann schmidt

ISBN 978-3-87439-975-3

Carol Wahler, Executive Director
Type Directors Club
The One Club for Creativity
450 West 31 Street
6th Floor
New York, NY 10001
T: 212-979-1900
E: tdc@oneclub.org
W: oneclub.org

Printed in Kracow, Poland

Acknowledgments

The Type Directors Club gratefully
acknowledges the following for their
support and contributions to the
success of TDC68 and 25TDC

Design
Tereza Bettinardi
terezabettinardi.com

Production
Adam S. Wahler
A2A Studio
a2a.com

Editing
Dave Baker
Super Copy Editors
supercopyeditors.com

Principal Typefaces
Donated and used in the
composition of The World's Best
Typography, TYPOGRAPHY 43 are
Laica A designed by Dinamo and
Proxy Cond by Commercial Type

° Signifies TDC member

6   TDC MEDAL Akira Kobayashi
12 IN MEMORIAM Gerrit Noordzij

18 TDC68
COMMUNICATION DESIGN
COMPETITION

20   Chairs' Statement
24   Meet the Judges/
       Judges' Choices
26,29 Student Awards
52   TDC68 Winners
54   Best in Show

290 25 TDC
TYPEFACE DESIGN
COMPETITION

292 Chairs' Statement
296 Meet the Judges/
     Judges' Choices
296 1st Place Student Award
312 Typeface Winners

340 ASCENDERS

342 APPENDIX

344 TDC Advisory Board
346 TDC Membership
348 General Index
354 Type Index

AKIRA KOBAYASHI

Akira Kobayashi was introduced to the possibilities of type while at school in his home country of Japan. Students were given regular poster art projects coinciding with civic initiatives, such as road safety week or dental healthcare week, and encouraged to use drawing and lettering to convey information. Kobayashi quickly realized the power of type and image put together. "As a child, I became aware of the importance of the form of letters," he says. "When I drew beautiful lettering for posters, it looked good, but when I drew beautiful pictures but the lettering was horrible, the poster would look horrible. That was the difference I sensed at the age of nine or ten."

Kobayashi was already learning Japanese calligraphy, so he had a basic understanding of what made for good form. He was unfamiliar with lettering, however. He remembers searching out newspaper headlines as a reference and teaching himself letter shapes by studying and copying them. As a teenager, he furthered his practice using lettering textbooks.

It's perhaps no surprise that Kobayashi went on to study graphic design at Musashino Art University in Kodaira, western Tokyo. His typography course there focused mainly on Japanese lettering and type, and he remembers that, at the time, graphic designers were considered the "stars" of the industry. But Kobayashi says he had his reservations about becoming one. He questioned whether designing advertisements for a product he'd never used, or a car he'd never driven, could be considered an honest job, and he worried if he'd feel like he was deceiving people. To add to this, Kobayashi found himself more interested in "pure type design."

In particular, he found himself fascinated by the work of Sha-ken, a Japanese type design and photo typesetting company. In 1983, he landed his first role with the business, which he describes as less like a graphic design studio and more like a factory, located

in Tokyo's suburbs. He'd arrive at eight o'clock every morning, put on his factory worker¬–style uniform, and draw letters until 4:30 p.m., using Sumi ink and white poster color. On an average day, he'd be creating anywhere from ten to twenty kanji characters. "It was quite a daunting task for a young designer in his twenties, but I really loved the job," says Kobayashi. "I worked for Sha-ken for six years, and during my career I learned to draw ten fine lines in one millimeter. I was trained like that."

While at Sha-ken, he discovered a book that would become enormously influential in his life. The company's type design department had a collection of titles about Western typography, including Hermann Zapf's About Alphabets. It took Kobayashi six months to finish it—he was learning English at the same time—but it sparked something in his mind.

"I realized that a type legend like Hermann Zapf, who could draw these beautiful letters, was also self-taught," explains Kobayashi. "He started to teach himself calligraphy, but he was told by someone that he was holding his pen at the wrong angle. So he was also a kind of layman when he started to learn calligraphy. If he started as a layman and designed a lot of beautiful typefaces, and did beautiful calligraphy, I thought I could follow in his footsteps. I didn't know anything about Western type design, but I thought maybe I could teach myself Western type design or calligraphy. So I decided to leave the company and go to London to study."

Kobayashi had never been abroad and says England was "kind of a culture shock"—full of things he'd never experienced in Tokyo, or even Japan. He'd learned to speak some English but had been taught by an Australian, so when he arrived at London's Heathrow Airport he struggled to understand what passport control was saying to him. Nevertheless, he made it to his apartment and enrolled in both an English course and an evening calligraphy course at the London College of Printing (now London College of Communication).

It was 1989, and he remembers it was extremely expensive to live in the capital. Kobayashi also says it was challenging for him to get to grips with the Latin alphabet—for example, understanding why the left side of a capital A is always thinner than the right diagonal. His calligraphy teacher suggested that he join a meeting of The Letter Exchange, a gathering of some fifty people from different disciplines. "There were stone cutters, calligraphers, also type

Akko Rounded Black · Akko Bold · Akko Rounded Regular · Akko Thin

Kürbiskernöl Baumkuchen Toastbrötchen Sahnepudding

DIN Next Heavy · DIN Next Rounded Bold · DIN Next Medium · DIN Next Rounded Light

Frankfurt a.M. Braunschweig Güldener Straße Saarbrücken Hbf

Neue Frutiger Heavy · Medium · Book · Thin

Gates 12–38 ←Departures Information→ Meeting point

1
Akko Rounded Black,
Akko Bold,
Akko Rounded Regular,
and Akko Thin.

2
DIN Next Heavy,
Din Next Rounded Bold,
DIN Next Medium,
and
DIN Next Rounded Light.

3
Neue Frutiger Heavy
Neue Frutiger Medium,
Neue Frutiger Book,
and Neue Frutiger Thin.

4
Type specimen for
FF Clifford Pro.

❀ FF Clifford Pro ❀

EIGHTEEN CAPS, ROMAN & ITALIC.

GRAY'S INN RD WC1

Bibliographical Society

Austin's Imperial Letter Foundry

Punchcutter to the Fry firm of Bristol

Furniture, Quoins, Shooting-Stick, Chase, &c.

NINE CAPS, ROMAN & ITALIC.

NEVILL COURT EC4

Wilson's Long Primer

Thorne's Fann Street Foundry

Transferred from Glasgow in 1834

London office of Stephenson Blake & Co.

SIX CAPS, ROMAN & ITALIC.

CHISWELL ST EC1

Justifying the head

10-11 Little Queen Street

Letter-cutting is a Handy-Work

Caxton Type & Stereotype Foundry

BORDERS.

"I DECIDED TO LEARN WESTERN TYPOGRAPHY BECAUSE I READ THE BOOK BY HERMANN ZAPF, AND IT WAS A DREAM COME TRUE," SAYS KOBAYASHI. "HERMANN ZAPF WAS LIKE A GOD SOMEWHERE FAR ABOVE ME..."

designers working for Letraset," remembers Kobayashi. "It was also a culture shock to me because when I was working as a type designer in Tokyo, that kind of thing—calligraphers and type designers in one room—was impossible."

At the end of the meeting, Kobayashi approached a stone cutter who invited him to a workshop in Norwich, where he used a flat brush to explain the anatomy of the Latin alphabet—including the thin left diagonal of the capital A that had been troubling him. Suddenly, says Kobayashi, things started to make sense.

It was also around this time that he received a letter from Letraset, to whom he'd applied for a job while still in Japan. The dry transfer lettering company was interested in one of Kobayashi's Arabic numeral designs that he'd made while still working at Sha-ken, which would become his first published typeface. Kobayashi called it Skid Row, after a song from the cult 1986 musical Little Shop of Horrors.

Kobayashi stayed in London for 18 months before returning to Tokyo, where some fellow former Sha-ken type designers were setting up a new type design studio, Jiyu-kobo. "A Japanese character set consists of kanji, hiragana, and katakana characters, and also Arabic numerals and Latin glyphs," says Kobayashi. "So they needed someone who was able to design Latin letters and of course kanji characters."

The '90s were an exciting time to be creating type, as things started to shift into the digital world. Kobayashi remembers being quite happy to work on a computer, but says he'd still use pencil and paper to visualize his ideas in the early stages of design—a practice he still uses today. After three years at Jiyu-kobo, Kobayashi joined TypeBank, where he was responsible for redesigning

and improving the Latin alphabet parts of the company's Japanese type designs. After another three years, he decided to go freelance, although he remembers that moving jobs this much was "quite unusual" at the time. "Of course, my parents worried about me, and one of the type designers in Tokyo who worked freelance warned me that a Japanese trying to Western type design was impossible," says Kobayashi.

Nevertheless, he was confident in his abilities. He'd already spent his free time and weekends designing Latin typefaces and successfully submitting them to ITC. These were published as ITC Woodland, ITC Luna, ITC Silvermoon, ITC Scarborough, ITC Japanese Garden, and ITC Seven Treasures. And in addition to working as a freelance type designer, Kobayashi taught Japanese and Western lettering at design schools in Tokyo.

In 1999, he submitted the Clifford typeface—one of his first Latin serif designs—to U&lc magazine's international design competition and won. Then in 2000, he repeated his success with Conrad, which also won. This caught the attention of Linotype, which offered him a job in Germany as type director. It wasn't a straightforward decision for Kobayashi, who didn't speak German and at this point was married with two children, one of whom had only just been born. In 2001 he decided to take the offer and relocate from Tokyo to Bad Homburg, where Linotype had its office. And his first job was a memorable one—no less than redesigning Hermann Zapf's Optima.

"I decided to learn Western typography because I read the book by Hermann Zapf, and it was a dream come true," says Kobayashi. "Hermann Zapf was like a god somewhere far above me, and then in 2001, I was able to work with him. Together we worked on

Optima, then after that Palatino, and other typefaces as well."

While at Linotype—which became part of Monotype in 2006—Kobayashi also worked with Adrian Frutiger, redesigning his Avenir typeface, released as Avenir Next in 2004, and Frutiger, released as Neue Frutiger in 2009. As well as collaborating with legends of the type world, Kobayashi directed the development of Monotype's first original Japanese typeface, Tazugane Gothic, and worked on major custom type projects for the likes of Sony, UBS, and Panasonic. He has also published several books explaining Western type design and typography to a Japanese audience—saying he believes one of his important roles is to "pave the way to Western type" for graphic designers and students in the country.

Now creative type director at Monotype, Kobayashi is seeing an increasing globalization of type. He says more Western companies are interested in Asian type, and more Asian companies are interested in Western type—meaning his role is in some ways circling back to the start of his career. While, at one time, Asian companies would have simply used Helvetica or Times New Roman, and Western companies would have paid little attention to the differences and qualities of Asian typefaces, Kobayashi says companies in both parts of the world are taking more care.

"I think I'm quite optimistic about the future of type design," he concludes. "We can use emojis and images instead of type, but I think people are more and more interested in the subtle differences in the visual images of brands or their information in type."

—*Emma Tucker*

5
Type specimen for Monotype's Neue Frutiger and its companion Tazugane Gothic.

6
Map designed using the typeface Tazugane Gothic.

5

Neue Frutigerに合う日本語書体

オリジナルのNeue Frutigerを108%拡大し、ベースラインを16/1000 em下げた。 The original Neue Frutiger typeface has been enlarged to 108 percent and the baseline has been shifted downward by 16/1000 em.

国東あアMonotype

Neue Frutiger

たづがね角ゴシックは、Monotypeの欧文書体、Neue Frutiger®に合う日本語書体として開発がスタートしました。Neue Frutigerのような（安心感）をもつヒューマニストサンセリフ体として、サイン・書籍・広告・Web等、用途を限定しない汎用性の高い製品を目指しました。日本語と欧文書体を組み合わせて混植をする時、漢字や仮名と比べてアルファベットが小さく見えることがあります。たづがね角ゴシックではそういった問題をできる限り回避できるように、あらかじめNeue Frutigerを拡大し、ベースラインシフトを施した状態で搭載しています。

The Tazugane Gothic typeface began as a project to develop a companion Japanese typeface for Monotype's Latin typeface, Neue Frutiger®. The aim was to create a humanist sans serif face possessing the steadiness of the Neue Frutiger typeface and nearly unlimited applicability in a broad range of uses, from signage and publishing to advertising and the web. When Japanese and Latin typefaces are used together in the same text, the Latin alphabet sometimes looks smaller in comparison to kanji and kana (hiragana and katakana). In order to avoid this problem as much as possible, the Tazugane Gothic typeface includes a version of the Neue Frutiger typeface that has been slightly enlarged and given a baseline shift.

Ultra Light　（見出し）

Regular　（本文）

Extra Black　（見出し）

Ultra LightからThin、HeavyからExtra Blackは見出し、用として大きく使われることを想定して、括弧類は過度にデザインしました。一方、LightからBoldまでは小さいサイズでもしっかりと見えるような太みを持たせています。

The Ultra Light, Thin, Heavy, Black and Extra Black weights were designed with slim parentheses, to allow for wide use as display type, while the parentheses in the weight range from Light through Bold have enough thickness to ensure legibility even at small point sizes.

Ultra Light
Neue Frutigerに合わせた和文書体たづがね角ゴシック

Thin
Neue Frutigerに合わせた和文書体たづがね角ゴシック

Light
Neue Frutigerに合わせた和文書体たづがね角ゴシック

Book
Neue Frutigerに合わせた和文書体たづがね角ゴシッ

Regular
Neue Frutigerに合わせた和文書体たづがね角ゴシッ

Medium
Neue Frutigerに合わせた和文書体たづがね角ゴシッ

Bold
Neue Frutigerに合わせた和文書体たづがね角ゴシッ

Heavy
Neue Frutigerに合わせた和文書体たづがね角ゴシッ

Black
Neue Frutigerに合わせた和文書体たづがね角ゴシッ

Extra Black
Neue Frutigerに合わせた和文書体たづがね角ゴシ

6

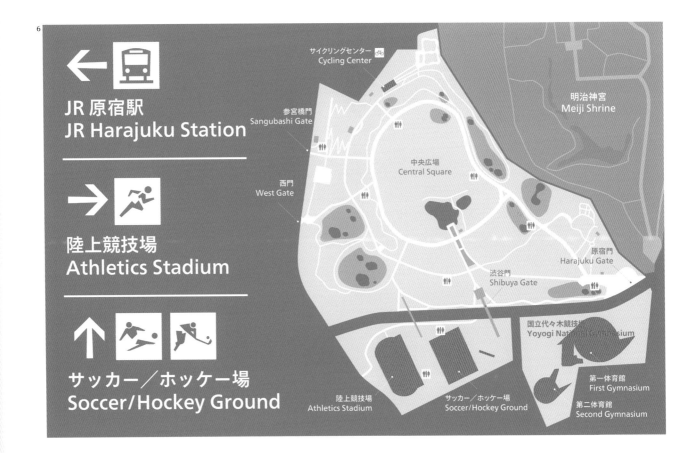

サイクリングセンター
Cycling Center

明治神宮
Meiji Shrine

参宮橋門
Sangubashi Gate

中央広場
Central Square

JR 原宿駅
JR Harajuku Station

西門
West Gate

原宿門
Harajuku Gate

陸上競技場
Athletics Stadium

渋谷門
Shibuya Gate

国立代々木競技場
Yoyogi National Gymnasium

サッカー／ホッケー場
Soccer/Hockey Ground

第一体育館
First Gymnasium

陸上競技場
Athletics Stadium

サッカー／ホッケー場
Soccer/Hockey Ground

第二体育館
Second Gymnasium

GERRIT NOORDZIJ

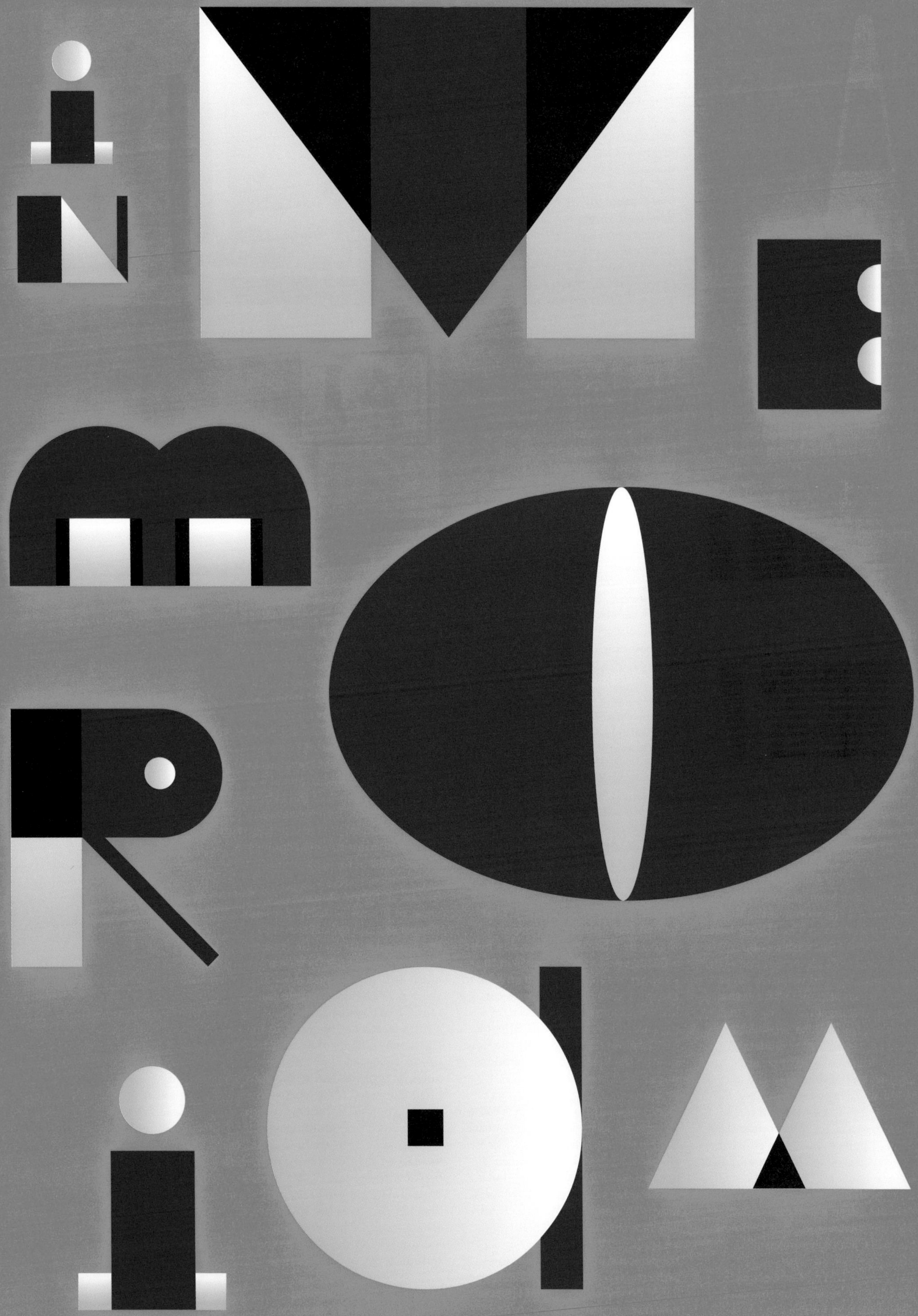

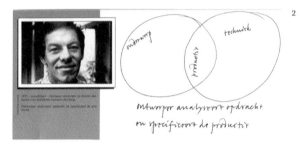

A

Arranger of the Type Universe
A personal in memoriam of
Gerrit Noordzij
(April 2, 1931–March 17, 2022)

In his speech, after being honored
In his speech, after being honored
with the 26th Type Directors
Medal at the ATypI Amsterdam
2013 conference, Gerrit Noordzij
modestly said he expected to
become famous, but not before his
death. 'New ideas of the sort that
could justify fame not only require
more than a lifetime to be accepted:
they also require a new point of
view. [...]: a new concept demands
a new generation', according to
Gerrit. He went on to say that the
TDC Medal changed his outlook
with the chance that he would enjoy
fame while still in this world. Of
course he did: Gerrit's theories and
teaching methods are embraced all
over the world. For example, The
Stroke: Theory of Writing has been
translated into many languages. In
this booklet Gerrit characteristically
describes typography as writing with
prefabricated letters.[1] Moreover,
there is the Gerrit Noordzij Prize
for extraordinary contributions
to the fields of type design,
typography, and type education.

It must have been in 1980 that Gerrit
entered his classroom of the Royal
Academy of Art in The Hague, better
known as KABK, with a copperplate
and burins. If I remember correctly,
he blinded a window with a sheet
of transparent paper to filter the
light and then started engraving.
Probably for Deliciæ, a collection
of 12 engravings after models
by the illustrious seventeenth-
century calligrapher Jan van den
Velde, which appeared in 1984. For
this edition it was decided not to
reproduce the original copperplate-
prints in offset, but to re-engrave
them (besides Gerrit there were two
other engravers). Gerrit did not shy
away from doing this exceptionally
delicate job in a noisy classroom,
because he never seemed to doubt
his skills, control, and insight.

Two years earlier, I had become
his student, actually by chance. I
did admission for the Fine Arts

department of the KABK, but the
committee on duty concluded that
I was more of a graphic designer. I
was familiar with figure drawing
and painting, but writing and
type design were completely new
to me. Gerrit was a striking figure
and a very passionate teacher: he
impressed my fellow students and
me with his extensive knowledge
and skills. I used to put sheets of
blank paper on my table for him
to demonstrate with broad tip,
pointed pen, and flat brush. If my
table was empty now and then,
Gerrit would use something else
to write on, such as a paper towel.
The result was always impeccable.

Gerrit often used texts from the
Bible for his examples –not only for
the ones he made for his students,
but also in type specimens. I
believe he was essentially Reformed
Protestant (my background too,
hence the recognition). Psalm 23
(The Lord is my shepherd) and
Isaiah 43:1 are quoted on the
obituary sent out by his family.
In general, the Bible plays an
important role in Gerrit's œuvre: he
designed the 1977 postage stamp to
commemorate the Delft Bible, the
first printed Dutch-language book,
dating exactly 500 years earlier. He
also designed Rembrandt en de
Bijbel, published in 1984, in which
religious work by the master painter
was combined with the biblical
texts on which they are based.

When I listen to the characteristic,
somewhat stubborn organ music
of Johann Ludwig Krebs, Bach's
favorite pupil, I sometimes associate
it with Gerrit's work. Listen, for
example, to Krebs' wonderful
and typical chorale arrangement
'Von Gott will ich nicht lassen.'[2]

Whatever the subject within his field
of vision, Gerrit became an expert. In
1979 Gerrit wrote Zeis en Sikkel: De
kunst van het maaien ('Scythe and
Sickle: The Art of Mowing'). That
he had really become a specialist
in this field became apparent when
a friend and I visited Gerrit in the
summer of 1982. To set up an ad-hoc
camping spot in an orchard near
his house, Gerrit drove ahead of us
on a small bicycle with a scythe on
his shoulder. Then he professionally
mowed the field where we pitched
our tents. Those were the days.

Gerrit was self-taught when it came
to mowing, as he also taught himself
to engrave –at least as far as I know.
He had become a type designer on
his own strength after obtaining a
bookbinder's diploma and a short
letters-oriented study at the KABK.
The fact that he had to discover a
lot for himself must have influenced
his personal arrangement of the type
universe. Gerrit made a classification
based on the contrast and contrast
flow from writing with the broad

nib (which he called 'translation')
and with the flexible-pointed pen
('expansion'): 'Contrast is governed
by the techniques of handwriting, but
it may be modified in design. A range
of drawings with gradually increased
and reduced contrast reveals all the
possibilities of typedesign.'[3] This idea
eventually culminated in his famous
cube, which includes all variants
from high to low: 'The ranges of sort
of contrast, increase of contrast
and reduction of contrast can be
set out on the dimensions of a cube
[...]. My description of the cube is
a mixture of technology, design,
cultural history, and psychology with
a flavor of cultural anthropology; a
square kind of fortune-telling.'[4]

In Zeis en Sikkel Gerrit's typical
sense of humor is clearly present:
'Blades of grass are attached to
the ground with their undersides,
so that they cannot be blown
away. But they are just loose at
the top.'[5] Another example can be
found in a booklet accompanying
a retrospective of his work in the
University Library of Amsterdam
in 1980, entitled Het verzamelde
misverstand van Gerrit Noordzij
('The Collected Misconception of
Gerrit Noordzij'). 'Putting things
upside down does not make them
always clearer, but often funnier', can
be read on the illustrated cover. Both
booklets were 'typeset' in Gerrit's
beautiful broad-nib handwriting. In
line, his classes at the KABK were
always laced with humor, which
was a good counterpoint to the
serious depth of his theories.

Gerrit strongly advocated
handwriting as the underlying

1
Photo from Vergeetboek
by Gerrit Noordzij
(1995) taken by William
Hoogteyling (who
probably owns the
copyright, I reckon).

2
From Het kader van
grafisch ontwerpers.
Lecturis 10' ('The
framework of Graphic
Designers'), a publication
intended to gain insight
in the views of Dutch
graphic designers.
Gerrit writes/illustrates:
'designer analyzes
task and specifies
the production.'

3
Cover design by Gerrit
Noordzij for a 'Magazine
for Graphic Culture' from
1979. The layout of the
entire publication was
in the humorous hands
of Gerrit, and he made
all illustrations as well.

3

spatie

Tijdschrift
voor grafische
cultuur waarin opgenomen

Orgaan
voor grafische
subcultuur
En Visuele Zelfbevrediging

force for type design. He was convinced that while developing an understanding of type through handwriting is not necessarily easy, it is the best way to make complex and subtle matters clear: 'Convention is no longer a restricting fence but a vast territory.'[6] This implies that writing explores the basic structure of type, on which the designer can develop his own specific idiom. The alternative method to gain more insight is to study existing fonts. However, this could severely limit the designer, as it will be difficult to imagine what is possible outside of the models examined.

Gerrit's students, whom he mentioned in his TDC-Medal speech, proved that writing is a solid foundation for type design. Teaching helped Gerrit to develop and refine his theories, but the results of his students also evangelized his ideas and methods. I remember how pleased he was with the small exhibition of the Letters] working group, consisting of former students who wanted to help and learn from each other, at the ATypI Basel conference in 1986. The displayed type designs provided solid proof of the quality of his teaching methods. These methods are used today by many of his former students and it is interesting to see how Gerrit's essentially recalcitrant ideas have been canonized by them.

As a personal side note and, in line with Gerrit, a bit contradictory with my tutor: while it is clear that handwritten models formed the basis for movable type, there is a quintessential difference between the two forms, which is that in movable-type characters need to be positioned on distinct rectangles. Although there was undeniably a direct relationship between roman and italic type and their handwritten precursors, the Renaissance punchcutters had to deal with all kinds of technical constraints that calligraphers were not aware of. This raises the question of whether certain details in roman and italic type are the result of these constraints rather than the interpretation of calligraphic models.

In 1987 an exhibition took place in the Museum Meermanno-Westreenianum. Work by five prominent Dutch type designers was on display, namely Chris Brand, Bram de Does, Dick Dooijes, Sem Hartz, and Gerard Unger. Gerrit's type designs were not present, only because the criterion was whether work was produced for a typesetting-machine manufacturer and thus available to the end-user market. I know Gerrit was negotiating with Monotype when I was his student. He once showed a relevant typeface of his hand and explained how he structured the capitals of the bold

to act as small caps for the medium weight. I do not know why the typeface in question was not licensed by Monotype in the end. I cannot rule out that Gerrit's stubbornness played a role in this. However, in the preface to the booklet accompanying the exhibition, John Dreyfus did not forget to mention Gerrit and his international significance as a teacher of type design.[7]

At the time, Gerrit mainly applied his typefaces to the numerous book covers he designed. For this, he had adapted a photo enlarger so that it was in principle comparable to Berthold's Staromat photographic headline setter. He used orthochromatic 35mm film on which the letters and their character widths were recorded. As with the Staromat, strips of photo paper were wetted with developer and the letters were positioned with a red filter before exposure. In the end, the paper was further developed and fixed. Gerrit used a small Aristo drawing board and a glue stick to position the final paper strips on the cover designs. He did this very quickly and efficiently, the proof of which I saw. Gerrit later digitized his type designs with Ikarus M: he clearly enthusiastically embraced the personal computer at an early stage. Eventually, his fonts became available exclusively in digital format through The Enschedé Font Foundry, run by his youngest son Peter Matthias.

Gerrit was very handy, not only as a bookbinder, and, like the aforementioned photosetter, often made his own tools. For example, he modified the refill of a Parker Jotter by removing the ballpoint and fitting a small diamond to the end, so that he could use the easy-to-carry pen for glass engraving. In addition, in the early eighties he used pressed solid polystyrene to create molds for type design, i.e., advanced French curves. In my opinion this creativity was exemplary of the way in which he always wanted to shape the world to his will.

Undoubtedly, sooner or later a biography will be in the making that will do justice to the idiosyncratic character and impressive œuvre of Gerrit Noordzij. The type designer's current profession would not have looked the same without him —certainly not to me.

—*Dr. Frank E. Blokland*

4

5

4
Calligraphy with brush on a paper towel, made by Gerrit during a class at the KABK around 1978/1979.

5
Calligraphy on a napkin, made by Gerrit during a diner in a restaurant in the mid 1980s.

NOTES

1   Gerrit Noordzij, *The Stroke: Theory of Writing* (London: Hyphen Press, 2005), p.49
2   https://youtu.be/7YuRTnmHO7o
3   Gerrit Noordzij, 'A Program for Teaching Letterforms', *Dossier A–Z 73: Association Typographique Internationale* (Andenne: ATypI, 1973), p.86
4   Gerrit Noordzij, 'The Shape of the Stroke', *Raster Imaging and Digital Typography II* New York: Cambridge University Press, 1991), pp. 34–42 (p.38)
5   Gerrit Noordzij, *Zeis en Sikkel: de kunst van het maaien* (Amsterdam: Uitgeverij Bert Bakker, 1979), p.65
6   Noordzij, 'A Program for Teaching Letterforms', p.86
7   Mathieu Lommen, *Letterontwerpers* (Haarlem: Joh. Enschedé en Zonen, 1987), p.17

6

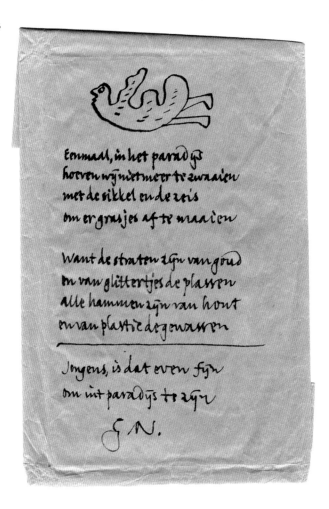

7

9

8

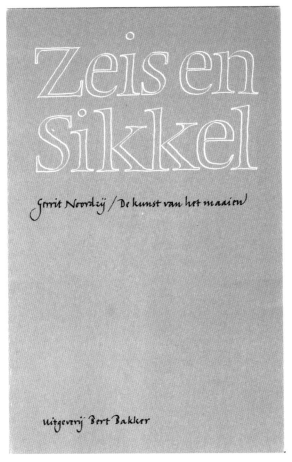

6
In 1984 I bought Zeis en Sikkel, and Gerrit not only signed the booklet, but also decorated the packing paper in his characteristic style.

7
Engraving by Gerrit from 1980 for Deliciae, which was published in 1984.

8
Signed French title page of Zeis en Sikkel.

9
Engraving by Gerrit from 1972, apparently after a model from Martin Schongauer (ca.1450–1491), and hand printed by him in 1975. (I bought this at an online auction a few years ago.)

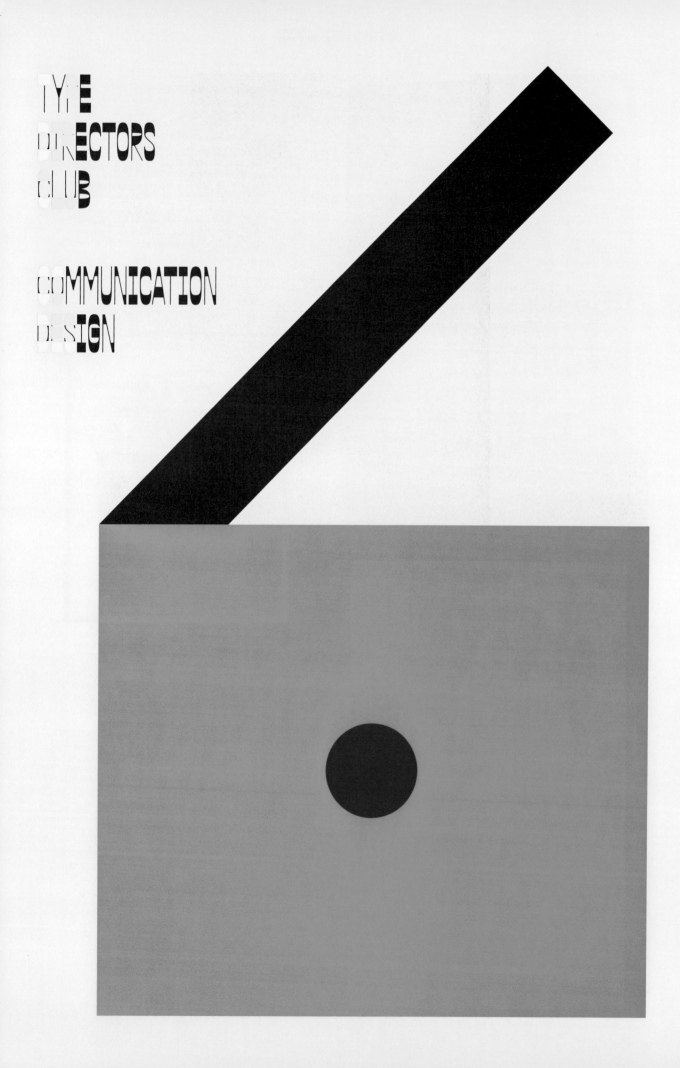

TYPE
DIRECTORS
CLUB

COMMUNICATION
DESIGN

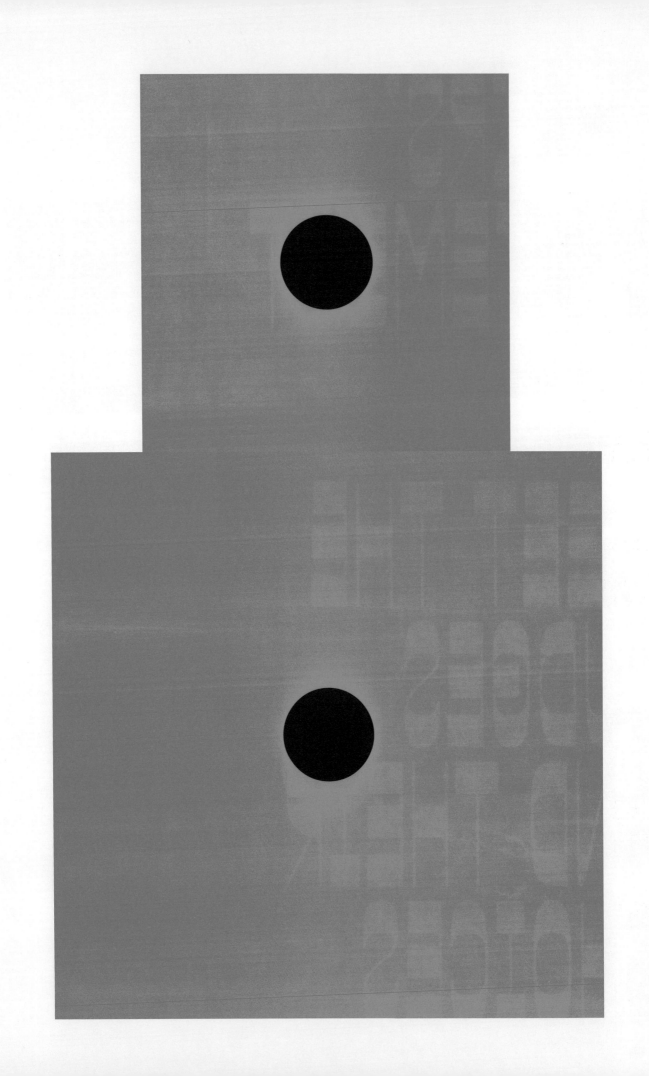

CHAIRS' STATEMENT

MEET THE JUDGES AND THEIR CHOICES

AS WE LOOK TO THE FUTURE, OUR CORE GOAL REMAINS: TO PROMOTE EXCELLENCE IN TYPE DESIGN AND TYPOGRAPHY. THE TDC COMMUNITY IS NO LONGER LIMITED TO THE FINITE CULTURAL SPACE OF NYC. WITH WINNERS FROM 34 COUNTRIES, THE BOOK YOU NOW HOLD TRULY REFLECTS THE WORLD'S BEST TYPOGRAPHY.

TDC was founded 75 years ago, in September 1946, bringing together an unprecedented group of professionals from New York's design community, including historic type icons Lou Dorfsman, Herb Lubalin, Bradbury Thompson, and Hermann Zapf.

Today, TDC is a global community, united by the shared belief that type drives culture, and culture drives type. Our membership from 42 countries is represented by an equally diverse Advisory Board.

The number of judges for the Communication Design and Type Design (see page xx) competitions has been significantly expanded to reflect that far-reaching community. Each judge brings a unique perspective, yet all share the same passion for type's ability to give form to meaning.

Our competition winners represent a celebration of typographic accomplishment, whether generated through personal experience, academic study, or visionary self-expression.

As we look to the future, our core goal remains: to promote excellence in type design and typography. The TDC community is no longer limited to the finite cultural space of NYC. With winners from 34 countries, the book you now hold truly reflects The World's Best Typography.

Manija Emran and Joe Newton, Communication Design co-chairs

MANIJA
EMRAN

JOE
NEWTON

ANTONIO
ALCALÁ

Antonio Alcalá runs Studio A, a small company working with museums and arts institutions. He art directs and designs postage stamps for the United States Postal Service, and loves teaching/lecturing at schools including the Corcoran College of Art + Design, SVA, Pratt, and MICA.

studioa.com
 antoniostudioa
 StudioAdesign

"IRREGULAR AND YET HIGHLY LEGIBLE. INTRIGUING, DIMENSIONAL (BUT NOT REALLY), AND COMPELLING. A BRILLIANT SET OF POSTERS. CONGRATULATIONS!"
— ANTONIO ALCALÁ

In an era when powerful digital tools are ubiquitous in design education programs, it is both surprising and thrilling to see students successfully embrace a low-tech approach for their annual exhibition: a rectangular, flat, thick slab of clay.

But by then pushing basic shapes into the printed clay surface, the typography is fractured and distorted in unpredictable ways that feel distinctly nondigital and a byproduct of human intervention. The basic typography becomes unexpected, vaguely mysterious, and exciting. Through the type, one senses various topographies in this simultaneously flat poster.

STUDENT
Hands On!

Design
Laura Hilbert and
Sarah Stendel

URLs
sarahstendel.com
laurahilbert.de

Professors
Catrin Altenbrandt
and Adrian Nießler

School
Hochschule für
Gestaltung Offenbach
Offenbach am Main

Principal Type
Stabil Grotesk

Dimensions
Various

Concept
"Hands On!" is the claim of the visual identity for the 23. Rundgang at HfG Offenbach, the university's annual group show. Because of the pandemic, many exhibitions had to be canceled or moved to the digital space, just like last year's Rundgang. To counteract the lack of haptics, we came up with the idea of producing the identity in an analogue way with our own hands. Every part of the visual identity is made from clay that was screen printed. We deformed the clay manually after the printing process, photographed it, and later edited the photographs digitally.

PHILIPPE APELOIG

Born in 1962, Philippe Apeloig studied arts in Paris. After two internships at Total Design in Amsterdam, he became graphic designer for the Musée d'Orsay in 1985. In 1987, he moved to Los Angeles to work with April Greiman. In 1993, he was granted a fellowship for the Villa Medici, where he created typefaces, and won the Tokyo Type Director Club's Gold Award in 1995.

He taught for seven years at the École nationale supérieure des Arts Décoratifs in Paris, then at the Cooper Union School of Art in New York (1999-2003), and was curator at the Lubalin Study Center of Design and Typography. In 2013 and 2015, two major retrospectives were held: "Typorama" at the Musée des Arts Décoratifs in Paris, with a book published in English by Thames & Hudson, and "Using Type" at the Stedelijk Museum in Amsterdam. In 2017, the GGG Gallery in Tokyo held an exhibition on his work.

Recently, he was commissioned by Hermès, Issey Miyake, the Manufacture de Sèvres, the Yves Saint Laurent Museum in Marrakech, or the Louvre Abu Dhabi, and also designed bespoke typefaces distributed by Nouvelle Noire in Switzerland.

"CONSTRUCTIVISM REPRESENTS THE REBELLION OF THOSE ARTISTS WHO DID NOT ACCEPT ONLY CLASSIC STANDARDS."
— PHILIPPE APELOIG

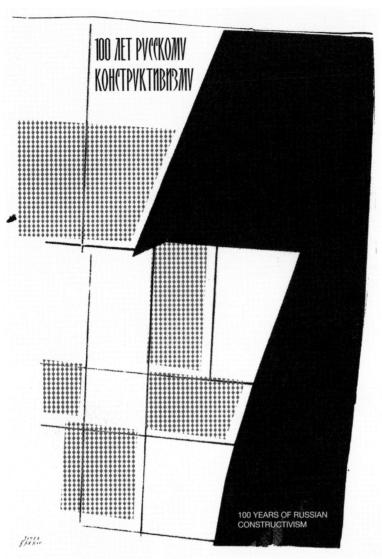

This poster series is a refreshing vision of Soviet Constructivism. How to connect the posters' patrimony and contemporary graphic design? This highly expressive style of composition challenges the structured typographical technique of classical poster. Born at the beginning of the twentieth century, Constructivism represents the rebellion of those artists who did not accept only classic standards. It's a reflection of the avant-garde of the twentieth century.

POSTERS
100 Years of Russian Constructivism

Design
Peter Bankov
Prague

Creative Direction
Kirill Karnovich-Valua

Design Firm
Bankov Posters

Agency
RT Creative Lab
Moscow

Principal Type
Avangarde by Bankov

Dimensions
23.4 × 33.1 in.
(59 × 84 cm)

Concept
Believe it or not, a hundred years ago, great ideas from Russia were revolutionizing global design. In the 1920s, Constructivism migrated from a young new country, the Soviet Union, to Europe, where it quickly spread, emphasizing geometrism, simplicity of form, rigor, and solidity. In our poster series (which launched an open poster contest as part of VKHUTEMAS.ACADEMY project), we aimed to catch the essence of Constructivism to connect it to our times. With ripped and raw shapes and black/red color accents, the posters tell a story of pioneering ideas that were eventually crushed and persecuted by the government. We hope peaceful times are not far away, and that new great Russian ideas will once again be appreciated and influence the world for good.

ANIL AYKAN

Anıl Aykan is a London-based graphic designer, originally from Istanbul. She holds a BA, MA in Graphic Design and a PhD in typography. Since 2014, she has been working at Barnbrook for internationally renowned clients such as Victoria & Albert Museum, Phaidon, Rizzoli, Thames & Hudson, and Somerset House. She is a member of the minimal electronic band Fragile Self.

barnbrook.net
@ anilaykan
anilaykan
Anilaykan

"I FIND IT INSPIRING WHEN STUDENTS BRING THEIR OWN INTELLECTUAL INTERESTS INTO A DESIGN PROJECT AND THEN ARE COURAGEOUS ENOUGH TO CREATE A WHOLE NEW VISUAL UNIVERSE OUT OF IT."

— ANIL AYKAN

It is the opposite of the commercially led work, which we see so much of. Such projects are done with passion and commitment that feed into the work. You have to enter into your own universe, into your own creative world, and link them together as a meaningful project that speaks to other people.

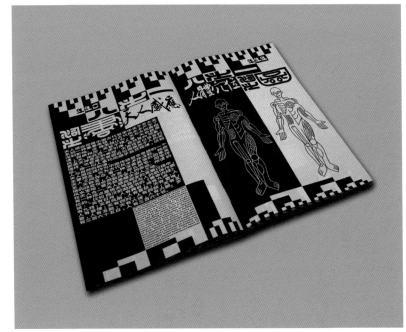

The Bagua diagram the design is based on has the capacity to symbolize complex ideas with basic symbols. In this project it was used to create a bold, striking design that is both historically based and absolutely modern. The design, content, and typography are integrated to create a standout visual language.

Student	Professor	Principal Type	Concept
THE CREED OF GCU	Tao Lin	Source Han Sans and Serif and custom	This is the bible of the fictional organization The Geomanist Club of Universe (GCU). It comprises twelve chapters, including Book of Changes (I Ching), Feng Shui, Eight Diagrams, Five Elements, Daoist Magic, and The Almanac. The 271 pages summarize the preliminary knowledge needed to join the GCU. The whole book adopts the layout design of the "Earlier Heaven" Bagua Diagram.
Design	**School**		
Chuye Chen	Shanghai University of Engineering Science Shanghai	**Dimensions** 11.4 × 7.5 in. (29 × 19 cm)	

GRAHAM CLIFFORD

"THIS ENTRY IS A WONDERFUL COMBINATION OF TYPOGRAPHIC DESIGN, CREATIVITY, AND TECHNOLOGY."
— GRAHAM CLIFFORD

Graham Clifford is a world-class, independent brand designer whose passion is brand development and consistency. His work stretches visual design across all forms of communication in a way that distinguishes a brand and sparks intense consumer connection.

As a brand designer, Graham uses his expertise in visual imagery to tell stories. He collaborates with creative agencies, as well as directly with businesses, in all aspects of visual communication including brand identity, advertising, and graphic design.

Graham's approach to visual brand consistency is both unique and exceptional. As a second-generation graphic designer with a foundation

as a typographer, Graham was trained by his father and then went on to work and continue learning at many of the world's most prestigious creative companies in London and New York, including: Collett Dickenson Pearce, Gold Greenlees Trott, Chiat/Day, and Ogilvy.

As Graham has honed his talent, he has been acknowledged by his industry and peers with almost every honor available today, including those from: The One Show, Communication Arts, Type Directors Club, and the Art Directors Club. In addition, Graham was voted President and Chairman of the Type Directors Club where he served on the board for more than a decade, and currently holds the title of Chairman Emeritus.

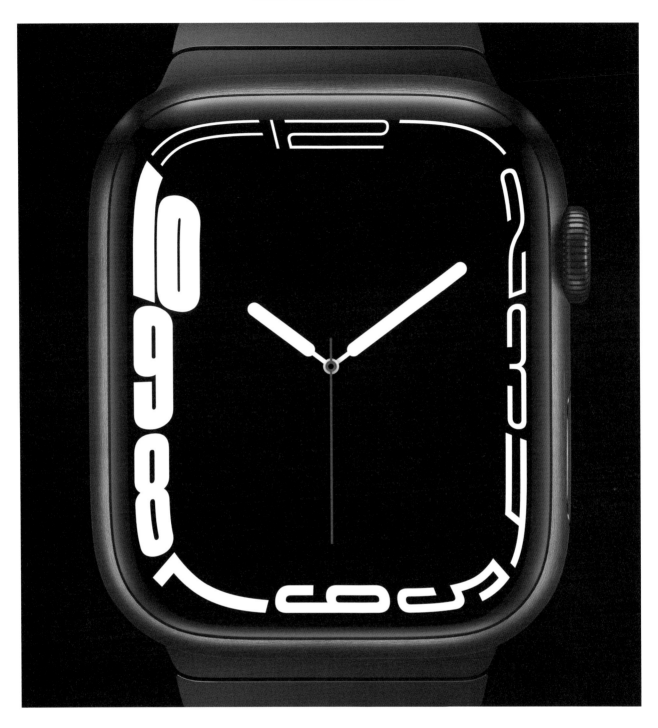

This entry is a wonderful combination of typographic design, creativity, and technology. I love how the design takes the dial right to the edge of the display and fluidly animates throughout the day, emphasizing the current hour. Bravo, Apple.

Digital Media
Contour Watch Face

Internal/
In-House Agency
Apple Design Team
Cupertino, California

Concept

We created a personalizable watch face that illustrates the passage of time and celebrates the full-screen, always-on display of Apple Watch Series 7.

Inspired by the passage of time, the contour face gradually changes throughout the day to highlight the current hour. The numerals are typeset from a custom font designed to fit into the edge of the display and transition in weight seamlessly from one hour to the next, celebrating the full-screen, always-on display of Apple Watch Series 7.

When the user raises their wrist, the numerals dynamically grow into focus, and then recede into a quiet, uniform composition when returning to rest. Turning the crown sends a wave of weight around the dial before resolving to the current hour. The face offers two type styles: Regular and Rounded. The color of both the numerals and dial can be personalized to complement the colors of Apple Watch bands.

ANA ANA BERNAUS GOMEZ

Ana is an award-winning illustrative lettering artist currently based in Los Angeles. Born and raised in Barcelona, her early work got influenced by Catalan Modernism. Its attention to detail and visual richness permeated her style filling her designs with dynamic and elaborated compositions.

In 2009 she moved to New York City, where she fell in love with typography. Barcelona brought her a taste for illustration, New York allured her with typography, and now both disciplines live in L.A., with expressive digital lettering.

Her current work feeds from both worlds and combines intricate pieces that live in contained and clean environments.

Her designs can be seen in a wide range of media, from film titles to advertising campaigns, apparel and editorial supports.

hello@anenocena.com
anenocena.com

"

THE MOEBIUS PIECE IS A PERFECT EXAMPLE OF HOW LETTERING HAS THE POWER TO COMMUNICATE THROUGH BOTH TYPOGRAPHY AND ILLUSTRATION."
— ANA BERNAUS

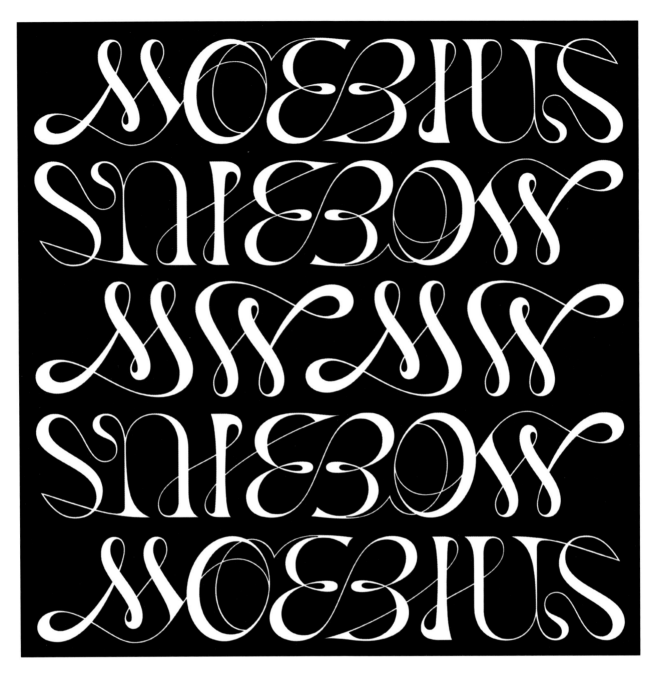

It perfectly conveys the concept of magic and infinity by treating the characters as a Moebius ring while keeping the legibility of the word. It also brings in ambigramic qualities in the way the "E" and "B" are treated as a rotational device, and the "M" and "S" swashes as reflective ones, giving the piece a dynamic feel. Compositionally, balance is achieved by intentional ornamentation of the characters, which not only gives it elegance but also guides the eye through the word. Conceptually, it visually connects with music via flowing forms that bring in rhythm through stroke weight variation and a combination of curvy shapes and sharp ends. It's a well-rounded lettering piece in which every decision has a purpose.

Logotype
Moebius

Design
Sanchit Sawaria
New Delhi

URL
sawariasanchit.com

Principal Type
Custom

Concept
Moebius is a musician and visual artist from India. He released his debut LP and, with it, a slice of nostalgia, rife with melodies evocative of dunes, nature, and constellations. The logotype created for Moebius is an embodiment of his intricate, fluid, and playful sound, which is sprinkled with themes of magic and infinity. At the beginning of the project, the client's intention was to create a single letter "M" monogram to illustrate the idea of infinity. We arrived at a drawing we liked, but it sparked new ideas about what a full logotype could look like, taking the same language forward. The final logotype was crafted with the intention of having no beginning or end.

GÖTZ GRAMLICH

Born 1974 in Heidelberg, Götz Gramlich studied at the University of Applied Sciences Darmstadt and graduated with a diploma in communication design. Before founding his studio "gggrafik" in Heidelberg in 2005, he was assistant to Niklaus Troxler / Studio Troxler in Willisau, Switzerland. Besides many international and national awards, Gramlich won the renowned Kieler Woche poster competition in 2017. He had a Guest-Professorship at Bauhaus University at Weimar. Götz Gramlich is member of the A.G.I. – Alliance Graphique Internationale.

gggrafik.de
🅞 instagggramlich

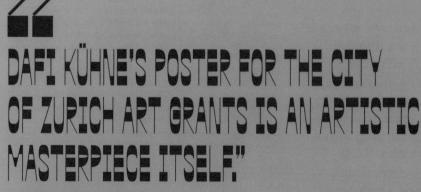

"DAFI KÜHNE'S POSTER FOR THE CITY OF ZURICH ART GRANTS IS AN ARTISTIC MASTERPIECE ITSELF."
— GÖTZ GRAMLICH

Dafi Kühne's poster for the City of Zürich Art Grants is an artistic masterpiece itself. Not only in form—the choice of colors and typeface, and how it is handled in context—but also in execution. In several passes with the same original, true art is created here by hand — for the artists.

Posters
Kunststipendien
der Stadt Zürich

Art Direction
Dafi Kühne
Näfels, Switzerland

URL
vimeo.com/575715409

Agency
Baby Ink Twice

Client
Helmhaus, Zürich

Principal Type
Berthold Akzidenz
Grotesk (digital) and
Helvetica (analog
metal typeface)

Dimensions
35.2 × 50.4 in.
(89.5 × 128 cm)

Concept
This is an exhibition poster for the official City of Zürich Art Grants 2021 at Helmhaus. The thirty-six names of the participating artists needed to be as big as possible, which is why I chose to work with perspective and overlapping type. The goal was to create a deep typographic cityscape of names. The edition of 300 posters has been letterpress hand-printed in twenty-three (!) print runs from laser-cut and engraved MDF and hand-set metal type. The colorful choice of tones and the super glossy letterpress printed ink on the matte dark blue paper support the contrast and depth of the typography. The posters were pasted around Zürich during summer 2021. I am honored that my work was chosen as a Judge's Choice by Götz Gramlich. Thank you.

EVA KELLENBERGER

> " SPINDLY ILLUSTRATIONS
> CONTRAST WITH BOLD
> TYPOGRAPHY, EVERYTHING
> IN BLACK AND WHITE.
> I STOP TO READ. I READ
> THE TEXT, AND THOSE
> ILLUSTRATIONS MAKE
> ME SMILE. "
> — EVA KELLENBERGER

Eva Kellengberger is co-founder of
Kellenberger–White, a London-based graphic
design studio, specialising in distinctive,
process-led design for industries including
art, architecture, food and fashion.

kellenberger-white.com
kellenbergerwhite

When you walk in the streets, thousands of images pass in front of you, seeming to blur into one another. Moments of friction can slow or stop this blur. I look for human interactions in the sea of images. Has somebody drawn on these stark, high-contrast posters? A response to these words? The graffiti nearby almost fooled me. I rarely go to the theater, but I'm intrigued by these posters. Perhaps they speak of some new form, not what I encountered when I was younger. There is a depth and lightness of touch at the same time—that is, for me, a successful visual marriage.

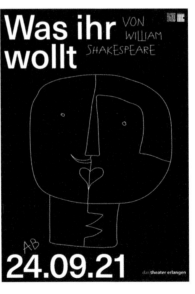

Posters
Theater Posters

Design
Sophia Döring and
Marina Huber

Art Direction
Nina Odzinieks,
Pit Stenkhoff, and
Johanna Zech

Design Firm
Neue Gestaltung GmbH
Berlin

Client
Theater Erlangen

Principal Type
Johanna I and Neue
Haas Unica Pro

Dimensions
23.4 × 33.1 in.
(59.4 × 84.1 cm)

Concept
In radical black-and-white or monochrome primary colors, Theater Erlangen's posters loudly announce the new productions. Ambiguous illustrations and bold typography stand out in the urban space. Via an app, the images start running and tell whimsical stories. The illustrations flow into life and reveal wondrously vivid stories by opening the immersive space with augmented reality. The design elements contrast negatively (white) with the backgrounds of the posters in a striking way. In the animations behind the posters, we use a wide range of stylistic devices: stop-motion, film, and collage.

FRITH KERR

"JOYFUL AND NON-HIERARCHICAL. THE MELTING OF BOUNDARIES BETWEEN THE TYPOGRAPHY, ILLUSTRATION, AND LAYOUT HERE CREATES A PIECE THAT IS AT ONCE CRITICAL AND CELEBRATORY. A HEADY COMBINATION."
— FRITH KERR

Frith Kerr is an award winning graphic designer and founder of Studio Frith celebrated for its original work and exceptional clients. 'the go-to graphic designer for creative clients' The New York Times. She is a member of the Alliance Graphique Internationale and a trustee of the Arts Foundation.

studiofrith.com
studiofrith

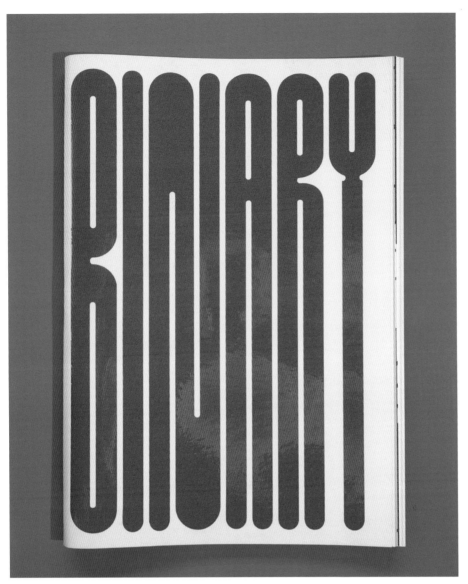

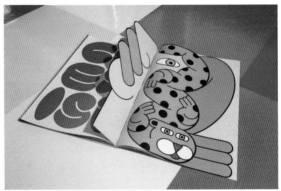

Student
Non/Binary

Design
Verena Mack

Instagram
@verenamack_

Professors
Prof Catrin Altenbrandt
and Prof Adrian Niessler

School
HfG Offenbach—
University of Art and
Design Offenbach,
Germany

Principal Type
Custom: WurstiType

Dimensions
11.7 × 16.5 in.
(29.7 × 42 cm)

Concept
The magazine shows the process from binary thinking to the nonbinary
spectrum. It starts with traditional double pages that resemble the
binary structure of society—a criticism of the binary system, hierarchical
structures, queerphobia, and the anthropocene. Later in the magazine, the
structure of the pages is extended into bigger formats and partly dissolved
using cut-outs. The need for acceptance and to dissolve hegemonic gender
roles and hierarchical structures becomes clear. The end of the magazine
shows the peaceful coexistence of all beings. By turning the pages, new
visual connections emerge and a new way of thinking presents itself.

HASSAN RAHIM

Hassan Rahim is an art director from Los Angeles, CA and based in New York City. His aesthetic deals in stark, esoteric imagery; it doesn't recoil from darkness. His direction and design have appeared on and ranged from magazines, gallery walls, record sleeves, concert stages, hats, street corners, and of course online.

Often as distinctive and boundary-troubling as he himself is, his work embodies far-flung but carefully steeped influences arranged into thrilling new harmonies. His willingness to forge new aesthetics rooted in but not tied to his own perspective has won Rahim venerable status as a thought leader, specifically among young black artists interested in nuance and subculture. As an autodidact, Rahim's work is all the more emboldening. His example is part and parcel of a movement which is affecting music, art, fashion, and culture in profound ways.

He has had the honor of working with clients such as; Netflix, Nike, Apple, Khalil Joseph, Herman Miller, Carhartt, Jason Moran, SSENSE, Tiona McLodden, NTS Radio, The Safdie Brothers, Marilyn Manson, and Nine Inch Nails to name a few.

In 2015 Rahim founded 12:01, a full-service independent creative studio; the name of which is a wry tribute to his tireless commitment both to aesthetics and the demands of his vocation.

hassanrahim.com

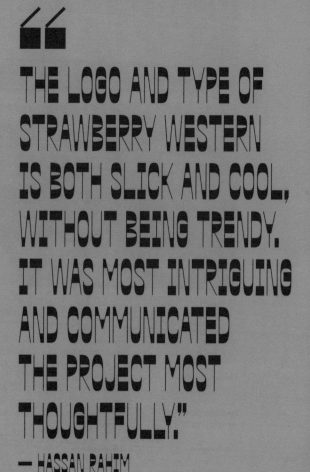

"THE LOGO AND TYPE OF STRAWBERRY WESTERN IS BOTH SLICK AND COOL, WITHOUT BEING TRENDY. IT WAS MOST INTRIGUING AND COMMUNICATED THE PROJECT MOST THOUGHTFULLY."
— HASSAN RAHIM

Ichigo M

...trawberry Western
is the anti-waste fashion
project of Kisa Sky
Shiga. With a DIY ethos,
Strawberry Western
knits together the global
energy of Kisa's hometown
of Queens, NY with the
traditions of craft
and preservation of her
Japanese and Irish heritage.

Strawberry Western is the anti-waste fashion
project of Kisa Sky Shiga. With a DIY ethos,
Strawberry Western knits together the global
energy of Kisa's hometown of Queens, NY with
the traditions of craft and preservation of her
Japanese and Irish heritage. In service of our
planet and all living things, Strawberry Western's
duty is resourcefulness, crafting precious pieces
out of unwanted old clothing, post-consumer
waste and scraps. Many SW pieces are one-of-a-
kind and handmade in th...

Ichigo S

Strawberry Western is the anti-waste fashion project of Kisa Sky Shiga.

Ichigo L

イチゴ-
ウェスタン

STRAWBERRY
WESTERN

Identity
Strawberry Western

URL
ryanbugden.com

Design Firm
R&M

Concept
This is an identity system for anti-waste independent fashion
label Strawberry Western. The identity fuses the eclectic
essence of Harajuku streetwear with kitsch Americana.

Design
Ryan Bugden°
Brooklyn, New York

Twitter
@rynbgdn

Client
Strawberry Western

Principal Type
Ichigo

MEHDI SAEEDI

Mehdi Saeedi is a graphic designer based in Philadelphia who was born and raised in Tehran. The design vision of Saeedi is influenced by his focus on contemplation of Eastern aesthetics, heritage, and tradition.

He uses his experience in graphic design, Persian calligraphy, type, and typography to transform Farsi letters into different forms and shapes, rendering unique conceptions in graphic design.

Saeedi's works have been exhibited in numerous well-known exhibitions, Biennials, and Triennials around the world.

A member of several national and international juries, he has won numerous awards in international graphic design competitions.

He is a Part-time faculty of graphic design at Towson University in Maryland USA, and he is an AGI member (Alliance Graphique Internationale).

mehdisaeedi.com
🅾 mehdisaeedistudio
🅕 mehdisaeedistudio

"THE WORK IS COLORFUL, HAS GOOD COMPOSITION, AND PLAYS WELL WITH TYPEFACES—AND WE CAN SEE THE CREATIVITY IN THE RESULT. SO I THINK THE PIECE WAS WELL DESERVED TO BE A WINNER."
— MEHDI SAEEDI

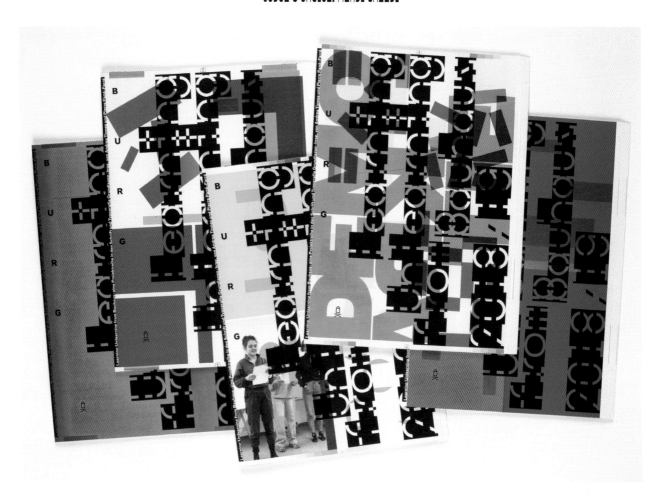

Editorial
Learning/Unlearning
from Bauhaus

Class
130 students of the
design department at
Burg Giebichenstein,
fall 2018–19

Printer
Burg Printing Workshop

Typographer
Pierre Pané-Farré
and Andrea Tinnes

URL
burg-halle.de/typoarchiv

Publishers
Pierre Pané-Farré and
Andrea Tinnes, and Burg
Giebichenstein University
of Art and Design
Halle, Germany

Principal Type
Allgemein Grotesk,
Amateur,
FF Bau, Corona, and
Neue Plak Condensed

Dimensions
11.7 × 16.5 in.
(29.7 × 42 cm)

Concept
The publication "Learning/Unlearning from Bauhaus"
shows student works created in the typography class at Burg
Giebichenstein University of Art and Design and puts them
together in an experimental printing process to create unusual
constellations and surprising chance encounters. For the cover,
the waste sheets from the printing process were recycled by
printing the title information on the front and the design grid on
the back of the cover in black ink. The changing color and motif
combinations result in a large number of variations. No two sheets
are alike, so that every cover in the entire edition is unique.

SCOFIELD
LAURA

" THIS TYPOGRAPHIC TWIST IS UNEXPECTED AND FRESH, WITH CLEVER USAGE OF ITS CIRCULAR COUNTER SPACES, AND IT LEAVES ITS VIEWERS WITH A LASTING IMPRESSION."
— LAURA SCOFIELD

Laura Scofield is a designer, strategist, and educator based in New York City. She work with brands & startups to help them create meaningful stories & experiences.

She is Sr. Design Manager at The Atlantic Re:Think, Part-Time Lecturer at Parsons and Design Professor at UNI-BH. Currently also serving as a board member of AIGA-NY (US). Previously, She worked at Pentagram and DesignStudio.

She has a MA from the School of Visual Arts in Design Research, Writing and Criticism (USA) a MA in Design (Brazil) and a BA in Graphic Design (Brazil). Laura is a devoted educator and loves being an active part of the design community in the US and Brazil.

She is part of AIGA-NY Mentorship Program helping designers with their professional goals while sitting on the jury of design awards such as Brazil Design Awards and Brazilian Graphic Design Biennial.

Laura's work has been recognized by D&AD, Cannes Lions, Red Dot, Print & How, iF and Brazil Design Awards. Her master research was awarded with Honorable Mention in Brazil and had projects showcased in Novum Magazine and Print Magazine.

laurascofield.com
⌾ laurascofield

In an age in which our eyes are fed the same aesthetic trends daily, original ideas that manage to deviate from the status-quo branding conventions become incredibly refreshing. And that is exactly why Strawberry Western stands out with its mesmerizing custom-type wordmark. Is it the merging of cultures ("eclectic Harajuku with kitsch Americana," according to the author) that fascinates us? Or is it its circular counter space that waters our mouth? This typographic twist is unexpected and fresh, with clever usage of its circular counter spaces, and it leaves its viewers with a lasting impression.

Logotype
Strawberry Western
Logotype

Design
Ryan Bugden°
Brooklyn, New York

Design Firm
R&M

Client
Strawberry Western

Concept
This is a bilingual logotype for independent sustainable fashion label Strawberry Western. Like the eclectic sensibility of Harajuku fashion, the logotype fuses multiple aesthetics: rationalized Japanese identity design and kitsch Americana.

OSMOND TSHUMA

Osmond Tshuma is the award-winning co-founder and creative director of Mam'gobozi Design Factory, a design studio that creates work and spaces that celebrate the Afrikan identity. His accolades include awards from the Pendoring Show, Loeries, New York One Show, and Cannes.

mamgobozidesign.com
☺ wakwatshuma
☺ mamgobozi

MY CHOICE AS A JUDGE GOES TO PLAY PLAY LAAAAAH, A PROJECT IN THE FORM OF A ZINE THAT CELEBRATES SINGAPORE'S HERITAGE IN A BEAUTIFUL AND FUN WAY. THE MODULAR-BUILT LETTERFORMS HAVE A PLAYFUL PERSONALITY TO THEM."
— OSMOND TSHUMA

My choice as a judge goes to *Play Play Laaaaah*, a project in the form of a zine that celebrates Singapore's heritage in a beautiful and fun way. The modular-built letterforms have a playful personality to them. One is drawn into the zine; it's a playground, with light brown pages equivalent to a sandbox, a canvas of creativity. You just want to hold the plywood pieces in your hands and create your own dragons. I believe it's an effective way of educating the younger Singaporean generation about their unique heritage. This is communication made playful.

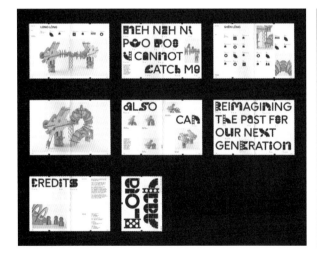

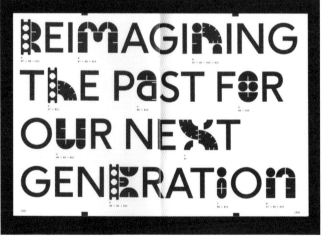

Editorial
Play Play Laaaaah

Creative Direction
Daisy Dal Hae Lee
and Joo Leng Lucien Ng

Design Firm
Studio Bang-Gu
San Francisco

URL
studiobanggu.com

Twitter
@StudioBanggu

Publisher
Social Species

Principal Type
Custom Modular
Typeface, F37 Ginger
Pro, and Monosten

Dimensions
6 × 8 in.
(15.2 × 20.3 cm)

Design Concept
Play Play Laaaaah is a zine about reimagining Singapore's most iconic playground for older Singaporeans to reminisce about their youth and the younger generation to learn their unique heritage. Built in 1970, the dragon playground is one of the most famous playgrounds in Singapore. These playgrounds were locally designed to instill a sense of national identity, but many have been demolished due to international playground safety standards. The zine is filled with a reimagined form of play that invokes people's memories of their youth. The form encapsulates Singapore's heritage and way of playing, inspiring future generations to be curious and imaginative.

DIEGO VAINESMAN

Diego Vainesman, design director.

He runs his own design studio 40N47 Design, Inc. in New York City.

Teaches "Type: Bridging Image and Context" for the MFA Visual Narrative program at the School of Visual Arts.

Judges competitions, gives talks and teaches design and branding workshops in Europe, Latin America and Asia.

Diego was the first Latin president of the Type Directors Club, and he developed Master classes for the different audiences. He was the Chairman of the TDC52's competition and he designed the 25th Annual of the TDC's competition. Actually he is the Club's Latin American liaison.

He recently published, through Kickstarter, the book *Logo: the face of branding*. He interviewed 40 designers from the five continents.

Clients include: American Express, Art Deco Society of New York, Canon, Hotel Palacio del Inka, Hotel Paracas, Hotel Tambo del Inka, IBM, New York State Democratic Committee, Pfizer, Print Magazine, Saturn, Subaru, The Bronx High School of Science, and Zenith Optimedia.

40n47design.com
facebook.com/diegovainesman
#type_is_alive
#diego_vainesman_design

THANK YOU, PLEA, FOR THIS PIECE, WHICH IS AN ODE TO THE LETTERPRESS PRINTING METHOD."
— DIEGO VAINESMAN

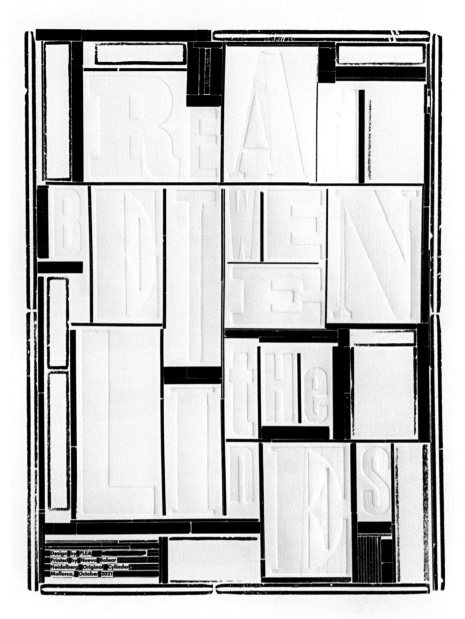

Typographically speaking, a line would be considered only horizontal. "Read Between the Lines" invites us to include the vertical ones. This poster pays homage to the "nonglamorous" silent visual elements that for many centuries have supported the letters and helped showcase their aesthetics.

This time the old Roman, Antique, and Gothic wood typefaces will have to wait. Today it isn't about you; today it is about those horizontal and vertical lines that have been creating the right amount of space for your families to communicate.

Congratulations to PLEA for rewarding these LEADing elements that have helped text's readability and legibility for many centuries.

Posters
Read Between the Lines

Creative Direction
Joan Canyelles Bestard
and Laureline Lavergne
Palma, Spain

Printer
Roberto Aguiló Mora,
Nueva Balear

Instagram
@plea.studio

Agency
PLEA

Principal Type
Old wood typefaces
(Roman, Antique, and
Gothic) and Futura
Bold lead type

Dimensions
13.90 × 19.5 in.
(35.3 × 49.5 cm)

Concept
A few years ago, we had the chance to print with letterpress for the first time. The technique opened up a new world of possibilities to us. We decided to self-initiate this project with the idea to reveal the hidden part of this technique. In this sense, "Read Between the Lines" is an ode to the letterpress printing method. To print any composition, the printer must build a functional structure that remains invisible. This part of the printing process involves a high level of detail. Our concept was to reveal this structure and make it the main protagonist of the poster.

KELLY KELLY
WALTERS

Kelly Walters is a designer, educator and founder of the multidisciplinary design studio Bright Polka Dot. In her ongoing design research, she interrogates the complexities of identity formation, systems of value, and the shared vernacular in and around Black visual culture. She is the author of Black, Brown + Latinx Design Educators: Conversations on Design and Race and co-editor of The Black Experience in Design (forthcoming February 2022). Kelly is currently an Assistant Professor and Associate Director of the BFA Communication Design Program at Parsons School of Design at The New School.

brightpolkadot.com
🅞 brightpolkadot

I WAS INSTANTLY DRAWN TO THE PLAYFUL TYPOGRAPHY AND THE WAY THE REPETITION OF LETTERFORMS SUGGESTED A SENSE OF VIBRATION AND SOUND."
— KELLY WALTERS

I chose the 2021 Music issue because of the amazing use of type, color, and texture. I was instantly drawn to the playful typography and the way the repetition of letterforms suggested a sense of vibration and sound. The layout was so dynamic that you could feel an underlying tempo stretching the form to its max. With the addition of the photography, there was an added a level of balance to the overall composition that made it both expressive and dramatic.

Editorial
The Music Issue,
March 14, Full Issue

Design
Matt Curtis and
Rachel Willey

Art Direction
Ben Grandgenett

Deputy Art Director
Annie Jen

Creative Direction
Gail Bichler°

Publication
*The New York Times
Magazine*

Principal Type
Generation Mono
and Söhne

Dimensions
8.9 × 10.9 in.
(22.6 × 27.7 cm)

Concept
Strong color and repeating typography filled the pages of the issue and created an adaptive and responsive design. The array of typographic elements and the textures they formed referenced the way that instruments of different tone, pitch, and vibration can come together to form a song

COMMUNICATION DESIGN WINNERS

WiN
NES
RS

IDENTITY: INTERNATIONAL CENTER OF PHOTOGRAPHY

Concept
The International Center for Photography (ICP)
in New York is the world's leading institution
dedicated to photography and visual culture.
Combining a museum, school, and archive,
ICP champions the idea of photography as
both an art form and an agent of social change,
with programming that explores the history
and future of image making. The designer
has created a new graphic identity for ICP
that captures the dynamic character of the
institution and of photography as a medium.

Creative Direction
Michael Bierut°

Associates
Todd Goldstein,
Delta Murphy, and
Jonny Sikov

Project Managers
Abby Matousek
and Susan May

Design Firm
Pentagram New York°

Client
International Center
of Photography

Principal Type
ICP Logo Generator,
Neue Haas Unica,
and Publico

ADVERTISING: CHINESE TRADITIONAL CULTURE POSTER

Concept
The goal was to restructure Chinese
fonts and reconstruct traditional ideas
with modern constructivism.

School
Communication
University of Zhejiang
Hangzhou, China

Client
Hangzhou Muke
Cultural Creativity

Principal Type
Cusongti

Dimensions
17.7 × 35.4 in.
(45 × 90 cm)

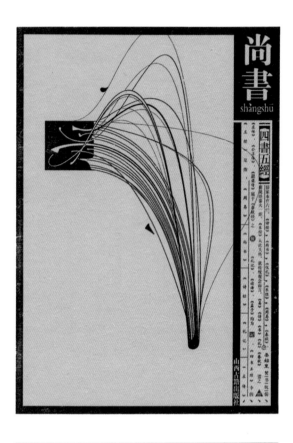

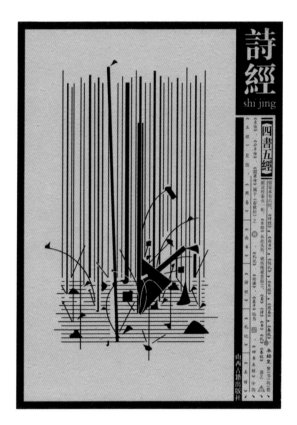

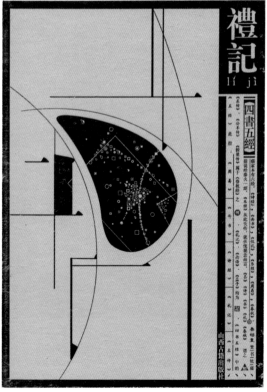

ADVERTISING: YOUFAB GLOBAL CREATIVE AWARDS 2021

Concept
This variable poster uses a unique cellular automaton algorithm. The algorithm, in which many cells laid out in space interact with neighboring cells and change their own state over time, is a simple rule, yet it behaves similarly to the life and death and the mechanisms of society. I cut out a moment of typography and printed it with an inkjet printer. By deliberately fixing the image on paper with physical properties, I aimed to create an organic visual that evokes the workings of life and a chain of thought, rather than staying in the digital realm of expression.

Design
Natsuki Isa and
Kohki Watanabe
Tokyo

Art Direction
Natsuki Isa and
Kazushige Takebayashi

Creative Direction
Sho Hosotani and
Natsuki Sagawa

Executive Creative Director
Toshiya Fukuda

Chief Technology Officer
Daiki Kanaoka

Digital Artist
Takayuki Watanabe

Freelancer
1002 inc.

Photography
Akihiro Yoshida

Programmer
Junichiro Horikawa

Printing Company
SHOEI INC.

Printing Direction
Shunichi Yamashita

URL
youfab.info/2021/

Design Firms
777CreativeStrategies,
Kitasenju Design,
Orange Jellies,
and SHA inc.
Toyko

Client
FabCafe and
Loftwork, Inc.

Principal Type
Custom

Dimensions
40.6 × 28.7 in.
(103 × 72.8 cm)

ADVERTISING: BUILT TO HOST

Concept
We created this dimensional lettering within a tuba's real-life intricate composition as part of a New Orleans Tourism campaign, building messaging into iconic Nola elements with hints of hospitality and contextual headline embedded into inviting photographic scenes, representing the historical jazz scene of the vibrant city. The concept was to build photorealistic typography into photographs, with the headline "Built to Host" as signature of the legendary cultural hub, positioning Nola as a unique destination for events hosting..

Digital Artists
Sean Freeman and
Albert Zablit
London and Montréal

Creative Direction
Andrew Hunter
New York

Illustration
Sean Freeman

Producer
Adrienne Darnell

Typographer
Eve Steben

URL
thereis.co.uk

Design Firm
THERE Studio
London

Agency
360i New York
New York

Client
New Orleans Tourism

Principal Type
Custom lettering

Dimensions
8 × 9.5 in.
(20.3 × 24.2 cm)

ADVERTISING: THE ISSUE WITHIN THE ISSUE

Concept

Typography was carefully considered when creating "The Issue Within the Issue." We wanted our typography to balance being bold and serious and being hopeful and uplifting. Aiming to create a powerful visual impact, we used strong and loud typography as an expression to illustrate the unignorable struggles that homeless LGBTQ+ youths face in New York City, and the significant efforts of the Ali Forney Center to combat the issue. While shedding light on a serious issue, we also wanted to represent the fun spirits, optimism, and tenacity of the LGBTQ+ community through our use of typography.

Design
Paul Martinez

Art Direction
Hamza Ali,
Julie Rosenoff, Rudy Troncone,
and Camille Walker

Chief Creative Officer
Dan Lucey

Chief Design Officer
Brian Lai

Executive Creative Direction
Bharat Kumar and
Marcelo Ramirez

Executive Producer
Melissa Tifrere

Director
Sal Migliaccio

Copywriting
Patrick Chase, Nick
Malone, Carlos Matias,
and Jp Winders

Editor
Oussama Zahr

Product Manager
Valentine Roche

Strategist
Alexis De Montaigu

User Experience Design
Janice Chen

Founder
Carl Siciliano

Agency
Havas New York

Client
Ali Forney Center/
New York Magazine

Principal Type
Bleeny, Dida,
Roboto, and Sen

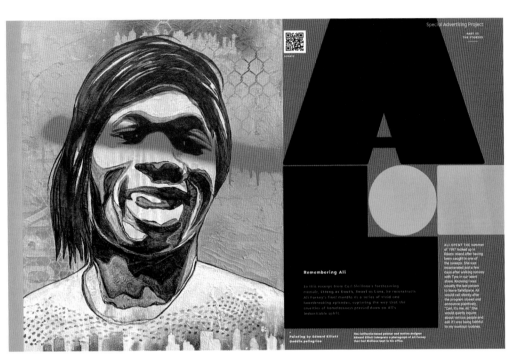

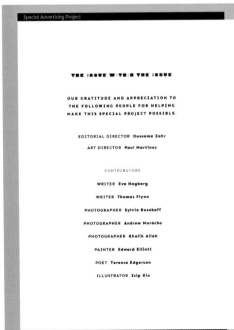

BOOK JACKETS: WITH TEETH

Concept
This design is meant to speak to the tone and contents of With Teeth by Kristen Arnett, using typography-as-teeth to transform the title into image.

Design
Lauren Peters-Collaer

Art Direction
Helen Yentus

In-House Agency
Lauren Peters-Collaer

Publisher
Riverhead Books

Principal Type
Custom type (title) paired with Martin (author name)

Dimensions
6.2 × 9.3 in.
(15.75 × 23.6 cm)

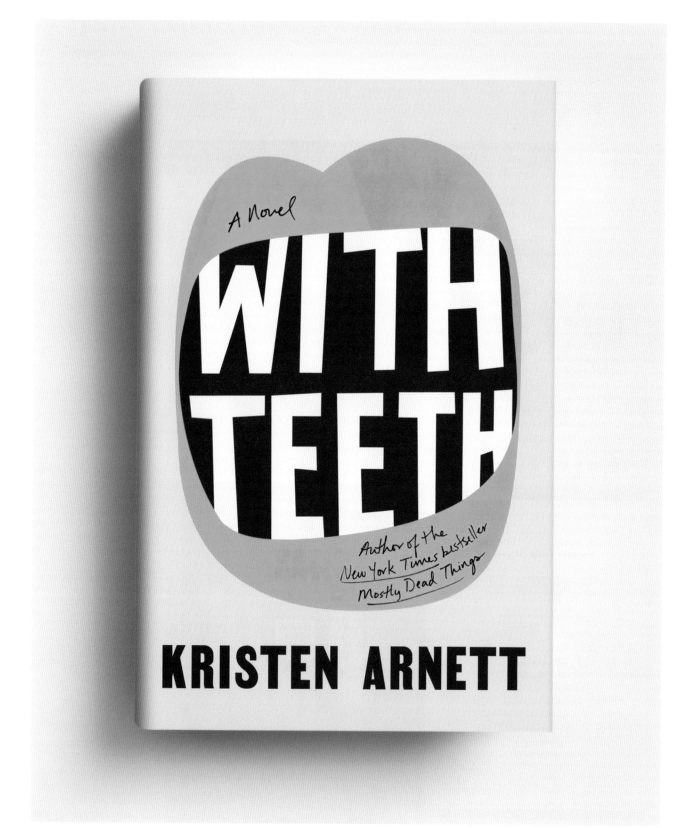

BOOK JACKETS: UIRAPURU

Concept
The book title is composed in a typeface
specifically designed for the project,
whose sharp triangles allude to fire.

Design
Thiago Lacaz
Rio de Janeiro

Principal Type
Uirapuru

BOOK JACKETS: GRANGER HIGH SCHOOL YEARBOOK COVER

Concept
Granger High wanted to make a memorable
cover for their yearbook. Inspired by 1920s
Art Deco, the 2021 Granger High School
yearbook reinvents Deco for the new '20s.

Art Direction
John Carlisle and
Addasyn Everill

Lettering
Kevin Cantrell

URL
kevincantrell.com

Twitter
@kevinrcantrell

Design Firm
Kevin Cantrell Studio
Mantua, Utah

Principal Type
Custom lettering

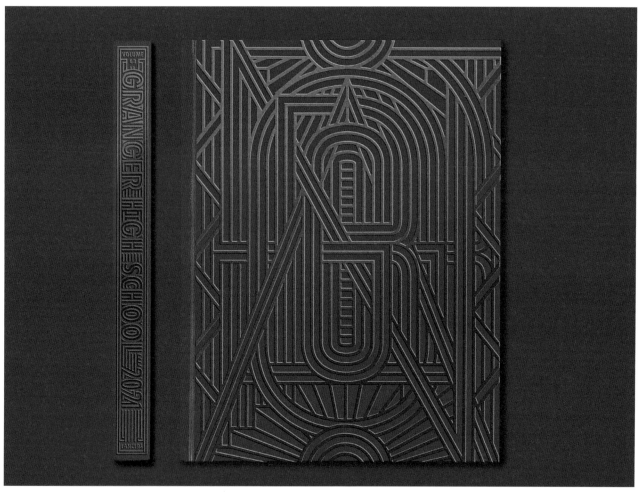

BOOK JACKETS: MY YEAR ABROAD

Concept
My Year Abroad is a provocative story about
a young American life transformed by an
unusual trip across Asia. I wanted the cover to
echo the energy and boldness of the book.

Design
Grace Han

Art Direction
Helen Yentus

Type Foundry
VJ Type
Paris

In-House Agency
Grace Han

Publisher
Riverhead Books
New York

Principal Type
Kobe Regular

Dimensions
6.3 × 9.3 in. (16
x 23.6 cm)

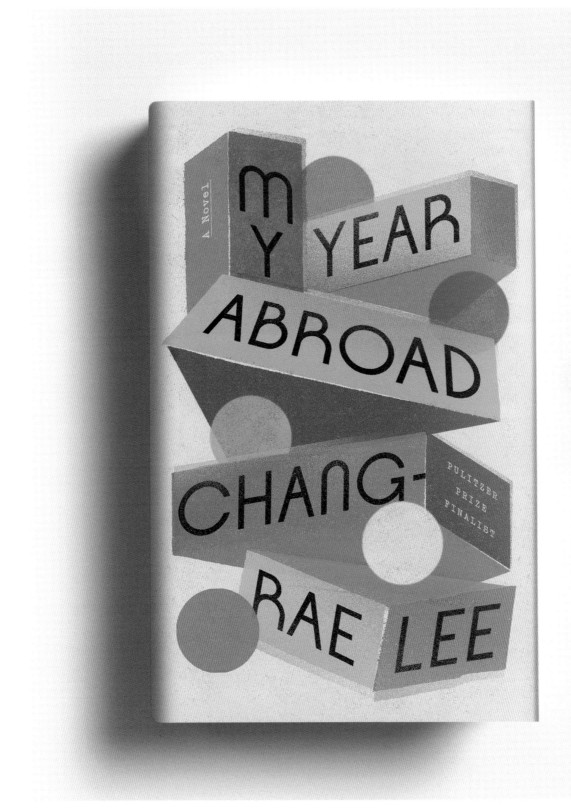

BOOK JACKETS: UNHEIMLICH

Concept
Unheimlich (uncanny) is a reference to Sigmund Freud's term.
Poet Artur Novikov asked me to make a design to embody his
description: "This book is about poetry, or should be. All the verses
in it are surrounded by a black shimmer, a black outline of ominous
consonances, or should be." This book is the author's attempt to say
goodbye to the leitmotif of the uncanny inside his being by transferring
the sound overpressure of this to paper. This book is a demonstration
of this transference process: It will be carried out before your eyes.

Design
Mikhail Lychkovskiy
Minsk

Client
Artur Novikov

Principal Type
Neue Montreal

Dimensions
5 × 8 in.
(12.7 × 20.32 cm)

BOOKS: PLAY PLAY LAAAAAH

Concept

Play Play Laaaaah is a zine about reimagining Singapore's most iconic playground for older Singaporeans to reminisce about their youth and the younger generation to learn their unique heritage. Built in 1970, the dragon playground is one of the most famous playgrounds in Singapore. These playgrounds were locally designed to instill a sense of national identity, but many have been demolished due to international playground safety standards. The zine is filled with a reimagined form of play that invokes people's memories of their youth. The form encapsulates Singapore's heritage and way of playing, inspiring future generations to be curious and imaginative.

Creative Direction
Daisy Dal Hae Lee
and Joo Leng Lucien Ng

Design Firm
Studio Bang-Gu
San Francisco

URL
studiobanggu.com

Twitter
@StudioBanggu

Publisher
Social Species

Principal Type
Custom Modular
Typeface, F37 Ginger
Pro, and Monosten

Dimensions
6 × 8 in. (15.2 × 20.3 cm)

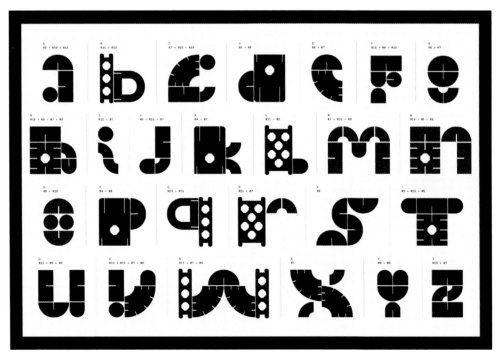

BOOKS: LETTERFORM VARIATIONS

Concept
This is a playful look at letterform construction using basic grid and shape-based systems and its potential to generate vast amounts of varying alphabetical outcomes.

Design Firm
Nigel Cottier
London

URL
letterformvariations.com/book

Publisher
Slanted Publishers
Karlsruhe, Germany

Principal Type
Letterform Variation 00,
Letterform Variation
01 IR, and Letterform
Variation 02 DFO

Dimensions
6 × 8 in.
(20 × 15.5 cm)

BOOKS: HERE—A WORLD POEM TISHANI DOSHI

Concept
HERE is a type specimen that celebrates cultural diversity through equity and inclusivity.

Creative Direction
Kai Bernau and Susana Carvalho

Creative Technologist
Ariel Walden
Modi'in Illit, Israel

Researcher/Writer
Karthik Malli
Bengaluru, India

Editor
Peter Biľak

Bookbinders
Benelux Boekbinders
Alphen, The Netherlands

Copy Editor
Johanna Robinson
Liverpool

Linguists
David Kamholz
and Ben Yang
San Francisco

Linguist and Technologist
Liang Hai
The Hague

Poet and Writer
Tishani Doshi
Chennai, India

Printer
Drukkerij Tielen
Boxtel, The Netherlands

URL
carvalho-bernau.com

Twitter
@at_cb
@typotheque

Design Firm
Atelier Carvalho Bernau
Porto, Portugal

Principal Type
Typotheque Lava, Typotheque November, and 4,000 other typefaces from the Typotheque collection

Dimensions
7.8 × 4.6 in.
(19.8 × 11.7 cm)

BOOKS: DAYDREAM

Concept
The book daydream provides a 678-page overview of the designer's graphic work over the past twenty-five years and is an expression of the living wellspring of his creativity, revealed in a multifaceted interplay of styles, forms, and content that all reflect his artistic thinking and experience. The compactly designed book looks like a solid brick but is very light and divided into nine corresponding chapters, which can be found quickly because they are marked with colored sticky notes, and each is preceded by a page printed in the color of the sticky note.

Design Firm
hesign Studio
Berlin

Principal Type
Grot12 Extended

Dimensions
7 × 10 in.
(18 × 25 cm)

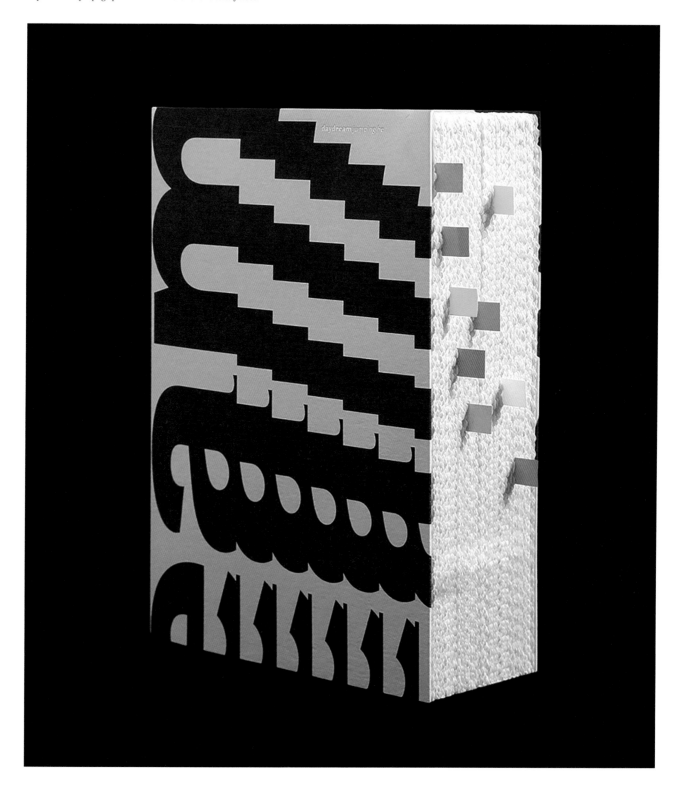

BOOKS: FORM OF LOVE

Concept
"What is love?" is a question that gives people a hard time, because there is no such thing as a model answer. There is more than one kind of love and more than one form of expressing it. Valuing a person is love, and so is cherishing a belonging. We made this zine to give the subject of what love is back to the audiences.

Design
Shuyao Bian and
Chen Xing

Art Direction
Xiang Li

Design Firm
STONES DESIGN Lab.
Beijing

Principal Type
Adobe Song, Helvetica
Now Variable, Hei
Regular, and custom

Dimensions
10.1 × 9.6 in.
(25.7 × 24.5 cm)

BOOKS: SUPPORT INDEPENDENT TYPE

Concept
The book is divided into six parts, each providing different insight into the current type design scene. The first part shows a photo series of design studios from around the world. The second part features essays and interviews from international greats in the world of type design. The third part features quotes from type designers and foundries about their work, offering insight into their thinking. Parts four through six show typeface specimens.

Editorial Direction and Design
Lars Harmsen and Marian Misiak
Karlshule, Germany and Poland

Forward
Paul McNeil

Publishing Direction
Lars Harmsen and Julia Kahl

Content Management and Research Instagram and PDF Section, Art Direction
Lisa Panitz

Research and Editing Support
Clara Weinreich

Retouching
Mahmoud Hamdy and Louis Hunt

Publisher
Slanted Publishers
Karlsruhe, Germany

Principal Type
Di Grotesk

Dimensions
8.3 × 11 in. (21 × 28 cm)

BOOKS: IT'S US AGAIN

Concept
In this book, parts of the cover are cut out. This allows you to look at the page behind and read the motto: "It's Us Again." The design of the cover takes up the idea of being opened again. A clear, strong graphic language and two Pantone colors ensure a recognizable restart of the new season of 2021–22.

Creative Direction
Davide Durante, Helen Hauert, and Barbara Stehle

Agency
collect
Stuttgart

Client
Ansbach Theater

Principal Type
Lausanne 300

Dimensions
5.7 × 7.9 in.
(14.4 × 20 cm)

BOOKS: THE BEST GERMAN BOOK DESIGN 2021

Concept

This is a book about books. Twenty-eight award-winning books are each presented in three double-page spreads. The reproductions are arranged variably in every chapter and are determined by the specific characteristics of each book. The metallic silver printing imbues the pages with a graininess, separating the images from their backgrounds. Meanwhile, the opacity of the lightweight paper used for the six chapter openers fuses the printing on both sides of these pages into singular motifs. The section that would perhaps be of most interest to designers is the facsimile of the original jury sheets.

Design
Jule Erner and Robert Radziejewski

Art Direction
Daniel Wiesmann

Writer
Elmar Lixenfeld

Editors
Carolin Blöink, Katharina Hesse, Josefine Kleespies, and Jana Mayer-Stoltz

Bookbindery
Josef Spinner Großbuchbinderei GmbH Ottersweier

Prepress Agency
farbanalyse Cologne

Printer
Gallery Print Berlin

Type Foundry
ABC Dinamo

URL
danielwiesmann.de

Design Firm
Daniel Wiesmann Büro für Gestaltung Berlin

Publisher
Stiftung Buchkunst Frankfurt am Main

Principal Type
Oracle and Oracle Triple

Dimensions
6.5 × 9.4 in.
(16.5 × 24 cm)

BOOKS: SOMETHING LIKE A PHENOMENON

Concept
Belgian artist Sharon Van Overmeiren's artistic practice of freely referencing a broad variety of historic and contemporary sources that are being transformed and amalgamated into her works is applied to the sphere of book design: The layout of each section/chapter typographically references an already existing book that is related in one way or another to Van Overmeiren's specific process and body of work. The cover is designed with a custom lettering consisting of shapes and forms from the artist's visual vocabulary.

Design
Hagen Verleger°

Writers
Koen Bulckens, Paul de Lange, and Václav Janoščík Belgium and Czech Republic

Editor
Gunther De Wit

URL
hagenverleger.com

Twitter
@HagenVerleger

Design Firm
Hagen Verleger— Typography, Book Design, Research Berlin

Publisher
Damien & The Love Guru Brussels

Principal Type
Monotype Baskerville, Bauer Bodoni, and FF Super Grotesk

Dimensions
8.3 × 11 in. (21 × 28 cm)

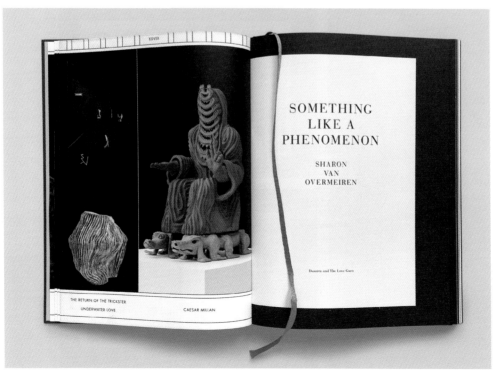

BOOKS: EUCLID—TYPEFACE MYSTERY NO. 1

Concept

Euclid—Typeface Mystery No. 1 is a multidisciplinary triptych
constructed from three main components that are skillfully interwoven
with one another: At the heart of the book is a mystery novel that
M. Michel has written specifically for this purpose. Hubertus Design
brought in Matthieu Gafsou. The Franco-Swiss artist contributed
a series of photographs that augment the book with a rich pictorial
layer. And then there's the Euclid typeface, which is used to set all text.
The combined outcome is just as beautiful as it is disturbing, and a
creation that cannot be categorized. A truly next-level type specimen.

Design Firm
Hubertus
Zürich

Client
Swiss Typefaces
Vevey, Switzerland

URL
swisstypefaces.com

Principal Type
Euclid

Dimensions
9.4 × 12.2 in. (24 × 31cm)

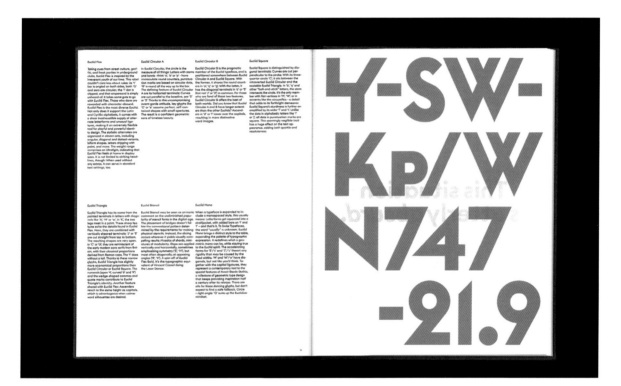

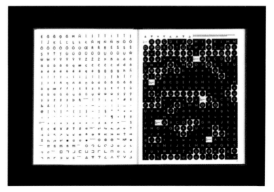

BOOKS: SUMMER READING

Concept

Summer Reading is an exhibition catalog. The book uses a system of bright colors, subtle type size shifts (changing line by line to always be fully justified without hyphenation), and peculiar page dimensions (a tall object, the book is about the width of a phone but takes full advantage of the printer's tabloid sheet size) to call the reader's attention to the act of reading. Each page's content is presented in a single, long column. Its screen-printed corrugated cardboard covers are made to easily ship through the U.S. postal system without additional packaging.

Design
Ben Denzer
Boston

Binding
Sarah Smith

Screen Printing
Melissa Guido

URL
centerforbookarts.org/
book-shop/catalogs/
summer-reading

Publisher
Center for Book Arts

Principal Type
Arial and JB Bingo

Dimensions
2.75 × 16.5 in.
(7 × 40.5 cm)

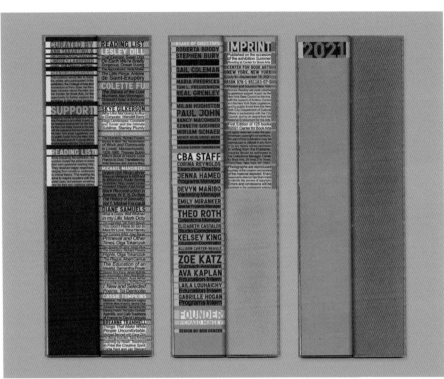

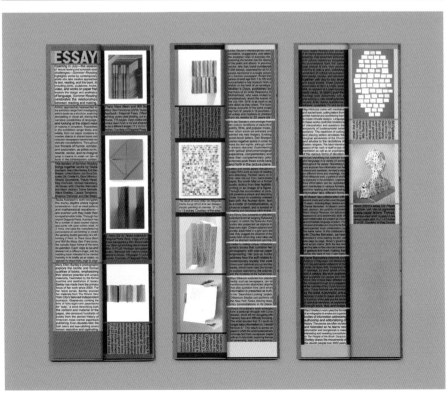

BOOKS: HANBOOKS 17

Concept
Thirty-four printed sheets in small format, separated by two paper colors and handmade burlap, express the concept of seventeen paths. The text layout of each book comes from the original book, while the multilayered presentation of the seventeen books includes the environment and people, book shadows, close-ups, and messages.

Design
Jin Huang,
Qing Zhao,
and Tao Zhu

Design Firm
Nanjing Han Qing
Tang Design
Nanjing

Publisher
Phoenix Fine Arts
Publishing

Principal Type
宋体 (Li Song Pro),
Helvetica, and
Times Roman

Dimensions
7.1 × 4.7 in.
(18 × 12 cm)

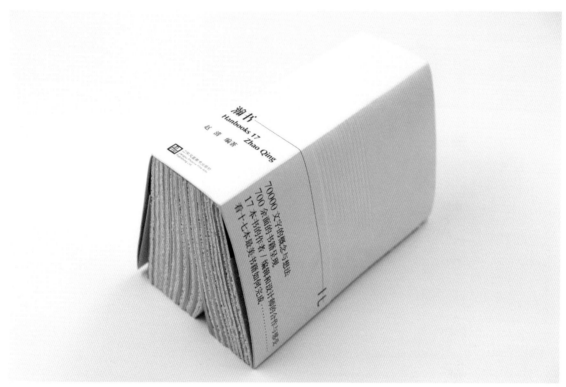

BOOKS: SHAPE GRAMMARS

Concept
Everything visible has shape. Everything can be reduced to its outline, a graphic figure, in black-and-white, light and nonlight. Grammar, on the other hand, is connected with language, something that is invisible as long as we do not put it in the form of letters. However, like linguistic formulations and sentences, graphic forms can also be constructed according to grammatical rules. If one can formulate the rules of a system, one can translate them into machine-readable code and thus let the drawing of countless variations be done by a computer. These rules are called Shape Grammars.

Design
Jannis Maroscheck

Advisor
Gertrud Nolte

Publishing Direction
Lars Harmsen
and Julia Kahl

URL
maroscheck.de

Twitter
@jannimaroscheck

Studio
Jannis Maroscheck
Berlin

Publisher
Slanted Publishers
Karlsruhe

Principal Type
Akzidenz Grotesk

Dimensions
7.3 × 9.25 in.
(18.5 × 23.5 cm)

BOOKS: SUEURS FROIDES COLLECTION—ÉDITIONS DENOËL

Art Direction
Raymond Lanctot

Creative Direction
Daniel Robitaille

Design Firm
Paprika
Montréal

Client
Éditions Denoël

Principal Type
Bâtard Grotesque

BOOKS: THE LYRICS, PAUL MCCARTNEY

Concept
We set out to create a confident, elegant, lively package that honored the bold nature of Paul McCartney's monumental influence in our culture. For both editions of the book, we used eye-catching colors, custom designed typography, handwriting from Paul's personal notebooks, and rich production finishes to achieve the look. We wanted the experience of looking at this package to feel like you were getting deeper into Paul's mind as you peeled off the layers from the clean typographic exterior to the grungy raw book boards. The spreads are designed to ensure legibility while infusing you with energy and excitement.

Design
David Heasty
and Stefanie Weigler
Triboro
New York

Exterior Art Director
Steven Attardo

Interior Art Director
Anna Oler

Typeface Design
Triboro with Omnibus

Publishers
Liveright and
W. W. Norton &
Company New York

Client
MPL
London

Principal Type
Rigby and Rigby Display

Dimensions
8.5 × 10.75 in.
(21.5 × 27 cm)

Rigby

RIGBY DISPLAY

Golden Slumbers
HELTER SKELTER
Lady Madonna
BACK IN THE USSR
Blackbird
YESTERDAY
A Fool on the Hill
CALICO SKIES
All My Loving

BOOKS: GUFTGU

Concept

The "Guftgu" title unit features a custom ligature and has the warm contours of a classic serif to offset the crisp countenance of Neue Haas Grotesk, which has been used throughout the rest of the publication. An industrial, unornamented aesthetic was maintained for the box, with holes in the spine, for ease of pulling from the shelf, and the choice of the cardboard material. The zines themselves were customized to each artist's work. The underlying grid system, and the classic, unobtrusive cover page design and typography were kept consistent.

Design
Ananya Khaitan

Design Firm
Novel
New Delhi

Client
Offset Projects

Principal Type
ITC Garamond and
Neue Haas Grotesk

Dimensions
6.5 × 10.7 in.
(16.5 × 27.2 cm)

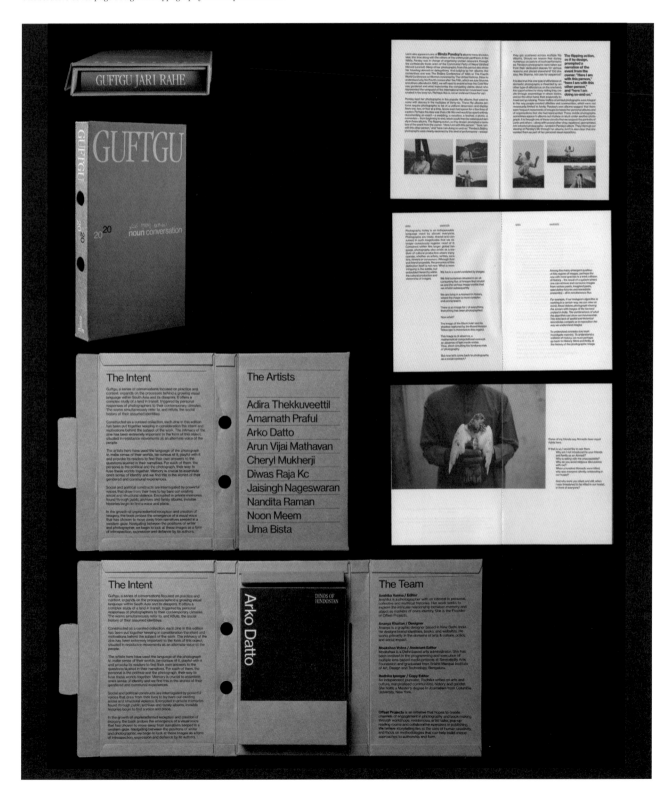

BOOKS: HISTORY OF CHINESE CHARACTER DESIGN

Concept
The title of the book uses seven Chinese characters to show the course of evolution. Black-and-white is the visual impression of Chinese character art. The cover is black with a rough texture, and the book box is white. The first page of each chapter is illustrated with Chinese characters.

Professor
Nan Chen

Design Firms
Research Center of Ancient Chinese Characters Art, Tsinghua University, and Six Sense Studio Beijing

Studio
Chen Nan

Principal Type
Hanzi Sheji Shi (the Chinese title on the cover is a typeface design that combines the collected ancient Chinese characters

from different historical periods corresponding to the Chinese title of the book), Fangzheng Baosong, and Helvetica.

Dimensions
31 × 43 in.
(78.7 × 109.2 cm)

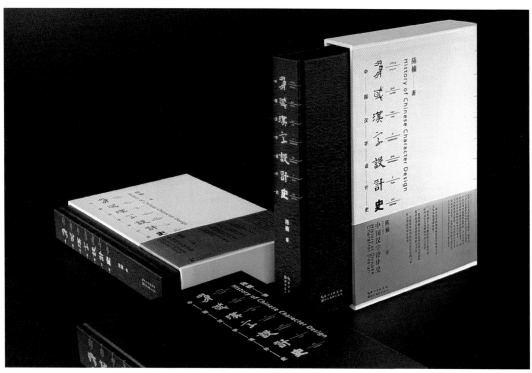

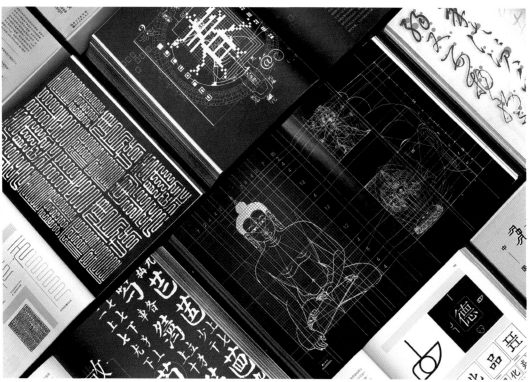

BOOKS: DATA CENTERS

Concept

Between black-and-white illustrated text articles on gray paper and in a uniform layout to create the appropriate impression of dry information transfer, four-color photo essays are inserted, which transfer the sterile aesthetics of the server stations into glossy photos—always one per page or double page. The asymmetrical text layouts with the footnotes running from left to right across the entire width in an unusual manner have an extremely dynamic effect. They do not always coincide exactly with the main text but give the impression of multilayered information that results in a stream of data flowing in regular cadence.

Design Firm
Hubertus
Zürich

Client
Monika Dommann,
Hannes Rickli, and
Max Stadler

Principal Type
Monument Grotesk

Dimensions
7.5 × 10.2 in. (19 × 26 cm)

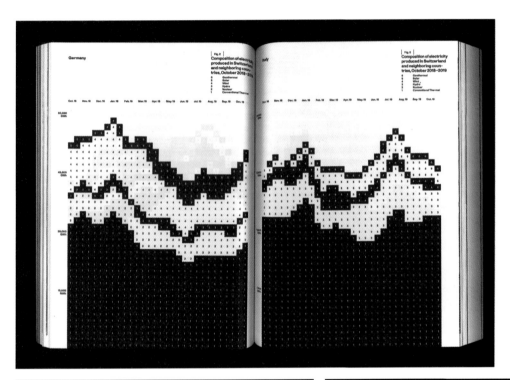

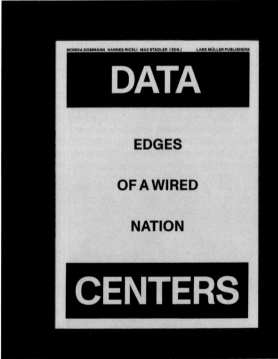

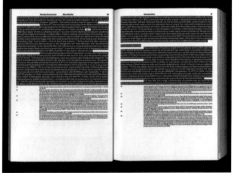

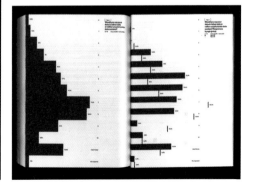

BOOKS: KOMPASS BY FRANK GERRITZ

Concept
The body of work from a minimal artist deserves a design concept following the same math-like principles: logical structures instead of expression.

Writer
Jadwiga Kamola

Editors
Christina Haas and
Jadwiga Kamola

Photography
Dirk Mabaum
Hamburg

Design Firm
Bank™
Berlin

Client
Galerie Michael Haas

Principal Type
Gramatika Bold

Dimensions
8.9 × 11.2 in.
(22.5 × 28.5 cm)

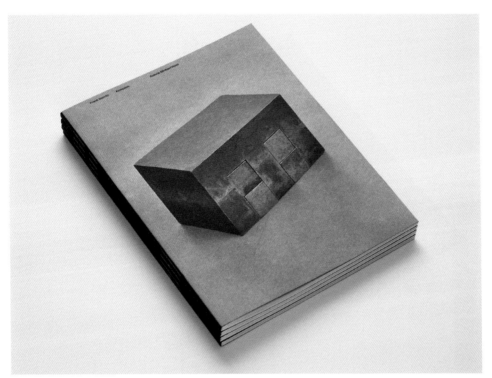

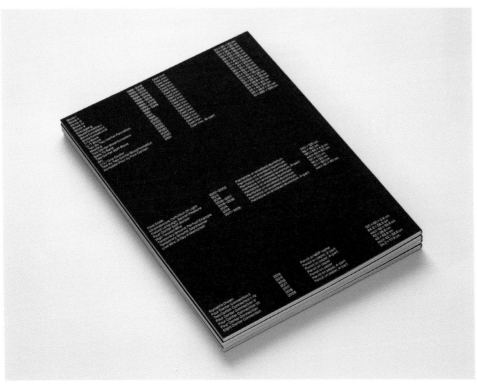

BOOKS: CRISIS OF NOW

Concept

The visuals for the exhibition series Crisis of Now (2018–2020) have been constantly developing over the past few years, though it is important to us that each year's exhibition form its own visual system. We switch colors, add new forms, and change the typesetting rules for each year and each publication. The only thing that stays constant is the elegant font composition. Burrow executed various visual elements for the exhibitions, which always included some silk screen-printed elements and the large-format publication with generously laid-out imagery.

Design Firm
Burrow
Berlin

Instagram
@imburrow

Client
IDOLONSTUDIO
(Chun-chi Wang)

Principal Type
Self Modern Italic and
Self Modern Regular

Dimensions
9.8 × 14.2 in. (25 x 36 cm)

BOOKS: BIFT GRADUATION WORKS BA, CLASS OF 2021

Concept
The redesigned Morse Code English font is applied on the cover of the book; the pulling structure formed by the fluorescent PVC and the book itself makes the words appear as abstract symbols. When the book is pulled out completely, we can see all the information on the cover, reflecting the connotation of the theme of the year's graduation season. Two dots in different forms represent "Eyes," and the image of the eyes is applied throughout the book.

Design Firm
Mint Brand Design
Beijing

Client
Bift

Principal Type
Hanyiqihei and F37 Jan

Dimensions
7.1 × 9.8 in. (18 × 25 cm)

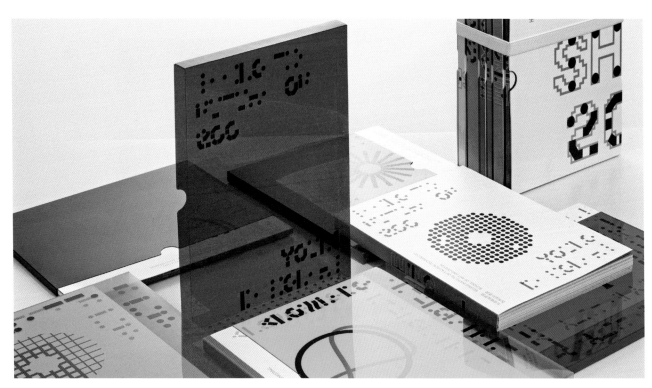

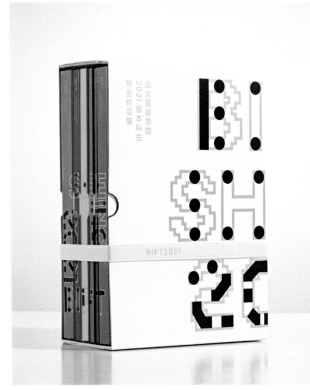

BOOKS: SEASON BOOKLET 2021-22

Concept

At last, the state of emergency seems to be over. But to what normality are we returning? Will the status quo be maintained? Or will new opportunities and possibilities open up? With exciting illustrations, we set the mood for a thrilling theatrical year. Each collage interweaves with the core of the play, opening up another nonverbal narrative level. The booklet repeatedly breaks with the visual expectations of the viewer. In addition to the theater texts in typographical New Objectivity, great ensemble portraits and lots of information complement the handy softcover. 168 pages.

Art Direction
Nina Odzinieks,
Flo Paizs, and
Pit Stenkhoff

Design Firm
Neue Gestaltung GmbH
Berlin

Client
Theater Erlangen

Principal Type
Neue Haas Unica
Pro and Rhymes

Dimensions
6.5 × 9.4 in. (16.5
x 24 cm)

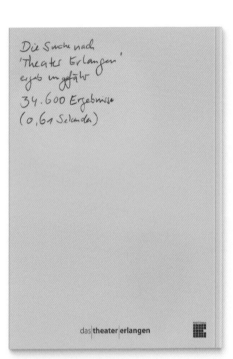

Was ihr wollt
Komödie von William Shakespeare
Premiere: 24.09.21
Markgrafentheater

Auf der erfundenen Insel Illyrien entspinnt sich ein Liebes- und Verwechslungsspiel mit viel Musik, in dem gängige Rollenklischees ausprobiert und schwungvoll über den Haufen geworfen werden: Vor der Küste erleiden Viola und ihr Zwillingsbruder samt Gefolge Schiffbruch. Im Glauben, ihren Bruder verloren zu haben, landet Viola in Illyrien und tarnt sich als junger Diener Cesario. Dieser wird zum Vertrauten des Herzogs Orsino und soll in dessen Auftrag um die Liebe von Gräfin Olivia werben, die allerdings sieben Jahre um ihren verstorbenen Bruder trauern will. Viola setzt sich in ihrer Männerverkleidung leidenschaftlich für Orsinos Liebe ein, in den sie sich jedoch längst selbst verliebt hat. Um das Chaos komplett zu machen, findet die Gräfin nun am Diener Gefallen statt an dessen Auftraggeber. Cesario/Viola soll Orsino die Abfuhr vermitteln und Olivia schnellstens persönlich über dessen Reaktion informieren. Die Wirrungen nehmen ihren Lauf.

In einem zweiten Handlungsstrang dreht sich alles um eine Intrige rund um Malvolio, Olivias Haushofmeister, eingefädelt von Olivias Kammerfrau Maria und zur Belustigung von zwei einfältigen Herren. Begleitet und beobachtet wird das Spiel von dem Narr Feste, der vielleicht als Einziger in

15

CALENDARS: A CALENDAR OF PLUTO

Concept

The calendar provides a time-oriented connection between us and Pluto. When we live on this plentiful Earth, let us release our soul to the far and silent planet that elapses us with its time. When we travel to the edge of our solar system and find residence on the planet that is astronomical units away from our original home of Earth, let us harmonize the times back to our starting point.

Creative Direction
Lobbin Liu
Shenzhen, China

Engineer
Junqing Qiao

Printing
Songwen Zheng

English Editor
Sissi Liu

Principal Type
Adobe Caslon and
Source Han Serif

Dimensions
23.6 × 4.8 × 7.4 in.
(60 × 12.2 × 18.8 cm)

CALENDARS: THE RING OF TIME CALENDAR

Concept

When all calendars are one page a day, they are not only boring but also environmentally unfriendly. In fact, the calendar can also be a story—a decorative, functional, environmentally friendly product. The year ring is a double-sided calendar designed with the ring as a source of inspiration. Besides the decorative and functional features of the calendar, the designers hope it can arouse people's thinking about time and bring life into the present moment.

Design and Art Direction
He Yuxuan (何宇轩)
Shenzhen (深圳), China

URL
hesign.cn

Studio
hesign Studio

Principal Type
FOT-UDKakugo
Large Pr6N,
Futura PT, and
Futura PT Cond

Dimensions
13.4 × 18.9 in.
(34 × 48 cm)

THE RING OF
TIME CALENDAR

THE RING 年輪 OF TIME 時間
TWO THOUSAND TWENTY-TWO
LIVE IN THE MOMENT 現在に生きる
日暦カレンダー CALENDAR

THE FUTURE IS NOW
現在就是未來

2022   HESIGN.CN   TWO THOUSAND TWENTY-TWO   THE FUTURE IS NOW 今は未来です

CALENDARS: 2021 ANOTHER CALENDAR

Concept
As the name suggests, we hope "another calendar" can be different from the conventional calendar system and reading habits. Our goal was to extend beyond the limited paper space using a graphical design language that considers the multidimensional properties of time, such as diversity, reversibility, and superposition. There seems to be a sense of rebellion here. Anti-rationality, anti-rule, anti-fixing.

Design Firm
out.o studio

URL
outostudio.com

Principal Type
Custom

Dimensions
12 × 10.4 x .7 in. (30.5 x 26.5 × 2 cm)

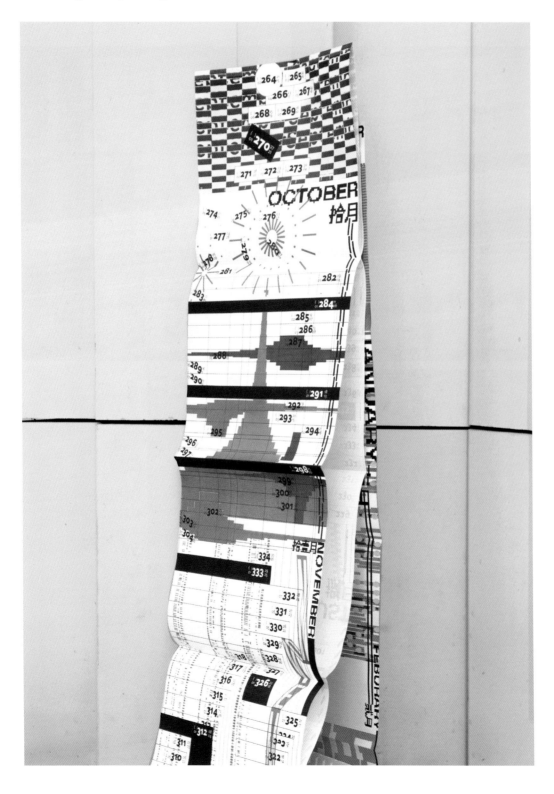

CATALOGS: STANFORD D. SCHOOL: TEACHING + LEARNING YEARBOOK

Concept

The d.school Yearbook is an annual publication for supporters of its Teaching & Learning program. With event and image availability limited during the pandemic, we instead commissioned photographs of empty d.school spaces. Paired with bold typography and a bright palette, the publication captures the team's innovative methods even through uncertain times. Lush, abstract photographs introduce each of the book's three sections, color-coded for easy navigation. 194 pages, perfect bound.

Design and Creative Direction
Daniel Frumhoff and Erica Holeman

Copywriter and Data Scientist
Megan Stariha

Editor
Carissa Carter

Photography
Patrick Beaudouin and Naila Ruechel

Typographers
Daniel Frumhoff and Erica Holeman

Type Foundries
Klim Type Foundry and OH no Type Company

URL
danielfrumhoff.com/ projects/stanford-dschool-teaching-learning-yearbook

Design Firm
Daniel Frumhoff Design New York

Client
Stanford d.school
Stanford, California

Principal Type
Beastly, Neue Haas Unica, and Signifier

Dimensions
8 × 8 in.
(20.3 × 20.3 cm)

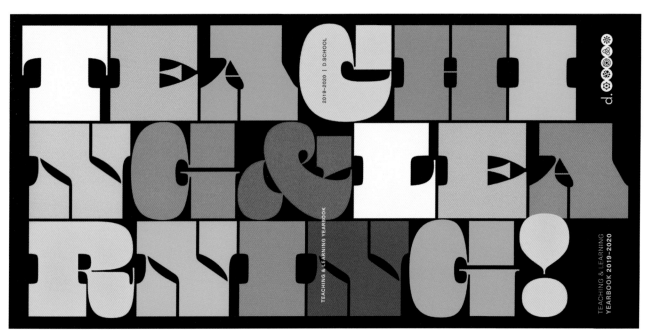

Artist **Naila Ruechel** conceived of and photographed the three section header photos in this yearbook. She created each image to match the specific theme of the section.

In her words:
I draw inspiration from everywhere, but I think on a subconscious level, my work is a direct reflection of my upbringing in Jamaica where I experienced a diversity of flora within a tropical environment. Deep, rich, vibrant colors and a warmth that embraced me like a blanket.

—*Naila Ruechel*

6

Behind
the *Curtain*

About:
Here's a sample of what happens behind the scenes of our curriculum and classes. Read on to learn about the topics that we've explored this year, the projects we've launched, and the feelings and learnings we've had along the way.

TEACHING AND LEARNING

DESIGN FOR SOCIAL GOOD: PLANTING BAMBOO IN THE SOUTH

Concept

The posters, designed with textual layouts, are rolled up and inserted into the bamboo forest surrounding the southern village, creating an artistic scene of a realistic bamboo forest that grows throughout the mountains to draw attention to the ecology and culture of this remote area.

Design Firm
By-Enjoy Design
Fujian, China

Clients
Half of the Mountain Art Space and Southern Living Arts Festival

Principal Type
Shu Song and Simplified Chinese

Dimensions
27.6 × 39.4 in.
(70 × 100 cm)

关中荆溪村位于荆溪镇西北八公里处，座落关源中心，距县城11公里，村东背靠福州市西北郊区（关东与西山关相对；隔山相连；毗邻六墩前；南洲村和仁村邻；全村耕地面积3,000余亩，山林

地面积1122亩，森林覆盖率80%以上达总户8600，全村27985游仙人，大源、石岩、里洋、下料、前元、安邦、王坂、村尾、然尾，11个自然村。

关中村地博适宜开种合综目业综合，发展农业，橄榄种植面积200余亩，2000水稻种植面积1500亩，面种植1500蔬菜种植5000亩发，资源优势，挥发竹木加工发展，日益人杰地灵。

与友好客，周边地点，里店白石屿，山坡徐洋山坡沙下洋，王廖，前园田，龙兄笠里，坑里，南尾榕树主，产品：李青豆，青干梅，桑南，莲藕，瓜子，小青。

DESIGN FOR SOCIAL GOOD: SOCIAL DISTANCING: ANIMATED TYPE

Concept
This is a typographic animation created to promote social distancing during the earlier days of the pandemic. It animates the concept of social distancing and staying home and away from others as much as possible to help prevent the spread of COVID-19.

Design, Animation, and Creative Direction
Daniel Frumhoff

URL
vimeo.com/429080292

Design Firm
Daniel Frumhoff Design
New York

Type Foundry
Lineto Type Foundry

Principal Type
Replica

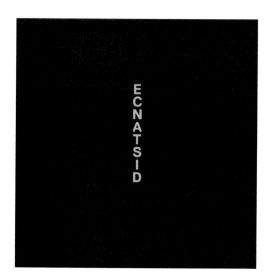
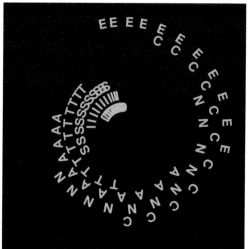

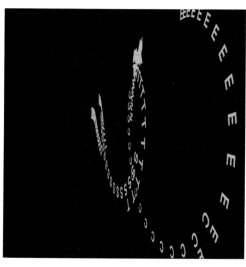
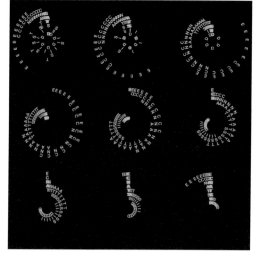

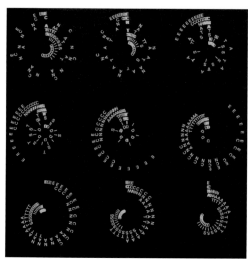
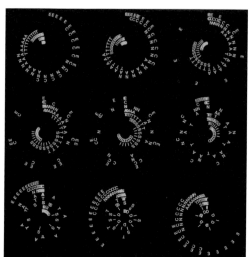

DESIGN FOR SOCIAL GOOD: THE ISSUE WITHIN THE ISSUE

Concept
Typography was carefully considered when creating "The Issue Within the Issue." We wanted our typography to balance being bold and serious and being hopeful and uplifting. Aiming to create a powerful visual impact, we used strong and loud typography as an expression to illustrate the unignorable struggles that homeless LGBTQ+ youths face in New York City, and the significant efforts of the Ali Forney Center to combat the issue. While shedding light on a serious issue, we also wanted to represent the fun spirits, optimism, and tenacity of the LGBTQ+ community through our use of typography..

Design
Paul Martinez

Art Direction
Hamza Ali,
Julie Rosenoff,
Rudy Troncone,
and Camille Walker

Creative Direction
Katharine Flynn

Chief Creative Officer
Dan Lucey

Chief Design Officer
Brian Lai

Executive Creative Direction
Bharat Kumar and
Marcelo Ramirez

Executive Producer
Melissa Tifrere

Director
Sal Migliaccio

Copywriting
Patrick Chase, Nick Malone, Carlos Matias, and Jp Winders

Editor
Oussama Zahr

Product Manager
Valentine Roche

Strategist
Alexis De Montaigu

User Experience Design
Janice Chen

Executive Director, Ali Forney Center
Alexander Roque

Founder
Carl Siciliano

Agency
Havas New York

Client
Ali Forney Center/
New York Magazine

Principal Type
Bleeny, Dida, Roboto, and Sen

DESIGN FOR SOCIAL GOOD: ONE MICHIGAN REBRAND

Concept

One Michigan is an immigrant-led grassroots organization based in Southwest Detroit. Their mission is to center youth and empower teenagers to become leaders in their community. One Michigan remains one of the few undocumented-led immigrant rights organizations in the country. I've learned so much from One Michigan over the years, and I am grateful to have had the opportunity to design their new visual identity. The new logo was inspired by the journey of immigration, as well as by the serpent, which carries symbolical meanings of dualism, transformation, and honor in cultures all around the world.

Design
Beatriz Lozano
New York

Client
One Michigan

Principal Type
Kawak Black and
Kawak Light

Dimensions
22 × 28 in.
(55.9 × 71.1 cm)

LED BY IMMIGRANT YOUTH & SUPPORTED BY STRONG ALLIES

DESIGN FOR SOCIAL GOOD: LET PARENTS STAY (HAN EMBROIDERY TYPEFACE)

Concept

Jinling Village is a poverty-stricken village with more than 2,000 "left-behind" children. When the designer got there, he was surprised to find that all the local people had mastered certain Han Embroidery skills, but their product did not sell well because of the old-fashioned style. So he worked with the Hubei Han Embroidery Association to help revive the local Han Embroidery culture..

Design and Art Direction
Yu Chen, China

URL
yuchen-creative.com

Client
Hubei Han Embroidery Association

Principal Type
Custom

DESIGN FOR SOCIAL GOOD: ALL POWER TO THE PEOPLE

Concept
The concept for this type is driven by resilience and
resistance of Black folks throughout the history of
Black freedom struggles. The type is gritty, raw, and
direct. Elements of Black movement work across
generations. In both the inspiration for the concept
and in its application, it is about and for the people.

Agency
Blackbird Revolt
Minneapolis

URL
blackbirdrevolt.com

Twitter
@BlackbirdRevolt

Principal Type
Stop Killing
Black People

Dimensions
12 × 12 in.
(30.5 × 30.5 cm)

DESIGN FOR SOCIAL GOOD:
NEW WAYS OF SEARCH READING MAGAZINES BY STUDENTS

Concept

As a typographic research student, I explore solutions to bridge gaps between design practice and empirical research to improve reading. This Ph.D. project aims to improve and innovate students' navigation in complex texts linked to index-typography by means of search tasks and reading comprehension. Especially in this era of digitalization and ever more fragmented, nonlinear reading, students need extended (search) reading possibilities. This pioneering set of magazine designs is used as test material for testing and educational purposes. It is based on my previous design research outcomes and three design preference tests among over 150 student participants thus far.

Design
Janneke Janssen
Maastricht, Belgium

Cultural Institutions
Research Foundation—
Flanders (FWO) and
READSEARCH
(MAD-Research &
Hasselt University)
Brussels and
Hasselt, Belgium

Principal Type
Suisse Int'l and
Suisse Works

Dimensions
52.8 × 87.4 in.
(13.4 × 22.2 cm)

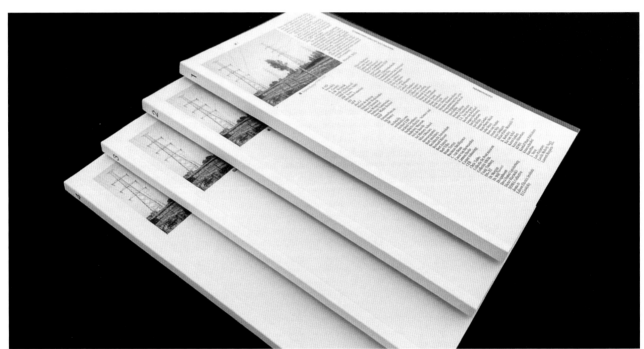

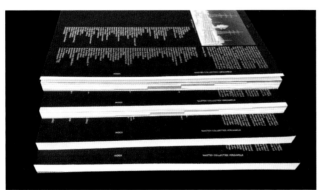

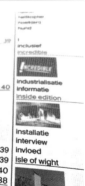

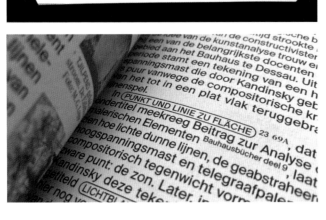

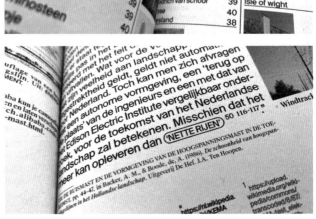

DIGITAL MEDIA: GALERIA INDEX WEBSITE

Concept

The objective of the website design was to convey the feeling of an index through organized layouts that can contain a vast amount of information. The website was inspired by the old yellow list books. The concept of the index appears with a list of artists in the A-to-Z style, employed to represent the zeitgeist of the local art scene.

Creative Direction
Marcos Mendes
Manente, Manufatura
Brasilia, Brazil

Production Company
FRONT

URL
galeriaindex.com

Type Foundry
Plau
Rio de Janeiro

Design Firm
Twoo®
Barcelona

Client
Galeria Index

Principal Type
Vinila

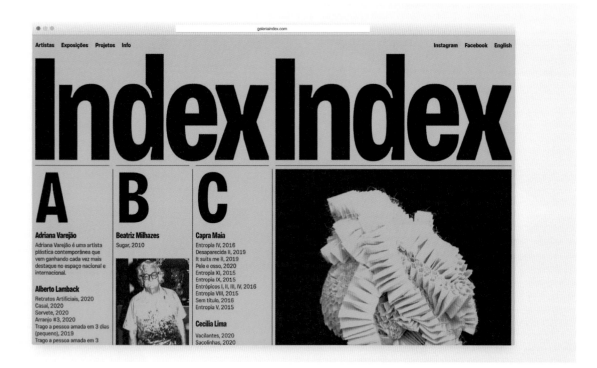

DIGITAL MEDIA: KHOJ WEBSITE

Concept

Khoj, an artists' association, has a quarter-century of programming that its website needed to house. To bring order to this sprawling body of work while keeping the artists and their work at the forefront, a clean and unobtrusive visual language was created. The mono-linear Roobert by Displaay Type, with its crisp and contemporary forms, was chosen as the primary typeface. It was also selected for its variable thickness, used throughout the site in conjunction with the user's scroll behavior. Cooper BT Light was chosen as the secondary typeface, appearing in tooltip instructions and as rotating badges.

Design
Hamsa Ganesh and
Ananya Khaitan

Developers
Ashwin Chandran
and Akshat Kedia

Design Firms
Novel and Thoughtput
New Delhi and
Pune, India

Client
Khoj

Principal Type
Cooper BT
and Roobert

DIGITAL MEDIA: HEY BARISTA PUBLISHING PLATFORM

Concept
Isometric collaborated with the Swedish oat milk company Oatly to design Hey Barista, an online publishing platform that reveals the dreams and aspirations of baristas, whether they are in it for good or are working hard to pursue other passions while supporting themselves financially through serving coffee. The visual identity and website highlight musings, art, and ideas from the barista community, serving as a love letter and a window into their lives beyond the coffee counter.

Design
Dan Abary

Creative Direction
Maria Loes and
Hannah Meng

URL
isometricstudio.com

Partners
Andy Chen and
Waqas Jawaid

Design Firm
Isometric Studio
Brooklyn, New York

Client
Oatly

Principal Type
GT Alpina

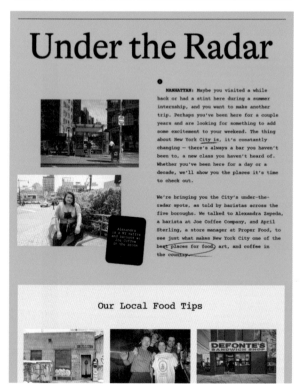

DIGITAL MEDIA: INTERACTIVE INFOGRAPHIC SCIENCE STACK: TOOLS WITHIN REACH

Concept

Low-cost and open-source tools are transforming the field of science, encouraging new users and generating data that will make a broader impact with new discoveries. These physical tools are significantly less expensive and expand participation to a larger community of makers. The design of open-source tools is made publicly available so that anyone can study, modify, distribute, make, and sell hardware based on that design. "Science Stack: Tools Within Reach" is an interactive infographic that demonstrates the diversity of open-source tools and low-cost hardware.

Design
Ting Fang Cheng
and Talia Cotton
New York

Partner
Giorgia Lupi

**Strategy and
New Business Lead**
Phillip Cox

Intern
Tara Magloire

URL
wilsoncenter.org/
sciencestack

Design Firm
Pentagram Design°

Client
Wilson Center

Principal Type
Libre Franklin and
Space Mono

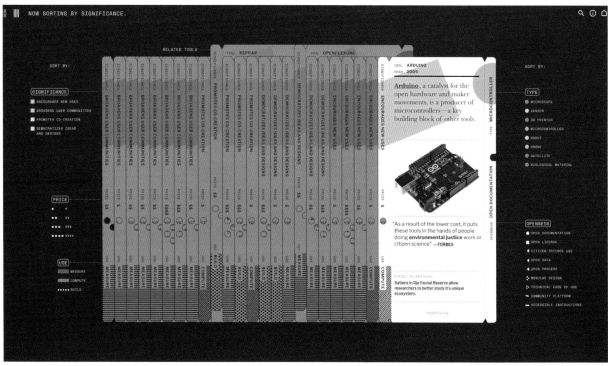

DIGITAL MEDIA: HELLO SCREEN SAVER

Concept
This design concept celebrates the introduction of the new iMac with an expressive, animated, three-dimensional greeting that nods to the legacy of the Macintosh.

In-House Agency
Apple Design Team
Cupertino, California

Principal Type
Various

DIGITAL MEDIA: WEBSITE DESIGN FOR SYROSFILMFESTIVAL.ORG

Concept

Cinema, workshops, talks, art, music, all combined in one festival. Syros International Film Festival is a multidisciplinary festival, and each part of it is reflected through a unique shape. Shapes that are peculiar, odd, interesting, mismatched, different, all together make a new identity and define the festival as a unique experience.

Design
Korina Gallika
Athens

Art Direction
Stefanos Andreadis

Creative Direction
Katerina Papanagiotou

Design Firm
MNP

Digital Agency
Tool

Client
Syros International
Film Festival (SIFF)

Principal Type
Helvetica

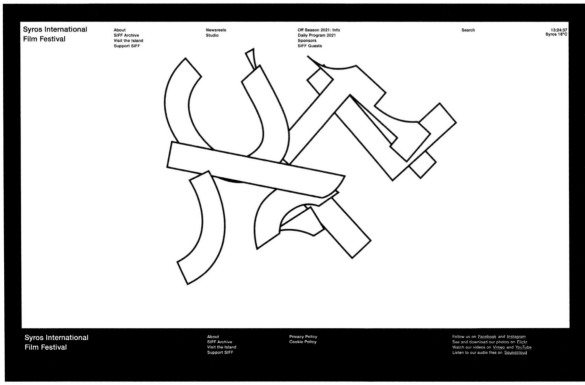

DIGITAL MEDIA: PLASTIC AIR

Concept
You can't see it, but plastic is floating in the air all around us. What happens to plastic items when we dispose of them? They degrade into smaller and smaller pieces called microplastics, which then end up within the air we breathe. "Plastic Air" is a web-based, interactive experience that vivifies a type of pollution that most people don't even know exists: airborne microplastic deposition, the result of ever-increasing global plastic production and consumption. The experience provides a lens through which to "see" and to explore the invisible plastic particles that are ever-present in the atmosphere around us.

Design
Ting Fang Cheng and Talia Cotton

Partner
Giorgia Lupi

Strategy and New Business Lead
Phillip Cox

URL
artsexperiments. withgoogle.com/ plasticair

Design Firm
Pentagram New York°

Client
Google Arts & Culture

Principal Type
Epilogue

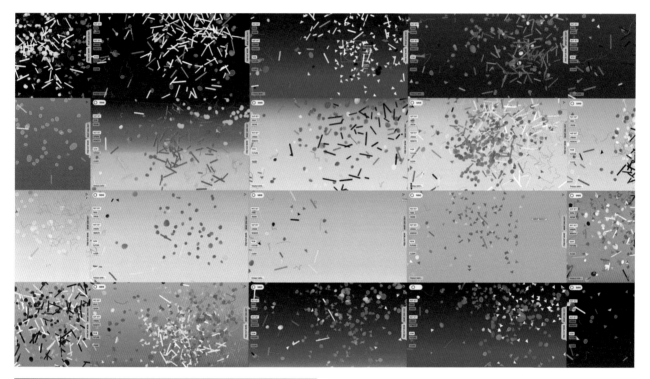

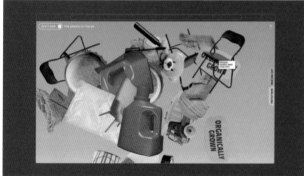

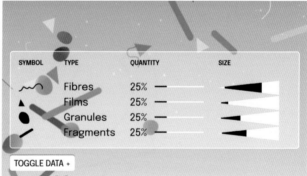

DIGITAL MEDIA: THE NEW PARACHUTE WEBSITE

Concept
Parachute's achievements were downplayed by its previous online presence. After two years in development, the brand wanted to deliver an elevated e-commerce experience and offer a transparent look into the world of Parachute Typefoundry. The website's grid structure, which combines a swipe-and-scroll experience, showcases full-screen animations of detailed typeface imagery and limited-edition goods in an environment that makes the beauty of the letterform stand out.

Design
Joshua Olsthoorn
and Kostas Vlachakis
Athens

Art Direction
Manos Daskalakis

Creative Direction
Panos Vassiliou°

Editor
Loukas Karnis

Web Development
Sofar
Zakynthos, Greece

URL
parachutefonts.com

Design Firms
Parachute Type
Foundry and Typical
Organization

Principal Type
Das Grotesk Mono,
Marlet, and Regal

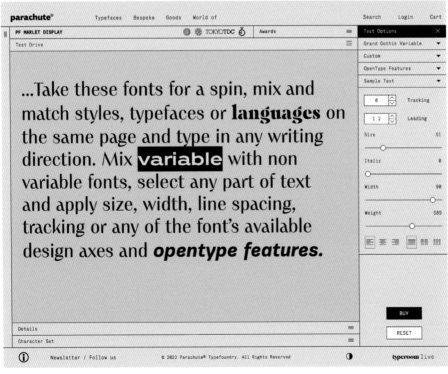

EDITORIAL: FESTIVAL RÜMLINGEN PROGRAMMBUCH

Concept
The Swiss author Robert Walser wrote texts in a tiny font he developed himself. At first glance, the pages look as if they consist only of grids and surfaces. The program book is oriented on these pages and aims to reproduce a similar aesthetic by incorporating the grid elements and the special layout.

Agency
Neeser & Müller
Basel

URL
neesermueller.ch

Client
Neue Musik Rümlingen

Principal Type
NN Rekja

Dimensions
5.9 × 9 in. (15 × 23 cm)

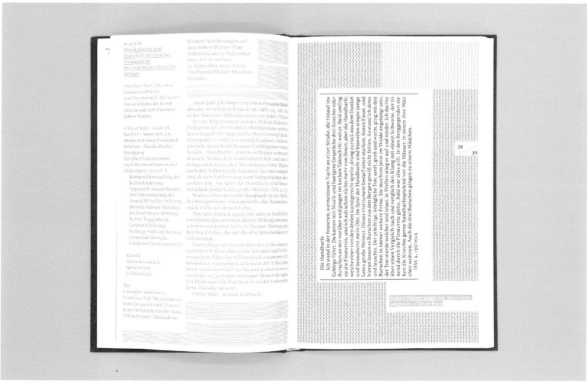

EDITORIAL: CHOREOGRAPHIE

Concept
The goal was to create a zine that would represent an ode to movement, using only type deconstruction. Rudolf Laban established choreology, the discipline of movement notation, by creating a system for recording and analyzing human movement: Laban Notation or Kinetography Laban. Laban Movement Notation (LMN) considers four factors in the analysis of movement: space, time, flow, and weight. These are the key concepts that encompass this publication.

Design
Maria João Vilaverde
Portugal

URL
linkedin.com/in/maria-vilaverde-951974186

Twitter
@maria_vilaverde

Principal Type
Gill Sans

Dimensions
5.1 × 7.1 in.
(13 × 18 cm)

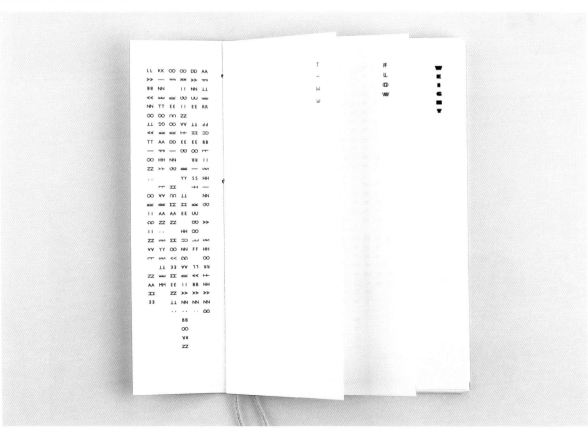

EDITORIAL: FASHION ISSUE TYPOGRAPHY

Concept

This is the guest typeface for Süddeutsche Zeitung commissioned by the great AD Birthe Steinbeck. Due to the pandemic, this fashion issue relied heavily on collage, and the twelve numerals (corresponding to twelve "weird" months) captured the spirit of collage by exploiting the tension of mixing hard and round forms together. The typeface itself is a revival of one of the oldest heavy sans on record, Zeitungs-Grotesque, which was published in 1874 by the Danzig-based Francke type foundry.

Design
A.A. Trabucco-Campos
Brooklyn, New York

Art Direction
Birthe Steinbeck

Publisher
Süddeutsche Zeitung
Munich

Principal Type
Zeitungs-Grotesque
(revival)

Professor Drosten, wann darf ich endlich wieder allein am Tresen sitzen und unglücklich sein, mir einen einsamen Drink nach dem nächsten reinstellen und dabei langsam immer weniger unglücklich werden, aber doch unglücklich genug bleiben, um die Welt mit empfindlichen Augen zu sehen, die klare Kälte draußen vor den Fenstern, den warmen Nebel im Innern, die Gesichter der Menschen, die miteinander reden und lachen und sich aneinanderlehnen und dabei ihre Aerosole ausatmen und verquirlen und sie zusammen mit den Seelencocktails aller Anwesenden wieder einatmen, ganz tief und frei von Angst, während die Musik den Raum über der Theke füllt, und jetzt kommt jemand rein, schon wieder einer mehr, schon wieder wird der Laden voller, schon wieder erst ein Lächeln mehr und dann ein Lachen, und voller werden auch die Köpfe, die unerhörte Dichte an Körpern geht durch Mark und Bein, und trotzdem bleiben manche allein, mit ihrem ewigen Scheiß, nie so ganz vermittelbar, nie so ganz dazugehörig, immer mitten daneben, wie das eben ist, auch im echten Leben, das tut schon weh, wenn es einem dämmert und gerade dann, wenn es dämmert, aber hier drin ist es leichter auszuhalten, denn die anderen sind doch da, ja: auch noch da – wann geht das wieder, Professor Drosten?
    —— Simone Buchholz

8

Die Lokalspezialität –
warum man die Einsamkeit in
Gesellschaft vermissen kann

LINKS OBEN: LOCHSTRICKPULLOVER UND HOSE MIT BUNTEN FARBSPRENKELN, VON DIOR. SCHWARZE SCHNÜRSCHUHE VON CHURCH'S. MITTE UND RECHTS: WEISSES KLEID MIT GEOMETRISCHEN CUT-OUTS, VON MARCO. HIGHHEELS VON LOUIS VUITTON. UNTEN: ROSAFARBENER JUMPSUIT MIT RAFFUNG, VON VÉRONIQUE LEROY. OHRRINGE »ELSA PERETTI DIAMOND HOOP« VON TIFFANY & CO.

46 SÜDDEUTSCHE ZEITUNG MAGAZIN

Das Miteinander-Gehen –
Herzen synchronisieren

EDITORIAL: TRICK OR TREAT?

Concept
In keeping with The New York Times' dedication to innovating in print, The New York Times for Kids produces these singular, visually driven, print-only broadsheet sections. The New York Times for Kids is published monthly, with a new issue in the paper on the last Sunday of each month. Since their inception in 2016, these sections have become a much-anticipated feature of the Sunday paper. This section aims to entertain and stimulate kids, to engage them creatively with the news while never talking down..

Design
Mia Meredith

Design Director
Deb Bishop

Senior Designer
Fernanda Didini

Photography
Keirnan Monaghan and
Theo Vamvounakis

Stylist
Jodi Levine

Cover Artist
Mark Ryden

Centerspread Artist
Amandine Urruty

Contributing Artists
Gary Baseman,
Paul Blow, Kelsey Dake,
Super Freak,
Renee French,
Eddie Guy,
Kyle Hilton,
Conor Langton,
Mikyung Lee,
Max Loeffler,
Travis Louie,
John Kenn Mortensen,
Christian Northeast,
Sara Tyson, and
Seo Young

Publication
The New York
Times Magazine
New York

Principal Type
Various

Dimensions
12 × 22 in.
(30.5 × 56 cm)

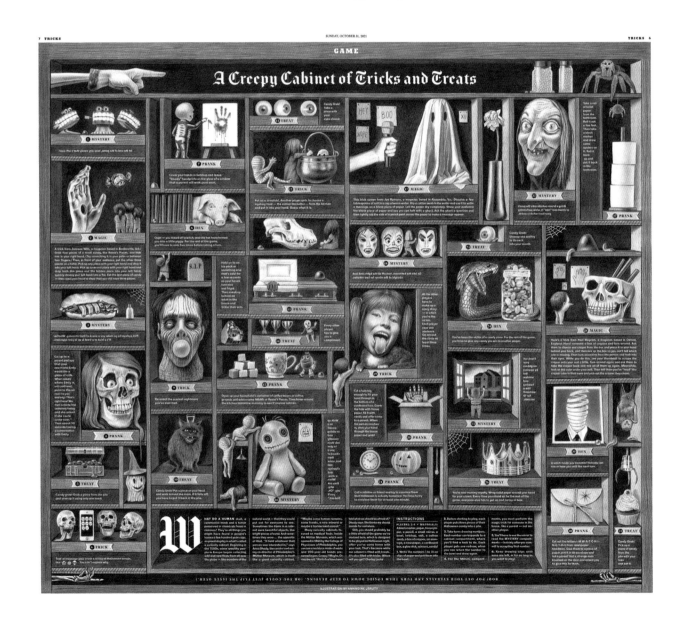

EDITORIAL: PITTOGRAMMA 01—CARATTERI INEDITI

Concept

Caratteri Inediti is the second issue of Pittogramma and features seven unpublished typefaces designed by type design students. Accompanying the type design projects the publication includes a text written by Michele Patanè and Alessio D'Ellena that describes the process and criteria that guided the selection of the projects, artwork by Collletttivo on the back cover, and a cover text written by type designer Joseph Miceli. The publication not only aims to showcase projects developed by promising talents but to map the current state of the type design discipline in the Italian territory.

Design

Fabio Mario Rizzotti
and Santiago Villa

Post-Production Company

CDcromo
Milan

URL

fmrizzotti.it

Typographers

Michele D'Ellena
and Michele Patanè
Superness, Milan
and London

Printer

Grafiche Veneziane
Venice

Principal Type

Adelphi, ABC Diatype,
Enea, Fano, Gesto,
Impressum,
AT Opale, Permanent,
and Pompilia

Dimensions

9.4 × 13.2 in.
(24 × 33.6 cm)

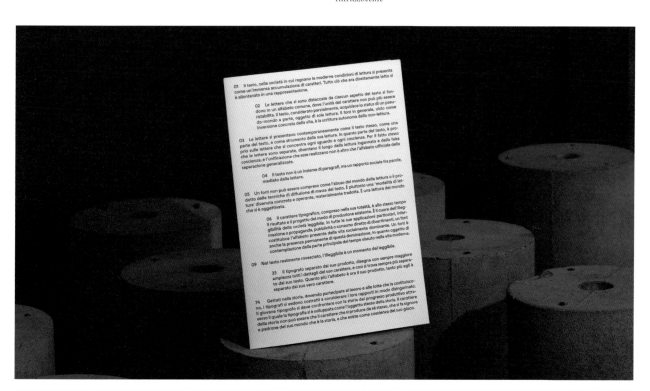

EDITORIAL: THE MONEY ISSUE

Concept
In keeping with The New York Times' dedication to innovating in print, The New York Times for Kids produces these singular, visually driven, print-only broadsheet sections. The New York Times for Kids is published monthly, with a new issue in the paper on the last Sunday of each month. Since their inception in 2016, these sections have become a much anticipated feature of the Sunday paper. This section aims to entertain and stimulate kids, to engage them creatively with the news while never talking down.

Design
Mia Meredith

Art Direction
Ken DeLago

Creative Direction
Gail Bichler°

Design Director
Deb Bishop

Photography
Brenda Ann Kennally and Diana King

Cover and Centerspread Artist
Tom Gauld

Contributing Artists
Raymond Biesinger, Paul Blow, Mishant Choksi, Greg Clarke, Kate Dehlr, Giacomo Gambineri, Jon McNaught, Cristina Spanó, and Tomi Um

Publication
The New York Times Magazine

Principal Type
NYT Mag Sans and NYT Mag Serif

Dimensions
12 × 22 in.
(30.5 × 56 cm)

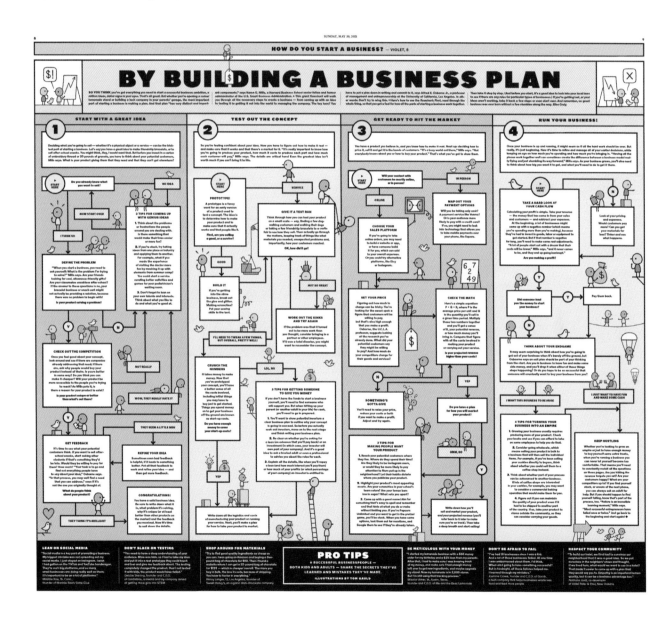

EDITORIAL: "THE EXCAVATIONS OF PEDRO ALMODOVAR" DECEMBER 19 OPENER

Concept
This opener design for a feature profile of film director Pedro Almodovar was inspired by the idea of film editing and memory.

Publication
The New York
Times Magazine
New York

Art Direction
Ben Grandgenett

Creative Direction
Gail Bichler°

Principal Type
NYT Mag Serif
Text Light

Dimensions
8.9 in. x 10.9 in.
(22.6 × 27.7 cm)

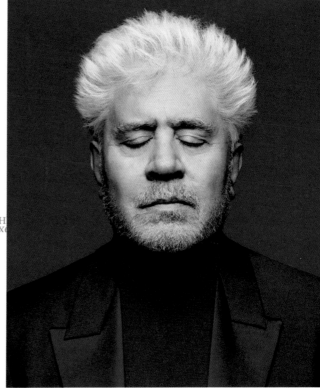

THE
EXCAVATIONS
OF PEDRO
ALMODOVAR

IN HIS NEW
FEATURE,
"PARALLEL
MOTHERS," THE
72-YEAR-OLD
DIRECTOR DIGS
UP SPAIN'S
MOST PAINFUL
HISTORY —
AND SEALS HIS
REPUTATION
AS THE NATION'S
MOST DARING
FILMMAKER.

BY
MARCELA
VALDES

Photographs by
Rafael Pavarotti

EDITORIAL: THE RETURN OF FOMO

Concept
The lettering celebrates the moment of reemerging from
quarantine in the beginning of summer 2021. The funky letterforms,
which seem to be dancing on the pages, convey the festivity,
and the vibrant colors speak to the joy of New Yorkers.

Creative Direction
Thomas Alberty and
Ellen Peterson

Design
Zuzanna Rogatty
New York

Publication
New York Magazine

Principal Type
Custom

Dimensions
8.9 × 10.9 in.
(22.6 × 27.7 cm)

EDITORIAL: SOCIOTYPE JOURNAL

Concept
Sociotype Journal is a reimagining of the conventional type specimen and a new platform for thoughts on arts, culture, and society. We believe typography should start conversations and spread new ideas. So rather than make our type specimens with the customary pangrams or pithy dummy copy, we've founded the Journal: a type specimen and so much more. Each issue, we'll invite interesting people to help us explore a single theme, inspired by (and typeset in) a particular type family from Sociotype.

Design
Alicia Mundy

Creative Direction
Nigel Bates
and Nic Carter

Editors
Nic Carter and
Henrietta Thompson

URL
socio-type.com

Design Firm
Socio
London

Type Foundry
Sociotype

Typographers
Joe Leadbeater
and Diana Ovezea

Publication
Sociotype Journal

Principal Type
Gestura

Dimensions
10.8 × 8.3 in.
(27.5 × 21 cm)

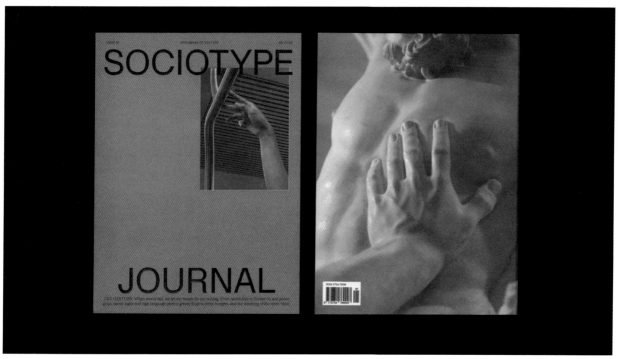

EDITORIAL: CANAL

Concept

Canal Street has been home of the Sunday Afternoon office for five years now. It's been a source of energy and inspiration. We've channeled it all in a broadsheet newsprint that pays homage to this wonderful New York oddity that is Canal Street. We've obviously called it Canal, and this is the inaugural issue. The magazine is designed with an AR filter that allows you to bring both the front and back cover to life for those who will have the physical print.

Design
Kee Wei Chin, Beatriz Lozano, Chandni Poddar, and Xiaoyu Xue

Executive Creative Direction
Ahmed Klink and Juan Carlos Pagan°

Photography
Ahmed Klink

Typographer
Beatriz Lozano

URL
sundayafternoon.us

Design Firm
Sunday Afternoon
New York

Client
Canal

Principal Type
Futura Extra Bold

Dimensions
13 × 19 in.
(33 × 48.3 cm)

EDITORIAL: FEW MAGAZINE

Concept
The aesthetics traditionally associated with the Roma is combined in FEW with modern interpretation through elegant photographs and a minimalist and experimental layout. The design of a separate logo and a font called FEW Display was commissioned for the visual identity. Highly unusual and difficult to read, the typographic elements symbolize the way in which minority cultures are often viewed by the majority as mystical and peculiar. It is almost as if the font is a foreign language in itself, challenging the reader to make a greater effort to understand it.

Design
Tino Nyman and Marina Veziko
Helsinki

Contributors
Claudia Cifu, Piia Emilia, Tiina Eronen, Emma Gillespie, Helmi Honkanen, David Jakob, Hanna Jämsenius, Arttu Kokkonen, Unni Leino, Eveliina Lempiäinen, Piia Lempiäinen, Kira Muesa, Sofia Okkonen, Ville Vainio, Ville Varumo, and Mickael Vis

Type Foundry
ABC Dinamo, Jaakko Suomalainen, and Matter of Sorts
Basel, Helsinki, and Collingwood, Australia

URL
few-mag.com

Publication
FEW Magazine

Principal Type
FEW Display, Monument Grotesk, and Quadrant Text Mono

Dimensions
9.5 × 12.7 in. (24 × 32 cm)

"Once I was stopped by the police and they happened to see my pistol in the glove compartment. Sure it was a large caliber 357 Magnum, that even the police can't get a license for... the police rushed halfway in through the window. Took the weapon and said that this goes now."

HARRY

FRIENDS OF

PART I.

FEW

WHEN IN ROMA

EDITORIAL: MOVEMENT RESEARCH PERFORMANCE JOURNAL #55

Concept
The layout system for MRPJ #55 was about "making space" in response to artists losing their space (physically and metaphorically) over the past few years. Each artist contribution received a "cover" page, where themes from the piece were translated to a typographic composition utilizing the space of the page. All contributions were treated equally with a full title page composed using the same type and size. On the cover: a full-bleed image of a make-ready test sheet from the previous issue; responding to another theme—the pandemic's temporal "glitch," where days, weeks, and months seem to loop in place.

Studios
Yotam Hadar and
Sean Yendrys
Brooklyn,
and Berlin

URL
yotamhadar.com

Publication
Movement Research

Principal Type
Terza Author
and Terza Reader

Dimensions
22.75 × 16.5 in.
(58 × 42 cm)

WHAT MY

ATOMS

ARE DOING

Mary Overlie

interviewed
by

Sylvère
Lotringer

edited by
Tony
Perucci

Mary Overlie performing The Figure (1977) at the inaugural Summergarden Dance series at The Museum of Modern Art, New York. Photo by Robert Alexander.

When Movement Research co-founder Mary Overlie was interviewed by Columbia University philosophy professor Sylvère Lotringer in 1977, she had only recently begun her work as a choreographer. She had not yet formed the Mary Overlie Dance Company, nor had she articulated her transformational approach to performance: The Six Viewpoints. Mary moved to New York to perform in Barbara Dilley's *The Natural History of the American Dance: Lesser-Known Species, Vol. 12–24*, at the Whitney Museum of American Art, but was already enmeshed in numerous collective enterprises: performing with Grand Union, the Judy Padow Dance Company, and the improvisation-based collective Dilley founded with dancers from her Whitney project; choreographing works by JoAnne Akalaitis and Lee Breuer for Mabou Mines; and co-founding Danspace Project. As Lotringer sought out SoHo artists to be interviewed for his journal *Semiotext(e)*, he was led to this iconoclastic artist, who had recently staged *Glassed Imaginarium*, the first of three works presented in the storefront windows of the Holly Solomon Gallery.

In the "Schizo-Culture" issue of *Semiotext(e)*, for which this interview was intended, Lotringer famously investigates a confluence of ideas that seemed to connect the radical Left social movements of the 1970s, the writings of French post-structuralist theorists (like Michel Foucault and Gilles Deleuze and Félix Guattari), and the work of Cage/Cunningham-influenced SoHo artists. He situates Mary Overlie among artists such as Douglas Dunn, Richard Foreman, Philip Glass, and Robert Wilson—who were staging a "breakthrough," a radical "deterritorialization of their senses that offered perceptions until then inconceivable."[1] In his interview with Mary, Lotringer proclaims her unique integration of conceptual, painterly and sensorial practice—her perceptual art—as having "far-reaching effects." Before Deleuze and Guattari's writings on the radical potential of "molecular" versus "molar" formations had been translated into English (and before French theoretical terminology was adopted by American artists as if it contained "some kind of career-enhancing) magic power"[2], Mary describes her aesthetics of the "molecular structure" and the dance of "atoms moving in accord with each other." She would continue to research performance materials through what she would later term "particulization," which was fundamental to the practice and pedagogy of The Six Viewpoints. Nearly three decades after this interview, Mary published her book, *Standing in Space: The Six Viewpoints Theory & Practice*, the fundamental principles of which were already evident in her conversation with Lotringer.

Unfortunately, Mary's interview did not appear in the "Schizo-Culture" issue, where it was slated to be followed (appropriately) by Marcel Duchamp's *Musical Sculpture*. It was later published (in translation) as "Was meine Atome machen" [What My Atoms Are Doing] in *New Yorker Gespräche* (1985), a German-language collection of Lotringer's interviews. Her interview appears in the exact middle of that book, fittingly between interviews with William S. Burroughs and Steve Reich. While Mary didn't seek out center stage, her unceasing curiosity and atomic brilliance meant that she was somehow always in the middle of everything.

—Tony Perucci

Mary Overlie died in June 2020 at her home in Bozeman, Montana.

1   Sylvère Lotringer, "Notes on the Schizo-Culture Issue," in S. Lotringer (ed.), *Schizo-Culture: The Book* (Cambridge: MIT Press, 2013), xbr.
2   Ibid., 9l.

EDITORIAL: THE ISSUE WITHIN THE ISSUE

Typography was carefully considered when creating "The Issue Within the Issue." We wanted our typography to balance being bold and serious and being hopeful and uplifting. Aiming to create a powerful visual impact, we used strong and loud typography as an expression to illustrate the unignorable struggles that homeless LGBTQ+ youths face in New York City, and the significant efforts of the Ali Forney Center to combat the issue. While shedding light on a serious issue, we also wanted to represent the fun spirits, optimism, and tenacity of the LGBTQ+ community through our use of typography.

Design
Paul Martinez

Art Direction
Hamza Ali,
Julie Rosenoff, Rudy
Troncone,
and Camille Walker

Chief Creative Officer
Dan Lucey

Chief Design Officer
Brian Lai

**Executive
Creative Direction**
Bharat Kumar and
Marcelo Ramirez

Executive Producer
Melissa Tifrere

Director
Sal Migliaccio

Copywriting
Patrick Chase,
Nick Malone,
Carlos Matias,
and Jp Winders

Editor
Oussama Zahr

Product Manager
Valentine Roche

Strategist
Alexis De Montaigu

**User Experience
Design**
Janice Chen

Founder
Carl Siciliano

Agency
Havas New York

Client
Ali Forney Center/
New York Magazine

Principal Type
Bleeny, Dida,
Roboto, and Sen

EDITORIAL: VARIOUS

Concept
In the redesign of the fashion magazine Vanity Teen, the publisher requested that I use only one typeface throughout the magazine. Given this restriction, I deconstructed the typeface Neue Haas Grotesk to create a more fluid and expressive visual narrative.

Creative Direction,
Cover and
You Rock My World
Niccolò Lapo Latini
Italy

Photography,
Cover and
You Rock My World
Emanuele Ferrari
Italy

Photography,
Distant Solitude
Florian Wellnhofer
Germany

Photography,
New Hope
Hector Tre
Spain

Photography,
The Clouds Go Soft
Cole Fawcett
United States

URL
faith.ca

Design Firm
Faith
Mississauga, Canada

Publication
Vanity Teen Magazine

Principal Type
Neue Haas Grotesk

Dimensions
9.25 × 13.5 in.
(24.5 × 34.3 cm)

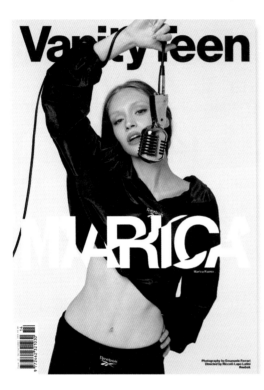

EXHIBITS: CHISINAU ADDRESS PLATES

Design
Anatolie Micaliuc
Chisinau, Moldova

Art Direction
Ilya Birman
Chelyabinsk, Russia

Principal Type
Suisse Int'l

Dimensions
15 in. high (38 cm)

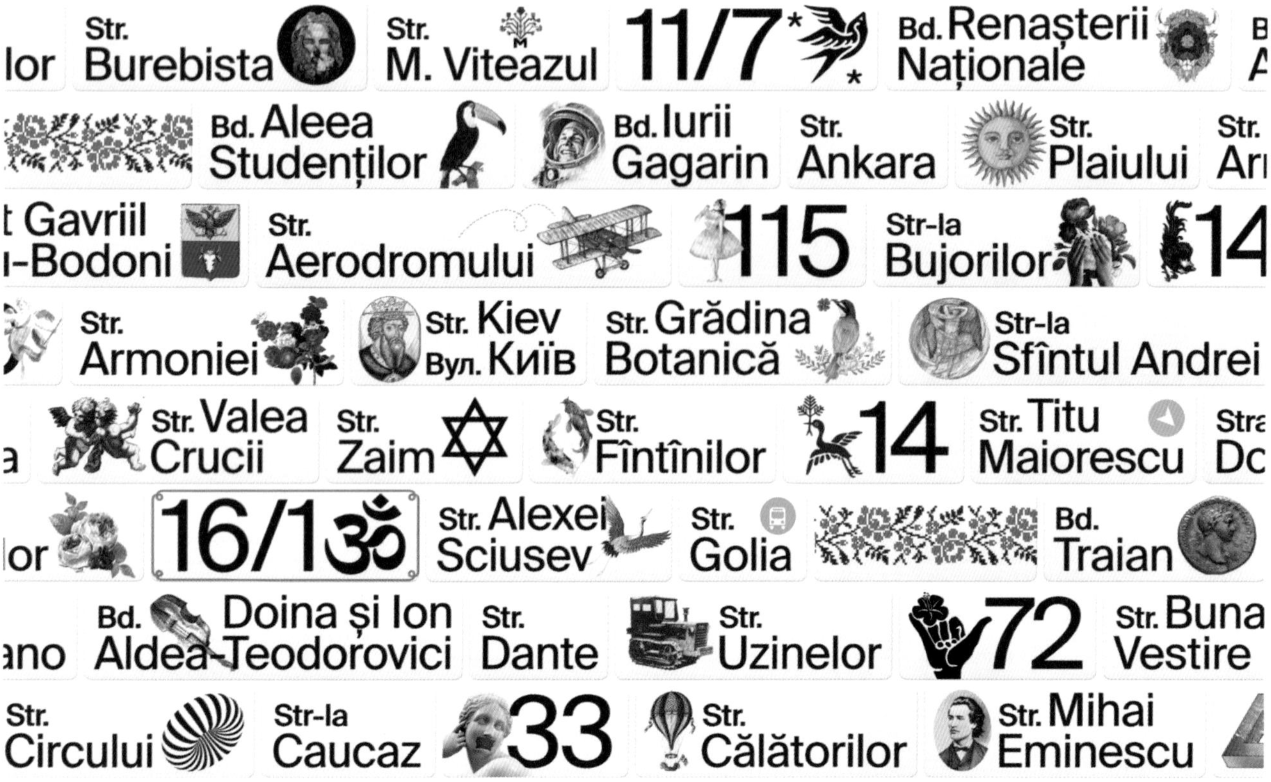

EXHIBITS: LETTERING LARGE: A BILINGUAL LENTICULAR MURAL

Concept
This project examines the intersection between typography and architecture. It employs innovative methods of making by fabricating a corrugated modular system to conceive monumental Arabic and English fonts. The mural, suspended on a building facade at Expo Dubai 2020, creates a grand lenticular viewing experience where the two languages live together and separately..

Design
Nada AlYafei, Jarrett Fuller, and Marian Misiak Wroclaw, Poland, New York, and Sharjah

Copywriter
Eman AlYousuf

Freelancers
Hala Al Ani, Bishoy Girgis, and Riem Ibrahim Sharjah

School
American University of Sharjah

Agency
Bureau Sepaen Paris

Client
USA Pavilion at Expo Dubai 2020

Principal Type
Custom

EXHIBITS: GWANGJU BIENNALE

Concept
Founded in 1995, the Gwangju Biennale in South Korea is Asia's oldest and most prestigious biennial of contemporary art. To commemorate its thirteenth edition, a transit kiosk for a major thoroughfare in Gwangju was commissioned. Built of typography, the bus shelter creates a distinctive urban landmark for the international exhibition.

Design
Jack Roizental and Jungln You

Partner
Paula Scher°

Project Manager
Emma Jung

Design Firm
Pentagram° New York

Client
Gwangju Biennale

Dimensions
7.7 × 2.3 × 3.1 yds.
(700 × 210 × 280 cm)

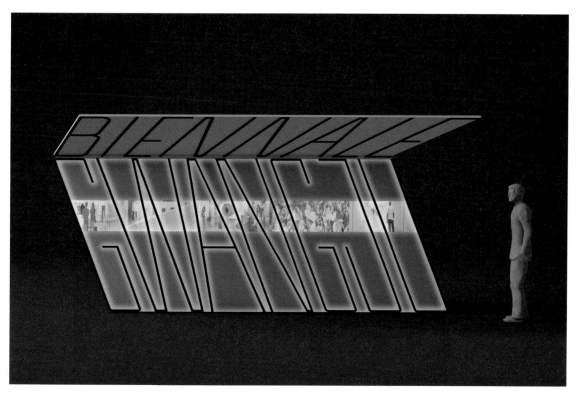

EXHIBITS: OMOTESANDO CURTAINS AND FLAGS

Concept

Omotesando is a tree-lined street in Tokyo. It stretches from Harajuku station up to Ayoma Dori and houses high-level fashion outlets with beautiful modern architecture. The street is popular with tourists and has many cafes and bars to explore. The new Omotesando restaurant on Miller Street in North Sydney evokes the spirit of its Japanese namesake with its tree-lined street below and Japanese food and atmosphere.

Design Firm
Harley Johnston Design
Sydney

Twitter
@harley_johnston

Client
Omotesando
North Sydney

Principal Type
Omotesando

Dimensions
External Flags:
24.4 × 47.2 in.
(62 × 120 cm)
Internal Curtains:
24 × 85.4 in.
(61 × 217 cm)

EXHIBITS: TUTTLINGEN DISTRICT COUNCIL OFFICES SIGNAGE SYSTEM

Concept

Simple designs might be said to fall out of nowhere: When you walk into Tuttlingen's district council offices, you find yourself in a large hall from which you can access all the other spaces. From the middle of the hall, you can see almost every potential destination—all the various departments, lined up alongside and above one another. All they needed was labeling in letters big enough to be legible from the hall below. And there it was, the finished design, out of nowhere. All we had to do was pick it up.

Design
Pehl Anika

Chief Design Officers
Carolin Himmel and
Andreas Uebele°

Design Firm
büro uebele visuelle
kommunikation
Stuttgart

Client
Stadt Tuttlingen

Principal Type
GT America

Dimensions
15.7 × 161.4 in.
(40 × 410 cm)

EXPERIMENTAL: CANAL

Concept

Canal Street has been home of the Sunday Afternoon office for five years now. It's been a source of energy and inspiration. We've channeled it all in a broadsheet newsprint that pays homage to this wonderful New York oddity that is Canal Street. We've obviously called it Canal, and this is the inaugural issue. The magazine is designed with an AR filter that allows you to bring both the front and back cover to life for those who will have the physical print.

Design
Kee Wei Chin, Beatriz Lozano, Chandni Poddar, and Xiaoyu Xue

Executive Creative Direction
Ahmed Klink and Juan Carlos Pagan°

Photography
Ahmed Klink

Typographer
Beatriz Lozano

URL
sundayafternoon.us

Design Firm
Sunday Afternoon
New York

Client
Canal

Principal Type
Futura Extra Bold

Dimensions
13 × 19 in.
(33 × 48.3 cm)

EXPERIMENTAL: TYPE CYPHER

Concept
Inspired by rap cyphers—an assembly of rappers taking turns spitting improvised verses/ freestyle rap—"Type Cypher" is a gathering of different letterforms, exchanging styles, forms, flows, and ideas with one another in a freestyle manner. These display letterforms are intended for use at large sizes for headings and titles and can be combined with one another.

Design
Jeth Torres
Cavite, Philippines

URL
jethtorres.com

Twitter
@JethTorres

Instagram
@jethtorres

Principal Type
Various

Dimensions
16.5 × 11.7 in.
(29.7 × 42 cm)

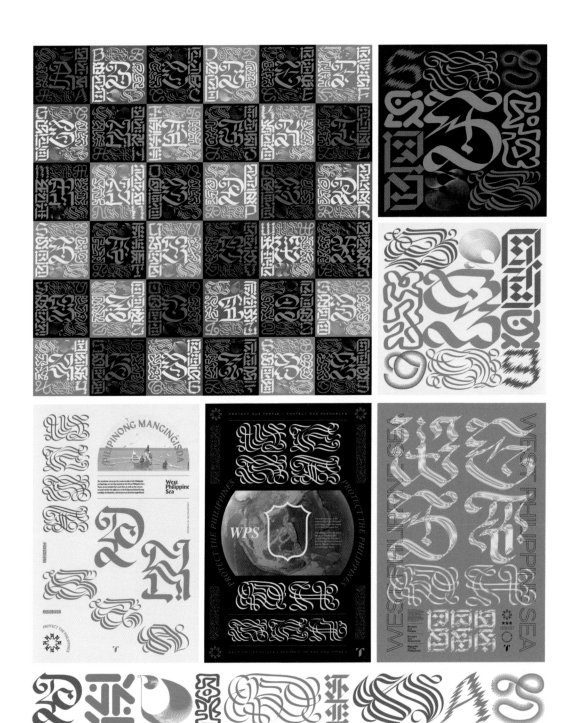

EXPERIMENTAL: PLAY PLAY LAAAAAH

aPlay Play Laaaaah is a zine about reimagining Singapore's most iconic playground for older Singaporeans to reminisce about their youth and the younger generation to learn their unique heritage. Built in 1970, the dragon playground is one of the most famous playgrounds in Singapore. These playgrounds were locally designed to instill a sense of national identity, but many have been demolished due to international playground safety standards. The zine is filled with a reimagined form of play that invokes people's memories of their youth. The form encapsulates Singapore's heritage and way of playing, inspiring future generations to be curious and imaginative.

Creative Direction
Daisy Dal Hae Lee and
Joo Leng Lucien Ng

Design Firm
Studio Bang-Gu
San Francisco

URL
studiobanggu.com

Twitter
@StudioBanggu

Publisher
Social Species

Principal Type
Custom
Modular Typeface,
F37 Ginger Pro,
and Monosten

Dimensions
6 × 8 in.
(15.2 × 20.3 cm)

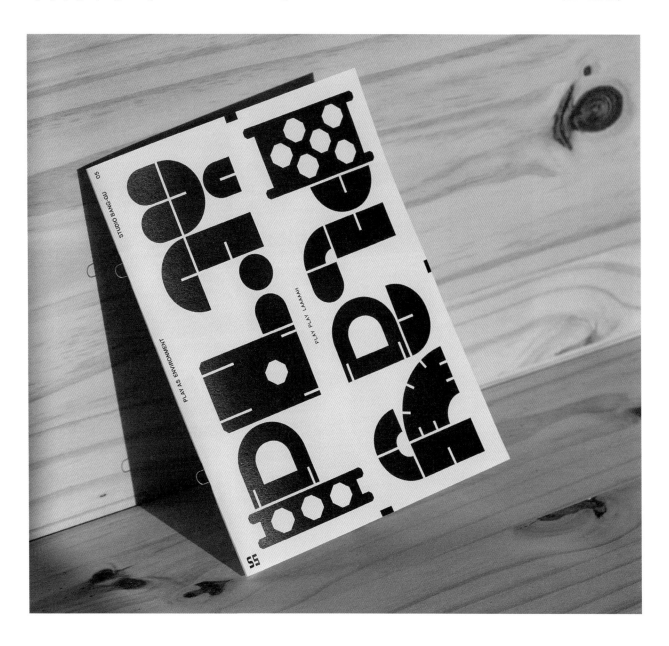

EXPERIMENTAL: 36 DAYS OF TYPE, 8TH EDITION

Concept
"It's the tool, not the hand, that makes the form." For the eighth edition of 36 Days of Type, I used my own custom-made tools, which I have been developing since 2018. The idea for these tools derives from geometric typefaces, which inspire me the most. I aim to use the possibilities that these brushes give me for making letter shapes. Therefore, I reject handling them just like any other drawing tool; instead, I embrace the restrictions. Letting the tools find their own visual language helps me explore new forms of letters.

Design
Saber Javanmard

Studio
Studio Saber
The Hague

URL
behance.net/
StudioSaber

Principal Type
Handmade letters

Dimensions
17.7 × 17.7 in.
(45 × 45 cm)

EXPERIMENTAL: MULTIGRAMAS

Concept
Multigramas started as a fun experiment, in which we tried to see how much we could push the mixture of textures and styles, plus intricate intertwining, and keep the letterforms recognizable. We ended up with a complex alphabet (from A to Z) where each of the letters works as a piece of art in itself.

Design
Leandro Senna and
Julio Zukerman
San Francisco
and São Paulo

Instagram
@senna_leandro
@tenisvermelho

Twitter
@leandrosenna
@tenisvermelho

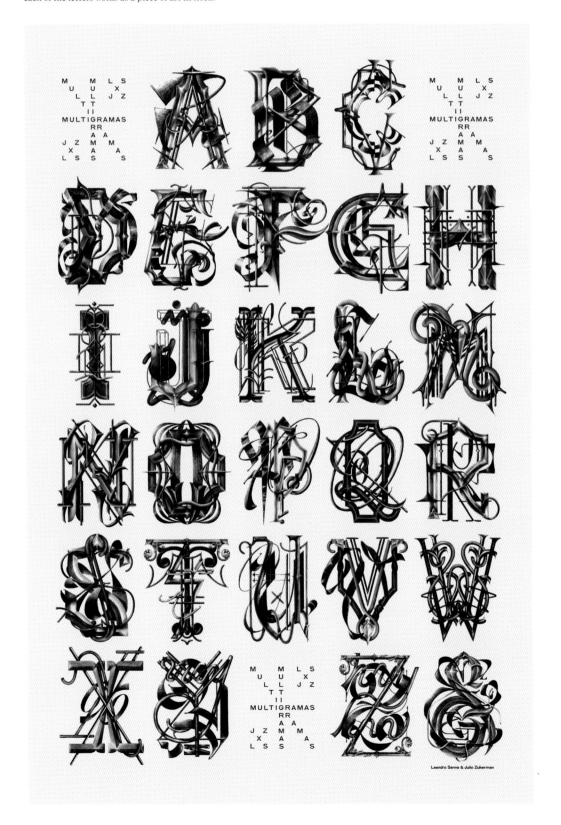

EXPERIMENTAL: NESPOR TYPE SPECIMEN BOOK

Concept

Nespor type specimen book is a visual overview of the typographic, grid-based project Nespor. A self-published book, designed and edited by Daan Rietbergen in 2021. The characters are designed as one family but also have the quality to stand on their own. The white space and margins are equally important as the shapes themselves. This typographic research started on screen and was then further explored on paper by drawing and painting the characters.

URL
daanrietbergen.com

Design
Daan Rietbergen
Utrecht,
The Netherlands

Printer
René Jongen,
Pantheon Drukkers

Lithographer
Marc Gijzen

Principal Type
Helvetica Neue LT
Pro—55 Roman

Dimensions
7.4 × 12.2 in.
(18.9 × 31 cm)

EXPERIMENTAL: DRINKING ALONE WITH THE MOON

Concept
Inspired by the poem "Drinking Alone with the Moon" by Chinese poet Li Bai, this experimental typography design expresses the juxtaposition of the tangible and intangible, virtual and real, using printing technique and visual form. Inspired by the visual imagery of moonlight and light and shadow, this type design references the waxing and waning of the moon. It also pays homage to the origin of Chinese characters as pictographs, treating each stroke as a visual element.

Design
Jan Hsieh
Kaohsiung City, Taiwan

Creative Direction
Cindy Wang
Singapore

Design Firm
cindymode
Taipei

URL
youtube.com/
watch?v=p5f6VuYagF8

Client
Taichung Blossom
Pavilion, Taiwan

Principal Type
Custom

Dimensions
15 × 20.9 in.
(38 × 53 cm)

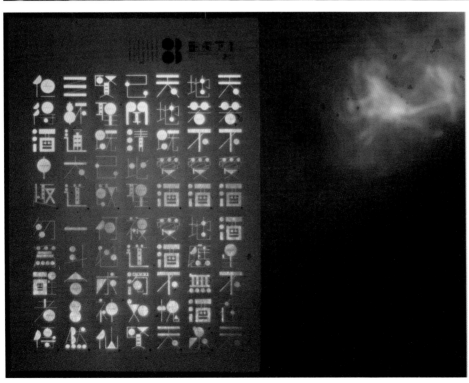

EXPERIMENTAL: 100 GRAPHIC DESIGN DIARIES

Concept
In the last three months of my study in London, I created 100 graphic design diaries on Chinese calligraphy exercise paper. As a graphic design student, I hope to record what I see in daily life and some design ideas through visual diaries.

Art Direction
Zhuohan Shao

Studio
Allergy Studio
China

Principal Type
Custom

Dimensions
7.4 × 10.4 in.
(19 × 26.5 cm)

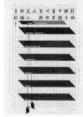

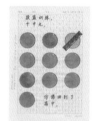

EXPERIMENTAL: HUNDRED FAMILY NAMES

Concept
This Chinese character typography design experiment presents Hundred Family Names of two dimensions in a three-dimensional wooden cube. There is only one best angle for each Family Name..

Design
China Academy of Art and Zhejiang Gongshang University Hangzhou

URL
adc1994.zjgsu.edu.cn

Client
Hanzi Club

Principal Type
Custom

Dimensions
27.5 × 39.4 in. (70 × 100 cm)

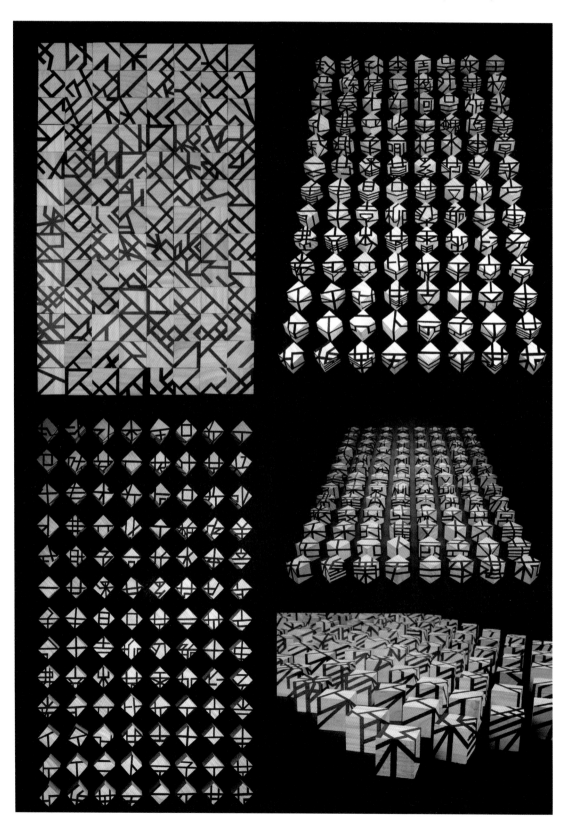

EXPERIMENTAL: 36 DAYS OF TYPE, 8TH EDITION

Concept
36 Days of Type is a project that invites designers, illustrators, and graphic artists to express their interpretation of the letters and numbers of the Latin alphabet. It is a yearly open call exploring the creative boundaries of letterforms, where participants are challenged to design a letter or number each day for thirty-six consecutive days as a global and simultaneous act showing the outcome of the ability to represent the same symbols from thousands of different perspectives.

Design
Khyati Trehan
New Delhi

Principal Type
Custom

Dimensions
33.5 × 33.5 in.
(85 × 85 cm)

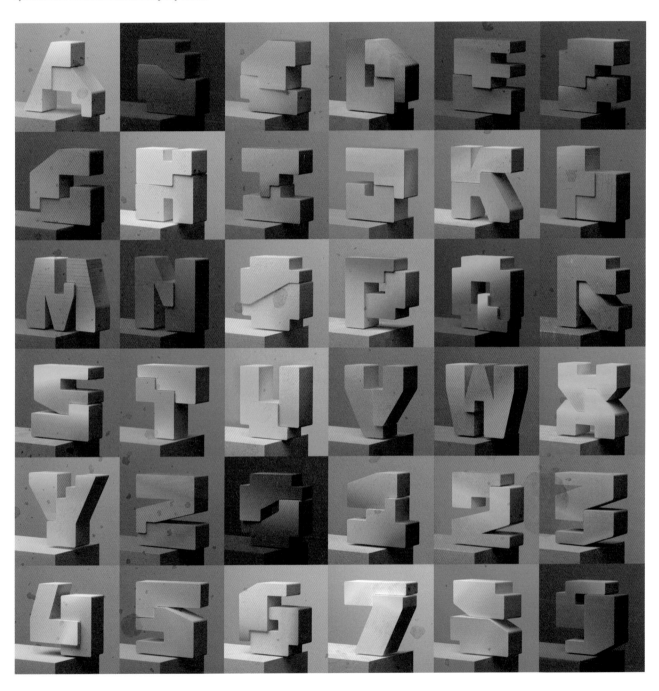

COMMUNCATION DESIGN

EXPERIMENTAL: BELIEVE

Concept
Do you believe in ghosts? Do you believe in magic?
Do you believe in miracles? Do you believe in
yourself? Adapting to strange times seems to
be the only way to survive today, being fluid and
in motion, pivoting through difficulties and
remaining hopeful under a warm and soft blanket.

Design
Valentina Casali
Jesi, Italy

Design Firm
Sunday Büro

URL
typophrenic.com/
believe-lettering-
blanket

Principal Type
Custom

Dimensions
72.8 × 59 in.
(185 × 150 cm)

EXPERIMENTAL: MOLECULAR TYPOGRAPHY LABORATORY

Concept

This is an experimental typographic research project called "Molecular Typography Laboratory." The laboratory examines the speculative premise that the characters of the Hebrew alphabet have a molecular structure. The research shows how this assertion affects the Hebrew alphabet, words, and language, and examines the discipline through the parameters of function versus aesthetics and content versus form.

Design
Kobi Franco Design
Tel Aviv

URL
kfdesign.co.il

Principal Type
Helvetica,
Molecular Round,
and Molecular Square

Dimensions
35.2 × 50.4 in.
(89.5 × 128 cm)

EXPERIMENTAL: ARCHITECTURAL TYPE STUDIES: LIGHT + SHADOW

Concept
While I visited Basel, Switzerland, I began photographing buildings, public spaces, and architectural moments of light and shadow as I walked through the city. These photographs served as memories of these buildings but also as a canvas for exploring forms. Having collected many photographs, I started to crop them into interesting moments that became almost typographic. Reducing the photos into single elements and focusing on formal qualities within the architecture manifested in transitions of light to dark. I explored how these transitions from light to shadow could be used to draw the interior and exterior spaces of letterforms.

Design, Creative Direction, Lighting, Photography, and Typographer
Daniel Frumhoff
New York

Design Firm
Daniel Frumhoff Design

URL
danielfrumhoff.com/
projects/architectural-type-studies

Mentors
Abraham Burickson,
Jason Mathews Gottlieb,
Ellen Lupton, Lili Maya,
Jennifer Cole Phillips,
and Elizabeth Sprouls,
Maryland Institute
College of Art,
Baltimore

Principal Type
Custom

Dimensions
11 × 17 in.
(27.9 × 43.2 cm)

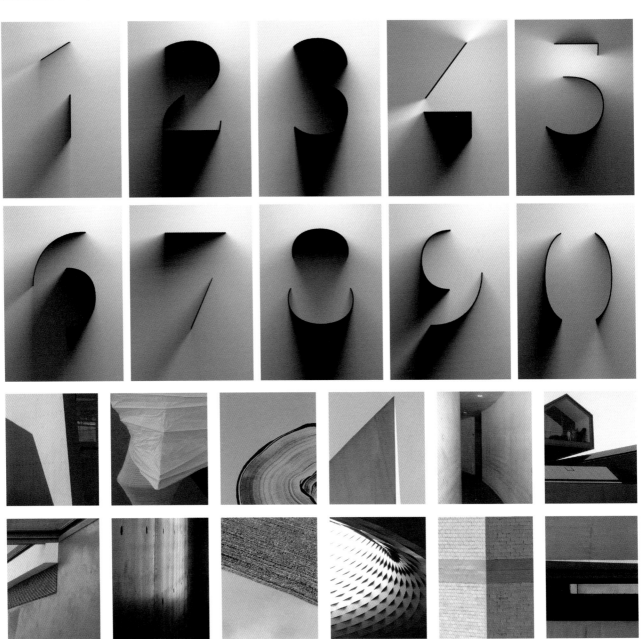

EXPERIMENTAL: BEAM

Concept
BEAM is a decorative font that tries to capture the spirits of futuristic lighting in city nightlife. You can also find the flavor of mathematics and space through the lines.

Design
Qiushuo Li
New York

URL
qiushuoli.com/beam

Foundry
Q-Create

Principal Type
BEAM

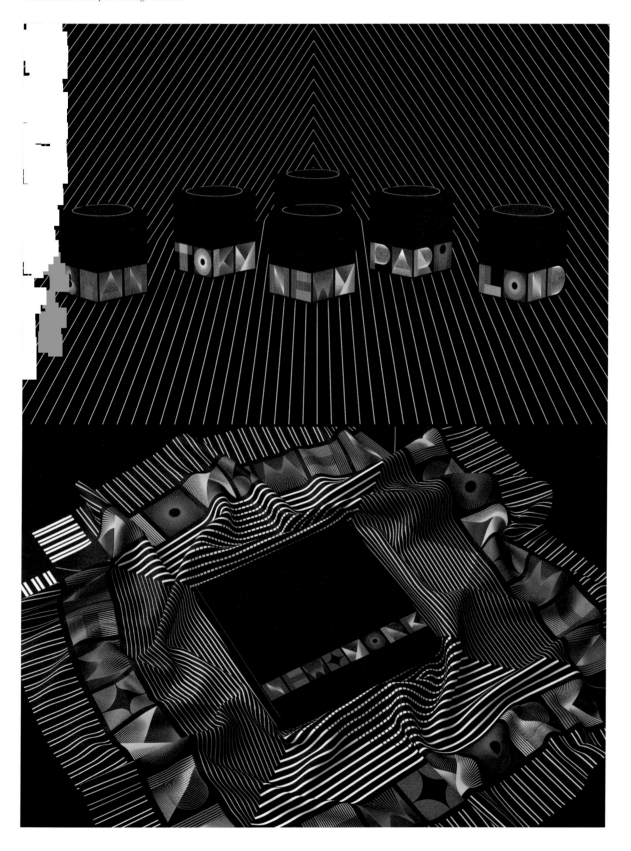

EXPERIMENTAL: CYBERDADA

Concept

Cyberdada is a response and a solution to the two changeless attitudes toward technology: tech = good and tech = threat. How can our society evolve to the next stage? We need creativity and evolution. The history of evolution has always been led by nonsensical pioneers. Art and design can promote the idea of engaging technology in a nonsensical way, which will inspire and ultimately provoke new attitudes toward the relationship between tech, humans, and our future. Cyberdada aims to transcend commonsense and establish new attitudes. We are Cyberdada, because the other attitudes toward technology are denial and despair.

Design
Yanwen Hang
Los Angeles

Principal Type
JUXTA SANS

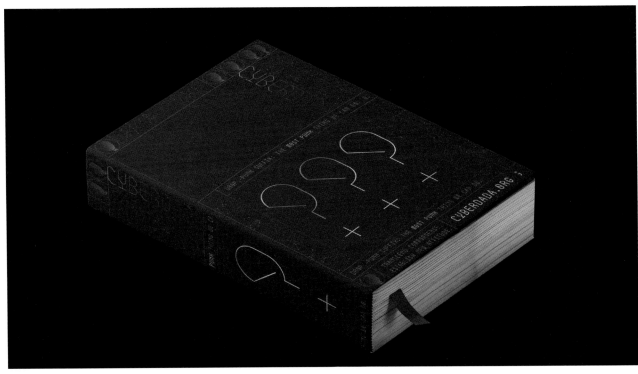

EXPERIMENTAL: DREAM BUBBLE

Concept

The inspiration was a liquid medicine called Voice Thickener from the Japanese manga Doraemon. Starting with the idea of building a physical speech-to-text system, a bubble type machine was designed to generate letters made of real bubbles. After observing and researching the physical property, bubble type was brought into the digital world using 3D software. Since the digital bubbles never pop, bubble type eternalizes people's dreams and wishes in the digital space, reminds us how fragile and precious they are, and delivers our goodwill to others in a more perceivable form..

Design
Rozi Zhu
New York

URL
rozi.fun/dream-bubble

Assistant Professors
Kyle Li and Richard The

Emeritus Professor
Anezka Sebek

Lecturer
Anna Harsanyi

School
The New School

Principal Type
Bubble Type

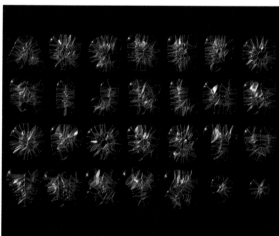

IDENTITY: MAH—MUSÉE D'ART ET D'HISTOIRE

Design Firm
Hubertus Design
Zürich

Client
MAH—Musee d'Art
et d'Histoire

MAH-Sans

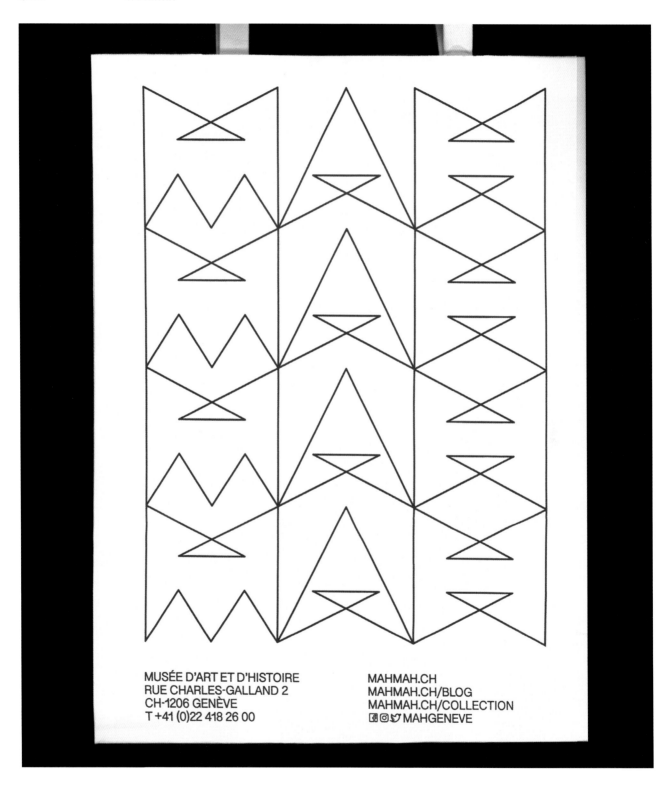

MUSÉE D'ART ET D'HISTOIRE
RUE CHARLES-GALLAND 2
CH-1206 GENÈVE
T +41 (0)22 418 26 00

MAHMAH.CH
MAHMAH.CH/BLOG
MAHMAH.CH/COLLECTION
🅕🅞🅨 MAHGENEVE

IDENTITY: FUN POT

Concept

We have built an immersive visual experience for the hot pot restaurant brand. The enthusiasm of hot pot culture is conveyed through the redesign of Chinese characters. The design is inspired by the ingredients and flavors of Sichuan hot pot—the hemp flavor will make the tongue stale, the spiciness comes from the stimulation of spices, and the umami flavor was usually obtained from fish and sheep in ancient times. The designer digs out the unique recognizability of Chinese characters, and through the deformation of the font, creates a vivid visual effect for the brand. The stretched font has unlimited imagination.

Design Firm
shanghai version
design group
Shanghai

Client
Fun Pot

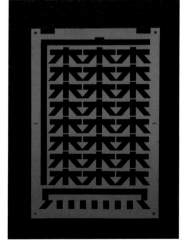

IDENTITY: FERGUS

Concept

The logo for Fergus was completely redrawn, inspired by the font Eckmannpsych by James T. Edmondson. We reduced the contrast, regularized the shapes, and adjusted the counter spaces to create a seamless, flowing wordmark. Typography plays an important role in the identity by combining the idiosyncratic, nineteenth-century grotesque-inspired warmth of FF Bau with the technical feel of Suisse Int'l Mono. Our goal was for Fergus to stand out in the homogeneous market that is organic online shopping and translate the pleasure of eating into a sustainable and unified language with just a touch of magic.

Design and Art Direction
Julien Hébert

Creative Direction
Bryan-K. Lamonde

Account Director
François Morin

Project Manager
Marie-Hélène Rodriguez

Naming and Editorial Content
Kristina G. Landry

Strategic Partner
Agence Souffle

URL
principal.studio

Design Firm
Principal
Montréal

Client
Fergus

Principal Type
FF Bau Pro and
Suisse Int'l Mono

Dimensions
Various

COMMUNCATION DESIGN

145

IDENTITY: BOURGIE HALL TENTH ANNIVERSARY

Concept
As part of its tenth anniversary, Bourgie Hall created a festive campaign that focuses on the musical genres that inhabit its museum space. In an intriguing collage exercise, the number 10 is created through the entanglement of various instruments.

Design
Marianne St-Pierre,
Vedran Vaskovic,
and Luc Verreault

Art and Creative Direction
Daniel Robitaille

Design Firm
Paprika
Montréal

Client
Arte Musica

Principal Type
Next

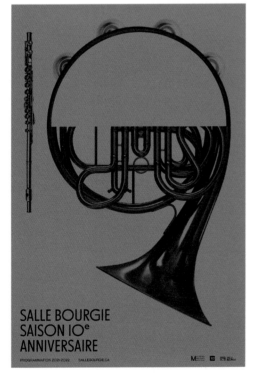

IDENTITY: ANONIMA—ART GALLERY

Concept

ANÔNIMA is a Brazilian gallery whose purpose is to break the commonplace, traditional art world and address the relationship between art and people who have always been on the margins: women (cis and trans) and nonbinary artists of color. The brand name is a reference to and a provocative confrontation with the lack of historical records and the devaluation these artists have endured over time. To convey this concept and the brand's authentic, brave, and bold Latin American essence, ANÔNIMA's visual identity is inspired by expressions of graphic and artistic resistance: underground media and textile arts.

Design Firm
Renata Moroni Design
Porto Alegre, Brazil

URL
renatamoroni.com

Client
ANÔNIMA—A
Galeria Herself

Principal Type
Custom font—Latin
American Artists
Alphabet and Typold

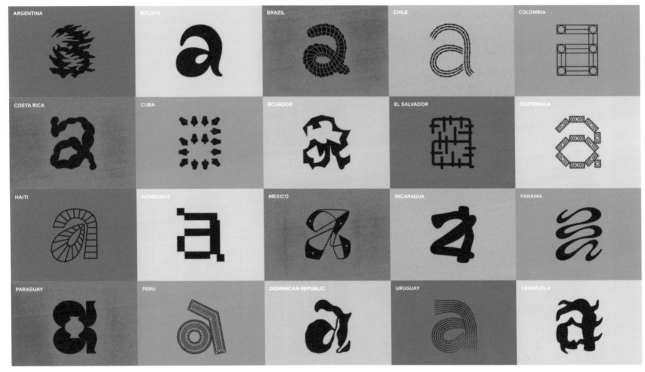

IDENTITY: SHORT WAVES FESTIVAL 2021

Concept

The visual identity version of the 2021 edition was based on the edition's slogan: MirrorMirror. The mirror not only reflects reality but also creates it, which shows the complexity of living in the present. The main theme of the entire visual identity—a mirror image in a box—looks at us, contemporary people. One reflection seems like a frame from the film, but the other remains unreadable: a reflection of reality, the ambiguity of the image, a deep journey into our psyche and much more, because everyone perceives the same reality in a different and unique way.

Studio
Uniforma s.c.
Poznan, Poland

Client
Short Waves

Principal Type
Sk Modernist Bold

COMMUNCATION DESIGN

IDENTITY: VESHCH! EXHIBITION VISUAL IDENTITY

Concept

Veshch! (Talking Objects) is an exhibition-installation held at the All-Russian Decorative Art Museum. It introduces some of the most vivid examples of twentieth-century Russian industrial design to the public and provides insights on how these pieces have inspired contemporary artists: from rethinking the folk-art traditions and Russian avant-garde to the design of the space race era, custom art design, sustainable development concepts, and high-tech smart home systems. Most importantly, there is an unmistakable dialogue between the objects of the twentieth and the twenty-first centuries that highlights the continuity of design ideas across generations.

URL
baklazanas.com/veshch

Design Firm
Design Studio
Baklazanas Moscow

Client
All-Russian Decorative
Art Museum

Principal Type
Futura PT and
VESHCH logo
typeface (logo)

IDENTITY: BERKELEY REP

Concept
The Berkeley Repertory Theatre in Berkeley, California, is one of the leading regional theaters in the U.S. and internationally renowned for creating ambitious theater that entertains and challenges its audiences. The organization needed a cohesive identity that would put Berkeley Rep front and center and promote the institution along with its individual productions. This new brand identity establishes a bold, contemporary visual language for the theater in line with its programming and reputation. The identity centers on a distinctive letter "B," with simple geometry inspired by the shape of a ticket, that dynamically extends across a range of brand expressions.

Design
Emily Atwood

Partner
Paula Scher°

Design Firm
Pentagram New York°

Client
Berkeley Rep

Principal Type
Obviously

IDENTITY: DUTCH DESIGN WEEK

Concept

For the new Dutch Design Week brand identity, we gave the almost twenty-year-old logo, DDW's tulip, a second life by styling it as the W in the event name. DDW's tulip is a constellation of rectangles and quarter circles. These elements were also used in typographic experiments from the 1920s that were revised in 1963 by the late Wim Crouwel for the poster he created for painter Edgar Fernhout. It is this poster that we took as inspiration for the new Dutch Design Week brand identity. We expanded the thirteen letters on the poster to produce an entire font..

Design Firm
Thonik
Amsterdam

Type Foundry
Foundry Types
London

URL
thonik.nl/work

Client
Dutch Design Week

Principal Type
Fernhout

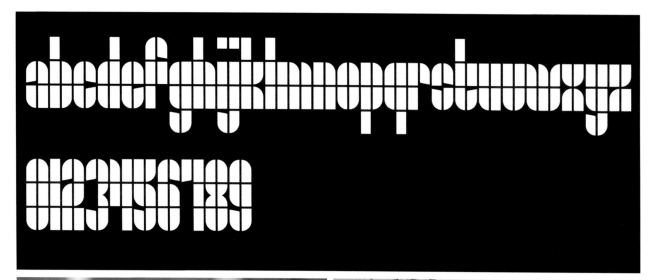

IDENTITY: OFFER OF ADMISSION GUANGZHOU ACADEMY OF FINE ARTS

Concept

Appearing at the entrance of the store, the words "WELCOME" scrolling on the LED screen are a warm greeting to new customers. I wanted to use this sentiment in the design of the admission letter of GAFA. The passionate dotted text, scrolling on the welcome material, makes the static font present a dynamic effect on the print media. The content of the internal material is set on the surface, thus creating the feeling of information rapidly passing by, and the interplay of text movement and stillness is like a moment of time frozen.

Design
Tian Bo, Chen Luyi, and Ling Hongdai

Art Direction
Tian Bo

Design Firm
TEN BUTTONS
Guangzhou, China

Client
Guangzhou Academy of Fine Arts

Principal Type
Helvetica Now Varible and Lanting Hei

Dimensions
Various

IDENTITY: PIEDMONT ART WALK

Concept
We created an iconic brand symbol and identity for a community-based event in Piedmont, California, called Art Walk. This was as simple as making the word "Art" walk. Through animation and witty interpretations of the logo and copy, it resonated with the community audience, both young and old, and created a memorable identity, recognizable for years to come.

Design
Hiuman Ng and
Cindy Zheng

Art Direction
Lyam Bewry

Creative Direction
Rob Duncan

Design Firm
Mucho
San Francisco

Client
Piedmont Art Walk

Principal Type
A2 Gothic

IDENTITY: DEEP FAKES

Concept

Visual communication for an extensive, multilayered exhibition at EPFL Pavilions in Lausanne Switzerland, following our new corporate design. The aim was to create iconic but simple solutions for basic applications, while having individual and multiple narrations with maximum artistic freedom for each exhibition. We combined the visual raw material of the contributors, a specific color scheme, and a set of grids together with simple but huge "Swiss" typography. That image is the base for all visual communication formats, from poster to advertising to on-site prints at the building.

Agencies
Lamm & Kirch
Leipzig and Berlin
Knoth & Renner
Halle an der Saale
and Berlin

Client
EPFL Pavilions

Principal Type
Dinamo Diatype

IDENTITY: LUBEZNIK CENTER FOR THE ARTS

Concept

We partnered with the Lubeznik Center for the Arts throughout the year to develop a comprehensive update, including a brand strategy, visual identity system, communication tools, and website redesign. This hidden gem in Michigan City, Indiana, is a world-class cultural hub that brings the local community together through eclectic programming and exhibits that foster meaningful connections—from poetry slams to educational programming. We knew early on that the visual identity needed to express as much personality as the center itself, so we designed a variable logo, typeface, and identity to reflect Lubeznik's character.

Design
Dean Sweetnich

Senior Director of Design
Will Miller

Associate Director of Development
Matt Soria

Director of Project Management
Megan DePumpo

Managing Director
Chantel Valentene

URL
lubeznikcenter.org

Design Firm
Firebelly Design
Chicago

Client
Lubeznik Center
for the Arts

Principal Type
Lubeznik Display
and Mabry

IDENTITY: SPARK THE NEW "CHOY"?

Concept
Our concept is to create a brand theme that brings temptation and happiness before and after every great treated meal, like going to a high-end restaurant. It includes wagging tails and happy ears inspiration for ink traps and Vietnamese diacritics, together with funny Gen Z copywriting supported by minimal and direct design layout.

Art Direction
Anh Pham

Creative Direction
Anh Nguyen

Executive Creative Direction
Duy Nguyen

Copywriter
Quan Nguyen

Photography
Wing Chan,
BITE Studio

Project Manager
Lan Mai

Producer
Quan Nguyen

URL
m-n.associates

Typographer
TypeType
Russia

Design Firm
M-N Associates
Ho Chi Minh City

Client
PetChoy

Principal Type
Fragen, Nunito, TT Trailers Petchoy, and VT 323

Dimensions
7 × 5 × 1.7 in. (18 x 12.6 × 4.4 cm)

BẾP ĐÃ TRỞ LẠI LỢI HẠI VÔ CÙNG

Available!

THỰC ĐƠN

THỊT CHIM CÚT, XƯƠNG GÀ,
GAN TIM GÀ, ĐẬU XANH,
KHOAI LANG TÍM, TÁO,
TRỨNG GÀ, BỘT YẾN MẠCH,
BỘT NGHỆ, BỘT CANXI,
BỘT AGAR, DẦU DỪA.

Gọi liền
089.687.8929
Boss yêu!

ĐIỆP VỤ ĂN TRĂNG

CÁ NGỪ ĐẠI CA

Chốt đơn!

MÓN MỚI HƠI BỊ NGON NHA!

petchoy.com

Mèo cưng
Hoàng thượng,
Cún cưng
Cat Tasty
Dog Protector
Snackie
Milk
Yogurt
Boss yêu!
Mèo cưng
Sen ơi,
Cún cưng

CHUYỂN NHÀ!

@mypetchoy

NEW HOME

Áá Àà Ảả Ãã Ạạ Ăă Ắắ Ằằ Ẳẳ Ẵẵ Ặặ Ââ Ấấ Ầầ Ẩẩ Ẫẫ Ậậ Đđ Éé Èè Ẻẻ Ẽẽ Ẹẹ Êê Ếế Ềề Ểể Ễễ Ệệ Íí Ìì Ỉỉ Ĩĩ Ịị Óó Òò Ỏỏ Õõ Ọọ Ôô Ốố Ồồ Ổổ Ỗỗ Ộộ Ơơ Ớớ Ờờ Ởở Ỡỡ Ợợ Úú Ùù Ủủ Ũũ Ụụ Ưư Ứứ Ừừ Ửử Ữữ Ựự Ýý Ỳỳ Ỷỷ Ỹỹ Ỵỵ.

TT TRAILER PETCHOY
****
DATE: 31/03/2021
COOKED BY TYPETYPE

AVAILABLE IN VIETNAMESE
DIACRITICAL DETAILS
FOR HEADLINE

IDENTITY: HOTEL BLÜ

Concept
As the Austrian emperor, Franz Joseph I played an important role in the historical development of Gastein and was a passionate admirer of the existing flora, we named the new hotel "Blü" (to bloom). It is an open-minded place dedicated to free development indoors and, of course, outdoors. To communicate this encouraging and flourishing feeling, we decided on a fresh mix of color, typography, and striking illustrations and created a distinctive approach, especially in the surrounding area.

Creative Direction
Kurt Glänzer and
Josef Heigl

Illustrator
Sebastian Curi
Los Angeles

Design
Bruch—Idee&Form
Graz, Austria

Client
Hotel Blü

Principal Type
Atak Regular and
LL Bradford Regular

Dimensions
5.8 × 8.2 in.
(14.8 × 21 cm)

IDENTITY: IDENTITY FOR HISTORISK MUSEUM

Concept
Historisk museum contains Norway's largest collection of ethnographic and historical artifacts. The architect of the museum, Henrik Bull, drew multiple versions of a monogram that adorns a variety of embellishments and details in the building. The monogram became a graphic focal point in the identity that can vary in size and clarity, which carries the history of the museum itself.

Design
Halvor Nordrum

Creative Direction
Svein Haakon Lia

Documentation Photography
Jan Khür

Project Manager
Marie Louise Steen

Strategist
Christoffer Nøkleby

URL
bleed.com/historisk-museum

Design Firm
Bleed Design Studio
Oslo

Client
Historisk museum

Principal Type
ABC Diatype

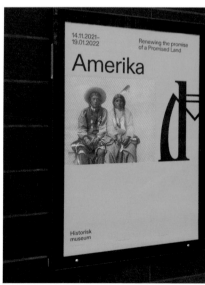

Concept

The logo for this teacher training college is a manifestation of the institution's soul: The shaping and arrangement of the letters say something about how people come together there and relate to each other. Each individual—each child, each teacher—has their own unique characteristics and quirks, expressed in the logo through the distinctive forms of the individual letters. The logo visualizes these personal differences fitting together, aligning and connecting, guiding and supporting one another. The distinctive, idiosyncratic design makes it instantly recognizable.

Design
Justyna Sikora

Chief Design Officers
Carolin Himmel and
Andreas Uebele°

Design Firm
büro uebele visuelle
kommunikation
Stuttgart

Client
University
College of Teacher
Education Tyrol

Principal Type
GT Eesti

PH TIROL
Pädagogische Hochschule Tirol
Zukunft mit Bildung

Wie gut

Montag,
10.01.2011, 17.00 Uhr
Pastorstraße 7

Wir freuen uns,
Sie zum Neujahrsempfang
der Pädagogischen
Hochschule Tirol
einladen zu dürfen.

Anmeldung:
Mag. Anna Rainer
Teamassistentin
anna.rainer@ph-tirol.ac.at

Neujahrsempfang

www.ph-tirol.ac.at

IDENTITY: EULJI-GIL

Concept

This project sought to provide communication so a sense of belonging could be felt among all hospital officials who walk with patients their whole lives as companions of the Eulji family. Illustrations formed by strokes depict the form of the Eulji family and indirectly acknowledge the identity of Eulji. The hospital name Eulji was expressed by implying the morphological characteristics (乙) of the Chinese character of Eulji and corporate value (love for Eulji family) into the concept of "a road." The typography, which deviates from standardized fonts to shape a road, is expressed using unique structures and geometric forms.

Design
Seung Yeon Ji, Ga Young Park, and Myung Jin Won

Creative Direction
Ja Kyoung Min

In-House Agency
Eulji University and Sejong University Seongnamsi and Seoul, South Korea

Client
Eulji Medical Center

Principal Type
Eulji Gil

Dimensions
23.4 × 33.1 in. (59.4 x 84.1 cm)

IDENTITY: ART + ENVIRONMENT CONFERENCE IDENTITY

Concept
Centered on the theme of Land Art, the 2021 Art + Environment Conference features a logotype and color palette that mirrors the stacked boulders of Ugo Rondinone's Seven Magic Mountains, while the "conference in a box," sent out to virtual attendees, embodies the rawness of the materials used to create the iconic earthworks. To reflect the monumentality of the sculptures, the system features bold, condensed typography across print, screen, and spatial media, including a 244-page catalog of Gianfranco Gorgoni's Land Art Photographs, a fold-out poster of Spiral Jetty, a multipanel calendar of events, and a hand-stitched program guide..

Creative Direction
Brad Bartlett

URL
bradbartlettdesign.com

Design Firm
Brad Bartlett Design
Los Angeles

Client
Nevada Museum of Art

Principal Type
Caslon Doric,
Caslon Doric
Condensed,
Caslon Doric Extended,
and Caslon Doric Wide

IDENTITY: PAIGE SMYTHE STUDIO

Concept

Paige Smythe is an artist from Charleston, South Carolina, specializing in paintings and collages. The brand for her studio represents her style: a contemporary twist on Southern, traditional themes. The graceful curves and tall x-height in the logotype form a fresh and approachable foundation for the brand. The monogram contrasts the cleanliness of the logotype, grounding the brand with a sense of authority. Its letterforms are inspired by historic wax seals, a reference to the papers used throughout the artist's work..

Design
Kristmar Muldrow
Charleston,
South Carolina

Client
Paige Smythe Studio

Principal Type
Custom

IDENTITY: CHINA SHADOW PLAY MUSEUM（中国皮影博物馆）

Concept
The beginning of civilization stems from the generalization of things and self-expression, just like the "pictographic" technique at the beginning of the formation of the writing system. Our inspiration came from Chinese character classification. We focused on "shadow" and used ink brush strokes to outline the flexibility of shadow puppets, overlapped the strokes to reflect the structures of shadow puppets, and used green and black as the main colors to enhance the recognition. In the generalization of traditional shadow puppets and the expression of modern styles, it honors the Chinese shadow puppets that have been passed down for thousands of years and spread across the country.

Design Firm
Liangxiang（良相设计）
Chengdu（成都）

Client
China Shadow
Play Museum
（中国皮影博物馆）

Principal Type
nothing（无）

Dimensions
11.7 × 16.5 in.
(29.7 × 42 cm)

IDENTITY: 2021 GUARDIAN ART BOOK FAIR

Concept

The image of the book fair focuses on two key points, one is "books," and the other is the "site of the book fair," the place where the sponsor is located, which is also the source of the visual differentiation of the image of the book fair. The exterior of the building is extracted into a stacked book image, with words surrounding the negative exterior of the "empty" building. The layout of words is arranged according to the external shape of the building, creating a new form. All visual images are then expanded accordingly.

Design Firm
Mint Brand Design
Beijing

Client
GUARDIAN

Principal Type
Akzidenz Grotesk
and Siyuan Hei

Dimensions
19.7 × 27.6 in.
(50 × 70 cm)

COMMUNCATION DESIGN

IDENTITY: NATIONAL WOMEN'S HISTORY MUSEUM

Concept
The National Women's History Museum is dedicated to telling the stories of the women who transformed the United States; displaying the collective history of American women; and offering a more complete view of U.S. history that will educate, inspire, and empower. Founded in 1996, the institution does this through a growing, state-of-the-art online presence as it looks forward to a future physical museum. This is a dynamic new visual identity for the museum that can evolve with the institution.

Design
Emily Atwood

Associate
Kirstin Huber

Partner
Paula Scher°

Design Firm
Pentagram New York°

Client
National Women's History Museum

Principal Type
Action Condensed Bold

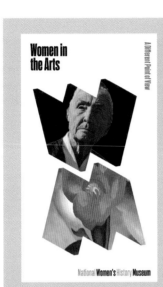

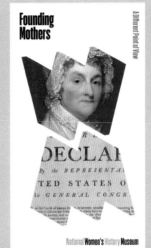

IDENTITY: PARADISE

Concept
This is the new logotype and brand identity for PARADISE.
We were invited to define and express a new visual identity that
highlights the company's marked innovation, emotion, and
visual dynamism. The newly designed logotype takes inspiration
from the 16:9 ratio medium and is set in a high-contrast
black-and-white color palette echoing classic cinematic title
design. The custom ligatures—created for the Adobe Originals
Willow typeface—maintain a concise footprint and evoke the
spirit of collaboration. Typographic moments are activated
as project stills float in and out of the anchored logotype..

Design
Catarina Freitas and
Lourenco Providencia

Creative Direction
Shannon Jager

URL
paradise.work

Design Firm
BRUTUS
New York

Client
PARADISE

Principal Type
Portrait and Willow
(customized)

IDENTITY: ROHRBACH GRUPPE BRAND

Concept
Rohrbach Architekten, Rohrbach Immobilien, and the property developer R+R Classic Bau are the three businesses of this family-run company. The logo system of the Rohrbach Gruppe is intended to unite all of the affiliated companies and strengthen them visually as a group. The family name is the company's trademark and is to be emphasized in the logo as well as in the company name—the "R" becomes a brand.

Design Firm
Ina Bauer
Kommunikationsdesign
Stuttgart

URL
rohrbach-gruppe.de

Client
Rohrbach Gruppe

Principal Type
Non Natural Grotesk

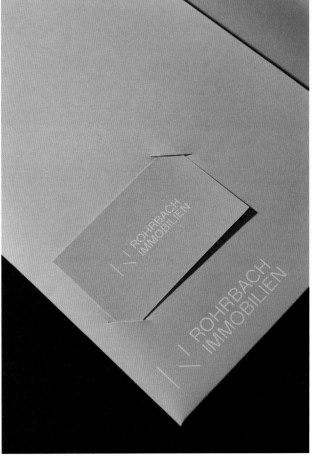

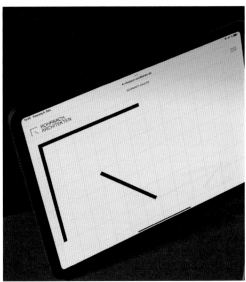

IDENTITY: DINO BURGER

Concept

Our brand wishes to convey a kind of "no make do," "no ordinary," "no surrender" life attitude. Who says a burger has to be junk food consumed quickly on the street? We say eating a burger can be like tasting a cup of coffee. Aside from the basic satisfaction of appetite, we hope that the moment customers open the box of burgers, they can be satisfied mentally and visually. To everyone out there, we wish the consumption of Dino Burger can offer a sense of "no make do" in your life.

Design Firms
Au Chon Hin, Untitled, and Witt Design
Macao

Photography
Rex Chang

Client
Dino Burger

Principal Type
Albertus Nova, Cako-Black, and Trois Mille Bold-25

Dimensions
24 × 36 in. (61 × 91cm)

IDENTITY: FOLK BRANDING

Concept

Folk crafts intricate textiles, taking care to source sustainable materials and dyes and only partnering with ethical weaving houses. The sans serif letterforms in the logotype were inspired by 1970s-era lettering, emphasizing each letter's simplest geometric qualities: paring down a complex idea to its essence. A thread conceptually ties the logotype together: from the horizontal stroke in the lowercase letter "f" to the horizontal stroke on the "k" that ends the logotype. These unexpected angles stand apart from stereotypical sans serif letterforms, tying the logo to the company's simple yet original designs.

Design
Kristmar Muldrow
Charleston,
South Carolina

Client
Folk

Principal Type
Custom

IDENTITY: 35A

Concept
Strong photographic references imbue the brand, 35A being the penultimate frame of a 35mm film roll. The pixel-based letterforms of the wordmark are inspired by film frame numbers. The bold orange color offers a contemporary reference to the sepia color of 35mm film. The rondel composition references lens specification markings. Copy callouts riff off photographic language with irreverence, contrasting the norm within an educational setting. Overall, the design retains a simple yet distinctive aesthetic that translates across key elements such as company collateral, emails, social, course, and promotional materials.

Design
James Powell

Creative Direction
Gideon Keith

Design Firm
Seven
Auckland

Client
35A

Principal Type
Untitled Sans
and custom

Dimensions
82.7 × 58.5 in.
(210 × 148.5 cm)

IDENTITY: LIPA ART COLLECTION BRAND IDENTITY

Concept
The collection features diverse art and artists, which we wanted to celebrate by producing a modular custom logotype, together with a varied color palette. At the same time, we also wanted to contrast the organic nature of the handmade art by going with strong, geometric graphics and simple color combinations, allowing the artwork itself to shine at times, and at others drawing attention with bold graphics and unexpected layouts. This idea of "controlled chaos," balancing and contrasting two opposing ideals, is at the center of a lot of the decisions we made.

Design
Domi Kramer

Typographer
Kurt Bullock

Type Foundry
Offhand Type
Malta

URL
behance.net/
gallery/133659055/
Lipa-art-collection-
Identity-System

Design Firm
Kumi Studio
Slovakia

Client
Lípa Art Collection

Principal Type
Diatype and custom

Dimensions
16.5 × 23.4 in. (42 x 59.4 cm)

IDENTITY: NEUFQUATRE EDITIONS

Concept
The concept was to capture the imperfect tension between two cultural poles. "In the southeast of Paris, from the ninety-four suburbs where the idea of creating our own publishing house was born to the bookstores stalls that we surveyed, our gaze is at the forefront of an intense cultural activity, fueled by the creative richness of our neighborhood and its proximity to the capital." —Theo Nestoret-Puyon, co-founder.

Design, Art, and Creative Direction
Tian Bai
Shenzhen, China

Client
Neufquatre
Editions Paris

Principal Type
Custom

Dimensions
23.6 × 35.4 in.
(60 × 90 cm)

IDENTITY: CHINESE NEW YEAR

Concept

The goal of this design was to create a happy and harmonious scene of Chinese New Year celebrations, reunion, and harmony; evoke people's memory of traditional Chinese New Year culture and Spring Festival rituals; and promote the rich historical culture and humanistic views of the Chinese New Year to the younger generation. The new year's door sign was inspired by the visual image elements of this exhibition. The traditional folk door sign was cut out of colored paper with rich, auspicious patterns and fringed heads on the bottom in festive colors. The New Year sign is posted on the door lintel to welcome the Spring Festival, which has a great charm when fluttering in the wind. The array of elements is active and smart, with a strong sense of space and full of beautiful meaning. The color system is combined with traditional clay sculpture colors, using positive red, pine cypress green, peach red, goose yellow, and other colors that have obvious New Year intentions, which fully presents a happy picture of the New Year's celebration in the sound of firecrackers.

Agency
China Academy of Art
Hang Zhou, China

Client
Crafts Museum of Caa

Principal Type
Source Han Sans

IDENTITY: CARNEGIE HALL BRAND IDENTITY

Concept
Carnegie Hall is synonymous with music. Its legacy of excellence in programming and world-renowned acoustics make it the most admired performance venue in the world, giving great significance to an artist's "Carnegie Hall debut." Champions worked closely with the in-house marketing and creative services teams to update the brand to help bring the transformative power of music to as many people in as many places as possible. The goal was to make everyone feel welcomed in the Hall without compromising on its standard of excellence.

Design
Taylor W. Hale

Design Direction
Bernard Hallstein and Michael McCaughley

**Assistant
Art Direction**
Raphael Davison and Cherry Liu

**Director, Publishing
and Creative Services**
Kathleen Schiaparelli

**Chief
Marketing Officer**
Sara Villagio

Illustration
Nina Carter

Graphic Design
Ephrat Seidenberg

Animation
Zipeng Zhu

Lead Strategist
Carina Sandoval

Marketing Associates
Michelle Stewart
and Amanda Zook

Project Manager
Haley Kattner Allen

**Senior Digital
Designer**
Hironi Park

Letterer
Jesse Ragan°
XYZ, New York

Typographer
Fred Shallcrass
Frere-Jones, New York

Partners
Jennifer Kinon and
Bobby C. Martin, Jr.°

Agency
Champions Design
New York

URL
championsdesign.com

Twitter
@heartgutsgrit

In-House Agency
Carnegie Hall Marketing
and Creative Services

Type Foundries
Frere-Jones Type
and XYZ Type

Client
Carnegie Hall

Principal Type
Cádiz and Fournier

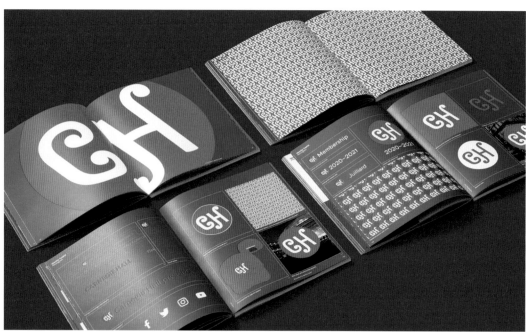

LOGOTYPES: RELICARIO

Concept

A reliquary as an object is a container for relics. It protects and keeps precious goods over the years. Based on visual language as a statement and as a way of approaching these precious objects, the type was created and inspired by the past, and temporal typography, with a contemporary approach. Old, timeless, and new, it creates a connection between an art language and graphics. The logo was created as a traditional stamp. And back to the pass as well—all the graphic materials were created with the stamp process print and scans.

Studio
SM Studio
Lisbon

Client
Fox TV Portugal

Principal Type
Relicario Type

175

LOGOTYPES: CARNEGIE HALL BRAND IDENTITY

Concept
Carnegie Hall is synonymous with music. Its legacy of excellence in programming and world-renowned acoustics make it the most admired performance venue in the world, giving great significance to an artist's "Carnegie Hall debut." Champions worked closely with the in-house marketing and creative services teams to update the brand to help bring the transformative power of music to as many people in as many places as possible. The goal was to make everyone feel welcomed in the Hall without compromising on its standard of excellence.

Design
Taylor W. Hale

Design Direction
Bernard Hallstein and
Michael McCaughley

**Assistant
Art Direction**
Raphael Davison
and Cherry Liu

**Director, Publishing
and Creative Services**
Kathleen Schiaparelli

**Chief
Marketing Officer**
Sara Villagio

Illustration
Nina Carter

Graphic Design
Ephrat Seidenberg

Animation
Zipeng Zhu

Lead Strategist
Carina Sandoval

Marketing Associates
Michelle Stewart
and Amanda Zook

Project Manager
Haley Kattner Allen

**Senior Digital
Designer**
Hironi Park

Letterer
Jesse Ragan°
XYZ, New York

Typographer
Fred Shallcrass
Frere-Jones, New York

Partners
Jennifer Kinon and
Bobby C. Martin, Jr.°

Agency
Champions Design
New York

URL
championsdesign.com

Twitter
@heartgutsgrit

In-House Agency
Carnegie Hall Marketing
and Creative Services

Type Foundries
Frere-Jones Type
and XYZ Type

Client
Carnegie Hall

Principal Type
Cádiz and Fournier

LOGOTYPES: CONNECTIVITY STANDARDS ALLIANCE

Concept

The Connectivity Standards Alliance (formerly the Zigbee Alliance), established in 2002, is the foundation and future of the Internet of Things (IoT). With wide-ranging global membership, the organization had evolved from its inception (focusing on Zigbee technology) to creating, maintaining, and delivering multiple IoT-enabling connectivity standards. With the Alliance having outgrown its original name, our challenge was to create a new brand that could represent the Alliance's reach and responsibility in enabling collaboration across the industry. Our goal was to capture the feeling of an organization that helps people truly work together, advancing the field of IoT.

Design Direction
Andrew Bellamy

Design Fellow
Eddy Lee

**Director of
Verbal Identity**
Blaine McEvoy

**Executive Creative
Director**
Oliver Maltby

**Executive
Strategy Director**
Andrew Miller

Consultant, Strategy
Yulim Heo

**Consultant,
Verbal Identity**
Rachel Loucks

**Senior Consultant,
Strategy**
Charlotte Li

**Senior Consultant,
Verbal Identity**
Jack Stiuso

Senior Designers
Liora Cher and
Spencer Seligman

Senior Client Manager
Engy Neville

Industrial Designer
Alexandre Nys

Agency
Interbrand
New York

Client
Connectivity
Standards Alliance

Principal Type
Assemble

Paving the way towards seamless connectivity.

Assemble, bespoke typeface

127 unique ligatures

127 unique ligatures

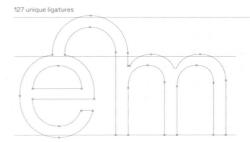

us → uß

we → we

LOGOTYPES: SPARK THE NEW "CHOY"?

Concept
Our concept is to create a brand theme that brings temptation and happiness before and after every great treated meal, like going to a high-end restaurant. It includes wagging tails and happy ears inspiration for ink traps and Vietnamese diacritics, together with funny Gen Z copywriting supported by minimal and direct design layout..

Art Direction
Anh Pham
Ho Chi Minh City

Creative Direction
Anh Nyugen

Executive Creative Director
Duy Nguyen

Copywriter, Producer, and Social Media Manager
Quan Nguyen

Photography
Wing Chan,
BITE Studio

Project Manager
Lan Mai

Type Foundry
TypeType Foundry
St. Petersburg, Russia

Design Firm
M-N Associates

Client
PetChoy

LOGOTYPES: KINEMA

Concept

Kinema is a new social cinema platform that makes it easy for anyone, anywhere to show movies and share in the proceeds. We devised a new brand identity for the company that centers around a bold wordmark and symbol. By combining the first two letters of the name, a graphic camera and/or projector icon is formed, putting technology and entertainment at the heart of the brand.

Art Direction
Lyam Bewry and
Luke Robertson
San Francisco and Paris

Creative Direction
Rob Duncan

Motion Design Studio
Gimmewings
Barcelona

Design Firm
Mucho, Inc.

Principal Type
Regola Pro and
Söhne Breit

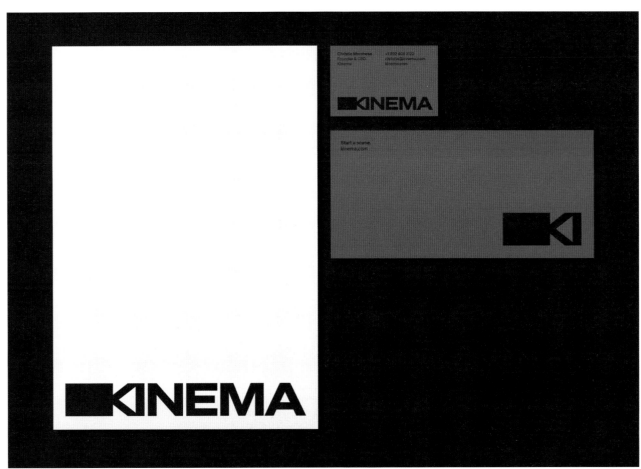

LOGOTYPES: AAPQ

Concept

The AAPQ's acronym draws a circle through its use of repetition and rotational movement. The organized circular arrangement of the logotype evokes a sense of gathering and speaks of an association that federates its members around common values. Its shape is also reminiscent of a seal that acknowledges the AAPQ's desire to have a visual identity that focuses on excellence. Different analogies, like one of a flower or planet Earth, can be drawn from the shape. The identity uses the typeface Fakt, designed by Thomas Thiemich..

Design and Art Direction
Julien Hébert
Montréal

Creative Direction
Bryan-K. Lamonde

Project Manager
Sarah Rochefort

URL
principal.studio

Design Firm
Principal

Client
Association des architectes paysagistes du Québec, AAPQ

Principal Type
Fakt

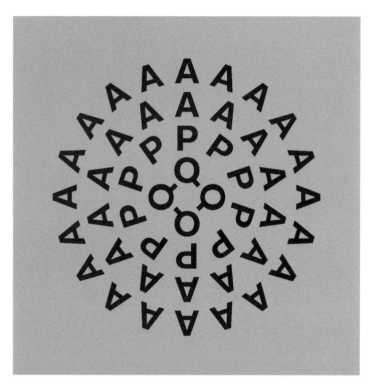

LOGOTYPES: PIEDMONT ART WALK

Concept
We created an iconic brand symbol and identity for a community-based event in Piedmont, California, called Art Walk. This was as simple as making the word "Art" walk. Through animation and witty interpretations of the logo and copy, it resonated with the community audience, both young and old, and created a memorable identity, recognizable for years to come

Design
Hiuman Ng and Cindy Zheng
San Francisco

Art Direction
Lyam Bewry

Creative Direction
Rob Duncan

Design Firm
Mucho, Inc.

Client
Piedmont Art Walk

Principal Type
A2 Gothic

LOGOTYPES: SQUIRRELS

Concept
Our strategic approach to the Squirrels brand idea was to rewind to the beginning of the Scouts story—Brownsea Island. It is the home to the birth of the Scouts movement 112 years ago (as well as a brood of ultra-rare red squirrels). We used the island's flora and fauna as inspiration for our visual language and created the squirrels logotype. The perfect balance between symbol and wordmark was achieved and proves a highly versatile component in the success of the brand.

Design
Rob Clarke°
Harpenden, UK

URLs
supplestudio.com
robclarke.com

Client
Squirrels

Agency
Supple Studio

Principal Type
Bespoke

LOGOTYPES: PARADISE

Concept
This is a new logotype and brand identity for PARADISE. We were invited to define and express a new visual identity that highlights the company's marked innovation, emotion, and visual dynamism. The newly designed logotype takes inspiration from the 16:9 ratio medium and is set in a high-contrast black-and-white color palette echoing classic cinematic title design. The custom ligatures—created for the Adobe Originals Willow typeface—maintain a concise footprint and evoke the spirit of collaboration. Typographic moments are activated as project stills float in and out of the anchored logotype..

Design
Catarina Freitas and Lourenco Providencia
New York

Creative Direction
Shannon Jager

URL
paradise.work

Design Firm
BRUTUS

Client
PARADISE

Principal Type
Portrait and Willow (customized)

LOGOTYPES: CHENGDU ART MUSEUM

Concept

The letter "A" and the letter "M" form a rotating poster stand. At forty-five rotation angles, you can see an abstract Chinese font, "Cheng," which represents "Chengdu, China." Different angles can be used as different sub-brands of the museum after being suspended. For example, ninety degrees can be used as a logo for an art store. After rotating to 180 degrees, it can be used as a logo for a public education space. The logo can be presented in different shapes in different sizes.s.

Design
Yiqiang Chen
and Jiao Teng

Art Direction
Xijiang Liu

Copywriter
Xiaoshuang Huang

Design Firm
Happy Brand
Chengdu, China

Client
Chengdu Art Museum

Principal Type
Letter Gothic Std

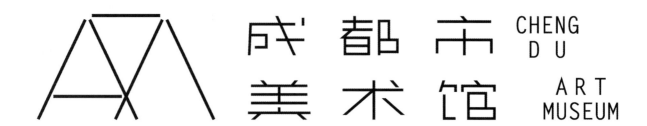

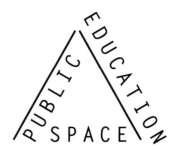

LOGOTYPES: ACRM

Concept
ACRM is an experienced architecture and construction company based in Athens. For the new logo, our main intension was to create a typographic "canvas" of the company principles and humane character as another layer behind the forms and precision of their actual work.

Art Direction
Laios Papazoglou
Athens

Creative Direction
Katerina Papanagiotou

Motion Design
Korina Galika and
Anastasia Melandinou

Project Manager
Spyros Acheimastos

Copywriter
Efthimis Filippou

Design Firm
MNP

Client
ACRM

Principal Type
Dromon CF Regular

```
A   C
R       M
Ask, Create,
Rotate, Make.
```

```
A       C   R   M
Athens, Cyan, Raw, Monolith.
```

```
A
C
R
M
Architecture,
Construction,
Revised,
Mixed.
```

```
A
C
R       M
Altruism,
Cubism,
Romanticism, Modernism.
```

```
A
C               R
M
Answers,
Centimeters, Revolutions,
Materials.
```

```
A   C   R       M
Alive, Curious, Romantic, Majestic.
```

```
A
C
R
M
Alive,
Curious,
Romantic,
Majestic.
```

```
A   C   R
M
Athens, Cyan, Raw,
Monolith.
```

```
A   C   R
M
Ask, Create, Rotate,
Make.
```

LOGOTYPES: MAKE

Concept
We developed a beautifully simple "M" monogram for Make that depicts a dovetail joint, a ubiquitous part of the furniture maker's craft. The logo can be elegantly applied to a number of applications, including digital material, uniforms, packaging, and signage, and it is even used as a maker's mark and branded into pieces of furniture, albeit discreetly.

Studio
Studio Garbett
Sydney

Client
Make

Twitter
@garbettdesign

Principal Type
Neue Haas Unica

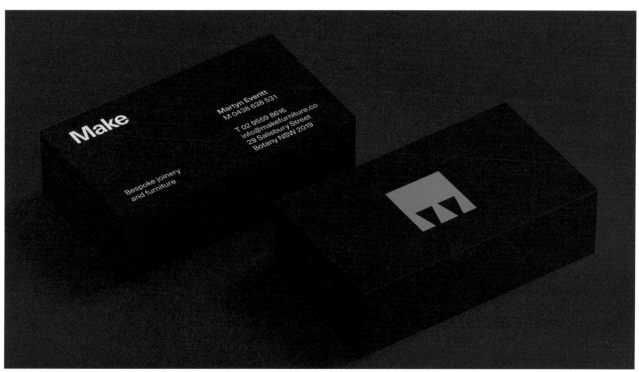

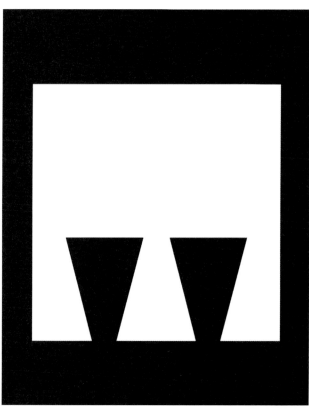

LOGOTYPES: HISTORISK MUSEUM

Concept
Historisk museum contains Norway's largest collection of ethnographic and historical artifacts. The architect of the museum, Henrik Bull, drew multiple versions of a monogram that adorns a variety of embellishments and details in the building. The monogram became a graphic focal point in the identity that can vary in size and clarity, which carries the history of the museum itself..

Design
Halvor Nordrum
Oslo

Creative Director
Svein Haakon Lia

Documentation
Photography
Jan Khür

Project Manager
Marie Louise Steen

Strategist
Christoffer Nøkleby

URL
bleed.com/historisk-museum

Design Firm
Bleed Design Studio

Client
Historisk museum

Principal Type
ABC Diaty

LOGOTYPES: THE WILDEST

Concept
Design Concept
As part of the brand identity for a new pet care editorial platform called The Wildest, we set out to create a logo that expressed both the wild side of pet ownership and at the same time conveyed trust in the expert advice the site offers. Our solution was a bespoke logotype grounded in a strong typographic sensibility (inspired by newspapers' old-style serifs) with an expressive, playful "W" that becomes a memorable brand gesture in its own right. This mark sets the tone of The Wildest's identity: trustworthy yet playful, honest yet lighthearted.

Design
Natalia Oledzka
and Hyejin Song
Brooklyn, New York

Creative Direction
Leo Porto and
Felipe Rocha

Animation
Giordano Caldas
and Rafael Morinaga

Project Management
Nicholas Schröder
and Claren Walker

Typography Refinement
Jesse Ragan°
XYZ Type

Design Firm
PORTO ROCHA

Client
The Wildest:
Jenna DiGiovanni,
Claire Falloon,
Tessa Gould,
and Emily Nesi

Principal Type
Plantin (customized)

LOGOTYPES: TCM LOGO

Concept
The TCM logo embraces the range of interpretations of a "Classic." When it is activated, the T and M letterforms act as a frame for the ever-evolving "C" in between, ultimately landing in its final state. The C is a storyteller with a vast series of interpretations. Our partnership and logo development for TCM extended past the main TCM logo and led to the creation of logos for TCM's on-air and in-person franchises, as well as the TCM Film Festival.

Design
Carla Dasso and
Claire Typaldos

Design Direction
Lauren Infante

Logo Design
Pam Olecki

Creative Direction
Kate Daniels

Chief Creative Officers
Mikon van Gastel
and Joe Wright

**Executive
Creative Direction**
Lauren Hartstone

**Executive Director,
Creative Strategy**
Anita Olan

Director of Production
Julie Bitton

Executive Producer
Joanna Fillie

Producer
Julia Oetker-Kast

Senior Animators
Lucas Bell and
Ben Nichols

**Senior Broadcast
Animator**
Jin Lim

Animator
Byunghoon Han

**Senior
Marketing Director**
Dexter Fedor

Writers/Producers
David Byrne and
Christian Hammann

Writer/Strategist
Allison Gutman

Agency
Sibling Rivalry
New York

Client
Turner Classic
Movies (TCM)
Atlanta

LOGOTYPES: F(U)=FORMULE CAFE

Concept

f(u) = formule CAFÉ is a coffee brand that follows a precise formula. The formula is also the design language of f(u) = formule CAFÉ. The veritable quadrilateral is the symbol of the infinite possibility of f(u) = formule CAFÉ. The graphics are all presented by the varying forms of the four letters "CAFÉ." As a result of the design idea, boundaries of the brand image are broken, the content is extended, and there is a plurality of forms of existence in random situations.

Design Firm
By-enjoy Design
Fujian, China

URL
by-enjoy.com/branding/
formuleCAFE.html

Client
f(u)=formule CAFÉ

Principal Type
Bodoni Oldstyle,
HarmonyOS Sans,
and Helvetica Neue

$$f(u) = \frac{form(u)le}{CAFÉ}$$

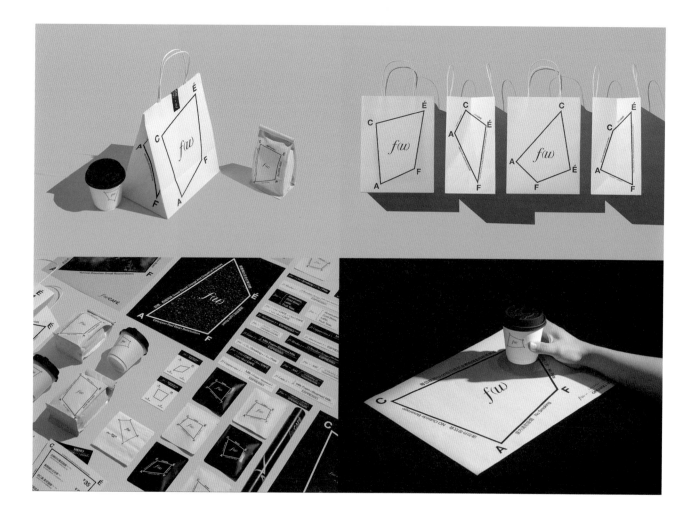

LOGOTYPES: FRANKIE'S BURGER BAR

Concept

The concept for the brand identity of Frankie's Burger Bar is based on those incandescent lines of the grill when the burger is on fire, which, when treated with different perspectives, transform the naming and generate a three-dimensional optical illusion that is carried to all online applications and offline, such as clothing, packaging, letters, web, etc., and of course to environmental graphics such as posters and signage, traveling and wrapping the space on the floor, walls, and ceiling, appealing to the diner with direct messages.

Chief Creative Officer
Carlos Sánchez
Valencia

URL
creatias.es

Twitter
@carloscreatias

Design Firm
Creatias Estudio

Client
Frankie's Burger Bar

Principal Type
Bebas Neue Pro Bold

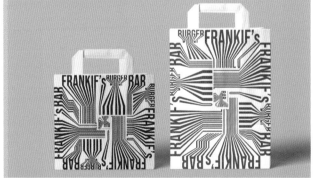

LOGOTYPES: XILANKAPU

Concept

Xilankapu is a traditional folk-art product of ethnic minorities in southwest China. The visual identity presented a modern, fashionable, and unique graphic logo by refining the classic colors and pattern structure of the traditional Xilankapu, using geometric figures to construct the Chinese and English fonts of Xilankapu, and then transforming the character into a visual graphic.

Art Direction
Mao Mao
Chongqing, China

Client
Sunac Folk Art

Principal Type
Custom

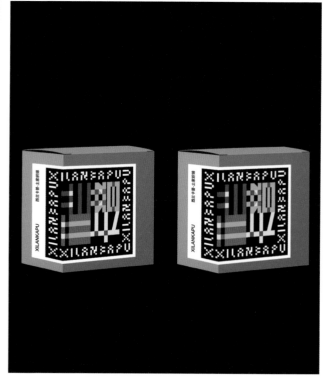

LOGOTYPES: KYOYO LOGOTYPE

Concept

Kyoyo is a joint project of creative workers, covering brand planning, graphic design, event planning, and event promotion, whose customers include a variety of industries and public welfare projects. We hope to give Kyoyo the meaning its name indicates, "sauntering in the cool autumn day." Relaxed and entertaining—an impressive brand image.

Design Firm
Chengdesign
Zhangzhou, China

Client
Kyoyo

Principal Type
Custom

LOGOTYPES: WUFANG ARCHITECTURAL DESIGN FIRM

Concept

Wu means emptiness or returning to zero, while
fang means rules and boundaries. 88
Wufang means freedom and infinity. Based on the original
spirit of architectural design, the work advocates the idea of
boundless design with the core of "being boundless." The names
of the guidance system are from Buddhist meditation terms,
which mean all things are empty and they are either dying
nor being born. They coordinate with the environment.

Design Firm
Jilin HOHA
Advertising Co., Ltd
Changchun, China

URL
hohachina.com

Client
Wufang Architectural
Design Firm
Shanghai

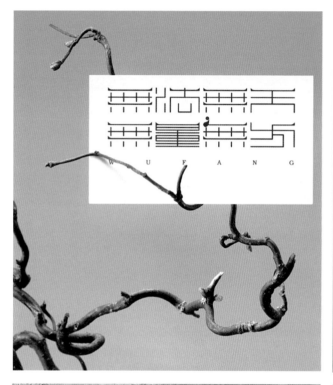

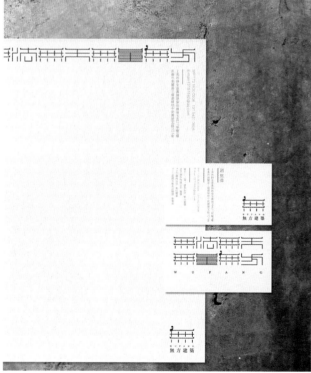

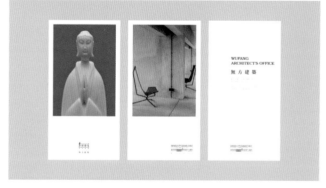

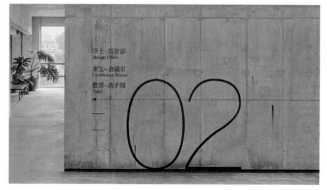

MISCELLANEOUS: PODCAST IDENTITY

Design
Trabucco-Campos
Brooklyn, New York

Client
SEARCH for Arts
Leadership

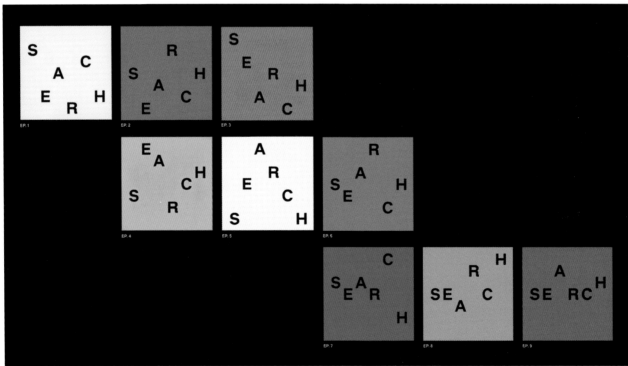

MOTION TV: RE:RISO NAUGHTY ROLL FEATURED WORKS EXHIBITION

Concept

The design concept of the trailer for the Riso exhibition is inspired by the instability of Risograph printing. The overall visual effect focuses on showing more different creativity and visual explosiveness brought out by the collision among graphic design works in different styles and contents influenced by the "instability" of Risograph. The font—the selection and design of which also aim to highlight the printing effect, dots, overprint, and imperfect nature of Risograph printing—jumps flexibly and dynamically over the whole trailer to express the flexible application and unique aesthetic features of Risograph printing.

Art Direction
Dan Ferreira
and Ieong Kun Lam
Macau

Animation
Ivan Sio

Illustration
Wakka Cheang
and Keika Leong

URL
indegodesign.com

Design Firm
indego design

Client
Naughty Roll

Principal Type
Aeonik

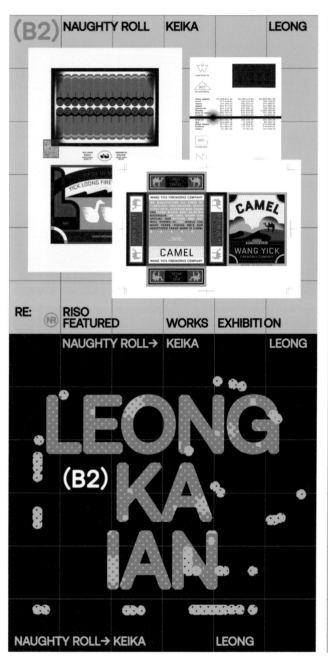

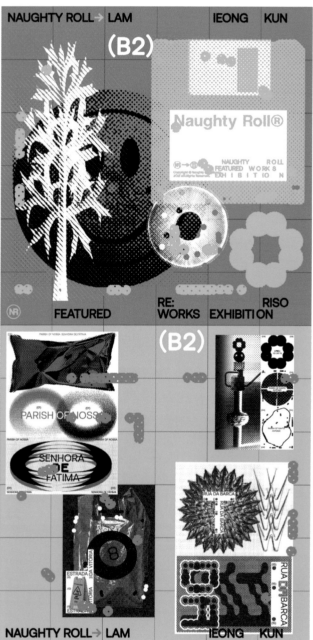

MOTION TV: MACHINE·LEARNING·GENERATED·AUDIO·REACTIVE·TYPE

Concept
This is audio-reactive, machine-learning-generated typography along a 512-dimensional axis. The type morphs from upper to lowercase, serif to sans, bold to italic, expanded to condensed, hairline to ultra black. It is typography that comes to life—something meant to be read is dancing instead. The experimental project is assisted by artificial intelligence, resulting in output that is impossible to create manually.

Design
Dev Valladares
Baltimore

Instagram
@devethanvalladares

Principal Type
Custom

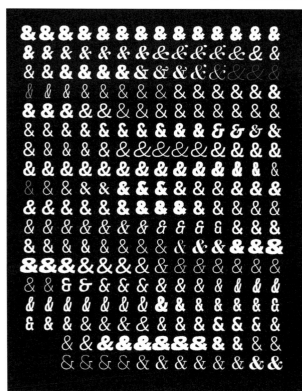

MOTION TV: WESTERN CALLIGRAPHY ANNUAL EXHIBITION: POP & ART

Concept
In response to the exhibition theme POP & ART, we designed these six modern English letters for the exhibition and invited the artists to write in Western calligraphy in the space reserved for the letters. In the video, the font has gradually evolved from a mysterious and elegant crystal texture to a metal texture with strong visual collision and full of illusory change in color, as the Western calligraphy, starting from traditional art, still bursts out different charm in the new generation.

Art Direction
Dan Ferreira and
Ieong Kun Lam

Animation
Koroh Lok

Typographer
Oliver Lao

URL
indegodesign.com

Design Firm
indego design

Client
The Lettering Artists
Association of Macau

Principal Type
Grand Slang Roman
and Nostra

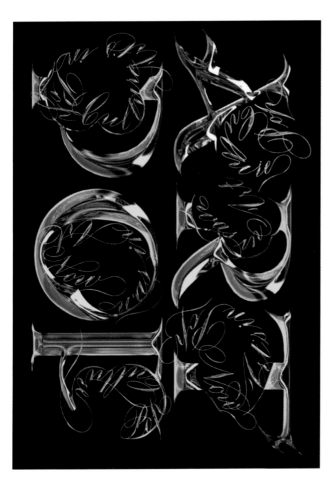

MOVIE TITLES OPENING: CASSANDRA

Concept
This project started a few years ago in a completely different format, a theater play later turned into a book. That book, also titled Cassandra, was designed in 2014. At the time, we came up with a design concept based on the fact that we had seven plays from seven Portuguese authors. Typography played a major role, and we wanted to keep it that way. The main challenge now was to get inspired by the book but at the same time create a unique motion piece that would represent all seven episodes and do that with a single graphic element: typography.

Motion Design
Nuno Leites
Porto

Art Direction
Sérgio Alves

Design Firm
Atelier d'Alves
and Nuno Leites

Production Companies
Take It Easy Films and
Cimbalino Filmes

Music Composers
Luis Fernandes
and Joana Gama

Principal Type
Rhode

PACKAGING: BEN'S BEST

Concept

The visual language of Ben's Best packaging is driven by expressive typography—all crafted within the safety requirements surrounding the product (the packaging is child-proof, opaque, and sealable). The product and packaging are adorned in a medley of the words of Black leaders, the work of contemporary Black artists and typographers, and calls to deschedule cannabis. The varied typographic and visual approaches capture the activist spirit of the brand in its packaging, speaking to the serious mission and messages at the heart of its work and expressing it through a crafted and engaging form.

Design
Raoul Gottschling

Artist
Dana Robinson

Partner
Eddie Opara°

Photography
Claudia Mandlik

Senior Designer
Jack Collins

Team Coordinator
Dana Reginiano

Junior Designer
Ruben Gijselhart

Design Firm
Pentagram New York°

Client
Ben's Best

Principal Type
Bayard, Eva Maria, and Martin

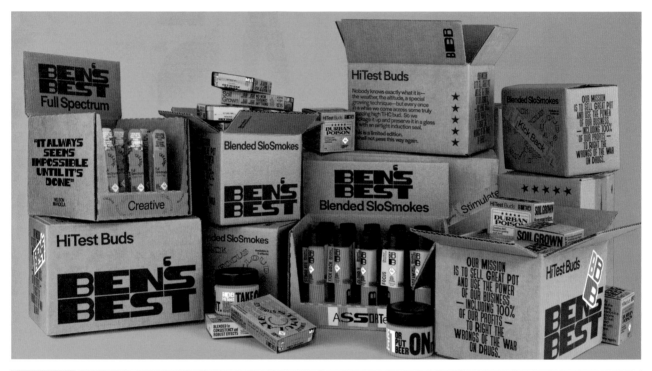

PACKAGING: FULL MOON TEA GIFT

Concept
The full-moon tea gift is composed of three years of white tea. We combined the meaning of the full moon with the brand concept, outlined the mountain scene under the full moon by cutting paper, and used concave and convex technology to show its cleanliness and delicacy appropriate to white tea. The white tea of different years is packed in three separate cartons and placed in sequence. The boxes also form a picture of the full moon on mountains and forests, with subtle aftertaste. Nowadays, gifts on the market often reflect the sense of quality using complex packaging. We sought to abandon redundant elements and use design methods to present the texture and brand temperament of the tea gift.

Design and Art Direction
Young Ho

URL
designbyao.com

Twitter
@designbyaodotcom

Design Firm
Design by AO
Shenzhen, China

Client
A Tea Store

Principal Type
Copperplate Gothic Std
and Source Han Serif

Dimensions
2.6 × 3.9 × 2.6 in.
(6.6 × 10 × 6.6 cm)
10.5 × 6.5 × 2.8 in.
(26.5 × 16.5 × 7 cm)

PACKAGING: SPARK THE NEW "CHOY"?

Concept
Our concept is to create a brand theme that brings temptation and happiness before and after every great treated meal, like going to a high-end restaurant. It includes wagging tails and happy ears inspiration for ink traps and Vietnamese diacritics, together with funny Gen Z copywriting supported by minimal and direct design layout.

Art Direction
Anh Pham

Creative Direction
Anh Nguyen

Executive Creative Direction
Duy Nguyen

Copywriter
Quan Nguyen

Photography
Wing Chan,
BITE Studio

Project Manager
Lan Mai

Producer
Quan Nguyen

URL
m-n.associates

Typographer
TypeType
Russia

Design Firm
M-N Associates
Ho Chi Minh City

Client
Pet Choy

Principal Type
Fragen, Nunito,
TT Trailers Petchoy,
and VT 323

Dimensions
7 × 5 × 1.7 in.
(18 × 12.6 × 4.4 cm)

PACKAGING: OFFER OF GAFA ADMISSION

Concept

Appearing at the entrance of the store, the words "WELCOME" scrolling on the LED screen are a warm greeting to new customers. I wanted to use this sentiment in the design of the admission letter of GAFA. The passionate dotted text, scrolling on the welcome material, makes the static font present a dynamic effect on the print media. The content of the internal material is set on the surface, thus creating the feeling of information rapidly passing by, and the interplay of text movement and stillness is like a moment of time frozen.

Design
Tian Bo, Chen Luyi, and Ling Hongdai

Art Direction
Tian Bo

Design Firm
TEN BUTTONS
Guangzhou, China

Client
Guangzhou Academy of Fine Arts

Principal Type
Lanting Hei

Dimensions
14 × 10.7 in.
(35.5 × 27.1 cm)

PACKAGING: BATIDOS MASA

Concept

Our job was not only to create the packaging but also to strategically decide how the Masa brand should look in large stores. Until now, Masa had only lived in its own stores. We decided to move away from common language with photographs found in supermarkets and created colorful packaging with striking typography that simulates the movement of fruits and vegetables in the blender. We also explain in a short and simple way the steps to prepare the smoothies at home.

Design
Nicolas Galeano

Art Direction
Felipe Osorio

Chief Design Officer
Oliver Siegenthaler

Design Firm
S&Co
Bogota

Client
Masa

Principal Type
Cactus and Feixen Sans

Dimensions
3 × 4.5 in.
(7.6 × 11.4 cm)

PACKAGING: SONOS ACCESSORIES PACKAGING

Concept

To complement the robust redesign of Sonos' next generation of packaging, we created a modular subsystem that allows for the growth and flexibility of new products and accessories as the Sonos product line expands. Creating a consistent system across many regions and even more products, we were able to maintain the spirit of the Sonos brand without losing sight of the sustainable, economical, and functional goals of the larger packaging system.

Design
Carl-Hampus Vallin

Art Direction
Olivia Ward

Art Direction, Packaging Experience and Visual Design
Ben Blanchard

Creative Direction
Brett Newman

Director, Packaging Experience
Michelle Enright

Executive Creative Director
Dora Drimalas

Principal Industrial Designer, Packaging Experience
Jeremy Etchison

Agency
Hybrid Design
San Francisco

Client
Sonos, Inc.
Santa Barbara, California

POSTERS: DRIFT

Concept
On the fifth anniversary of the Elbphilharmonie Hamburg, the internationally sought-after artist duo DRIFT is staging its most extensive presentation in Germany to date at the MK&G. From January to May, DRIFT will transform the MK&G into a sensual experience space on 350 square meters with three spectacular kinetic sculptures.

Design Firm
Fons Hickmann M23
Berlin

Client
Museum für Kunst und
Gewerbe Hamburg

Principal Type
Scto Grotesk

Dimensions
33.1 × 46.8 in.
(84.1 × 118.9 cm)

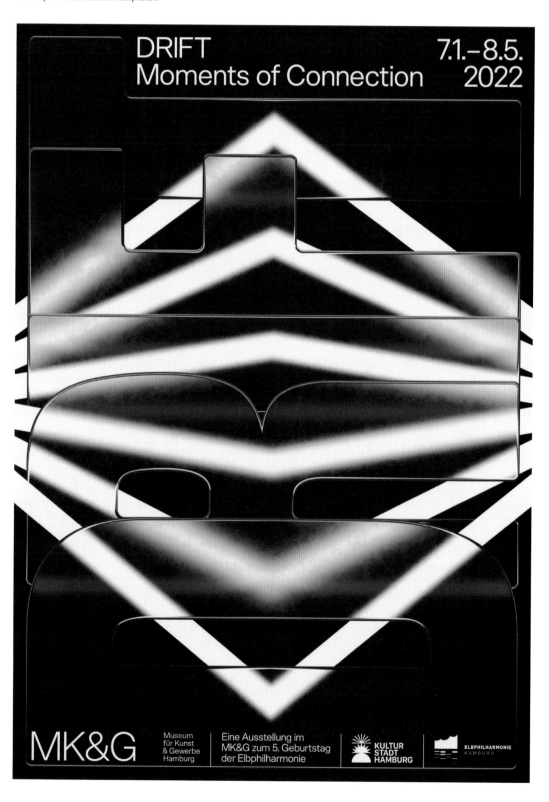

POSTERS: THE FIVE GREAT MOUNTAINS OF CHINA REVAMP

Concept

The Five Great Mountains of China posters convey a message of discovering with knowledge—read thousands of books and travel thousands of miles. The posters show the Chinese names of the five great mountains of China yet present the well-known unique geomorphic characteristics of the five great mountains: East—Mount Tai (泰) is like sitting, South—Mount Heng (衡) is like flying, West—Mount Hua (华) is like standing, North—Mount Heng (恒) is like walking, and Center—Mount Song (嵩) is like lying. The mountain forms the type, and the type shows the mountain.

Design
Jingyi Huang

Creative Direction
Jordan Ou Zhuopeng

Design Firm
Centre Design
Zhongshan, China

Client
Caobu Public Library

Principal Type
Custom

Dimensions
21.9 × 33.1 in.
(55.5 × 84 cm)

POSTERS: FLIBBERTIGIBBET

Concept
The party series flibbertigibbet takes place at locations that are not officially communicated. Accordingly, the poster had to develop a clearly recognizable formal language that could be shared on social media as an animated icon and serve as a signpost in the urban space. Like the party series, the poster has become a (typographic) experiment: the typeface is interrupted by an undefined element, almost element, almost dissolving in places, thus becoming louder, more urgent, more inescapable—like its namesake, flibbertigibbet.

Design Firm
Siyu Mao
Berlin

Principal Type
Roumald

Dimensions
23.4 × 33.1 in.
(59.4 × 84.1 cm)

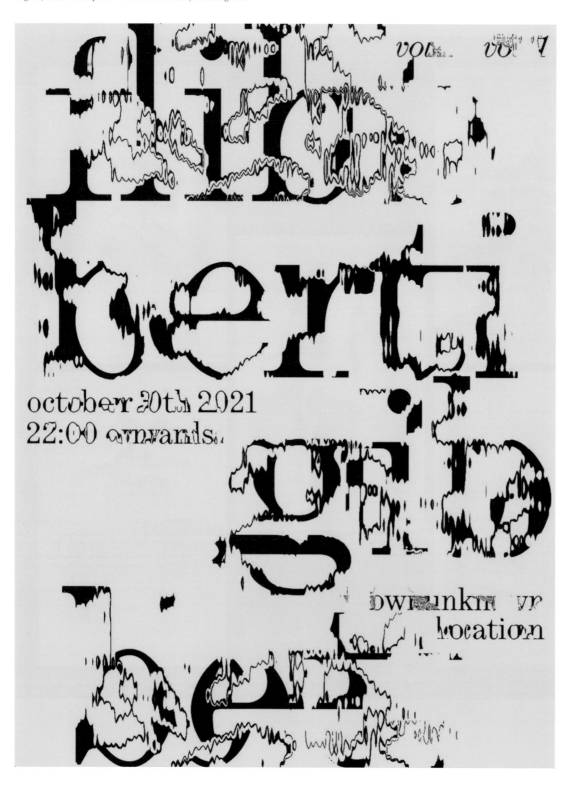

POSTERS: THE 52ND TOGAKUSHI SOBA FESTIVAL

Concept
This typography was inspired by
vaudeville characters.

**Design and
Art Direction**
Tatsuya Nishi
Togakushi,
Nagano, Japan

Studio
Nishigraph

Client
Togakushi Soba Festival
Executive Committee

Principal Type
Futo Go B101 and
Rosewood Std Fill

Dimensions
28.7 × 40.6 in.
(72.8 × 103 cm)

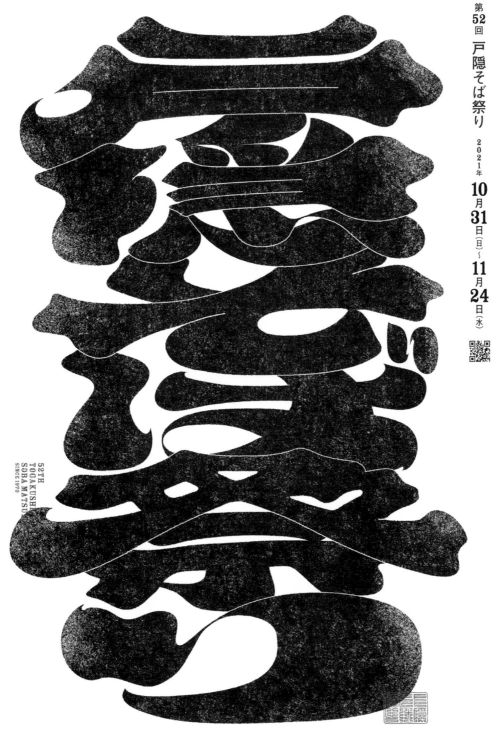

第52回 戸隠そば祭り

2021年 10月31日(日)〜11月24日(水)

52TH
TOGAKUSHI
SOBA MATSURI
SINCE 1970

https://sobamatsuri.com

主催／戸隠そば祭り実行委員会　お問い合わせ／長野市商工会戸隠支所 TEL.026-254-2541、(一社)戸隠観光協会 TEL.026-254-2688　共催／長野市商工会、(一社)戸隠観光協会　後援／長野市、(公財)ながの観光コンベンションビューロー

POSTERS: PROSPERO

Concept

This diptych poster series is at the heart of the campaign promoting Théâtre Prospero's 2021–2022 program of shows. It aims to reflect the creative process of the institution based on an experimental, daring, and surprising approach that always questions conventions and explores new forms. The typographic layout system is broken up by a few spaces to disturb the rhythm and add tension to the compositions. Within each diptych, one of the posters focuses on the main actor photographed through a distorted lens—referencing the season's recurring theme of consciousness/unconsciousness—while the other is strictly graphic, packing all the main information.

Design
Nick Losacco

Art Direction
Bryan-K. Lamonde
and Nick Losacco

Creative Direction
Bryan-K. Lamonde

Project Manager
Justine Crépeau-Viau

Account Director
Mathieu Cournoyer

URL
principal.studio

Design Firm
Principal
Montréal

Client
Théâtre Prospero

Principal Type
Futura and Superpose

Dimensions
24 × 36 in.
(61 × 91.4 cm)

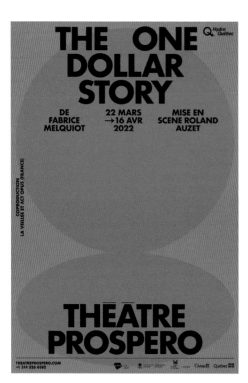

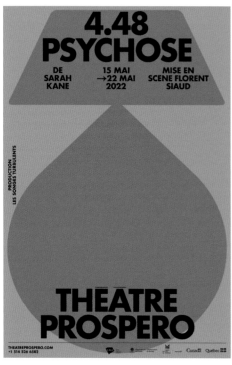

POSTERS: U&I

Concept
This is a poster for "What Unites Us 2," an international poster exhibition in Turkey. This year's topic was "Stronger Together." I used block letters U and I, tied together with an ampersand bow.

Creative Direction
Jan Sabach°
Northampton,
Massachusetts

URL
codeswitchdesign.com

Design Firm
Code Switch

Client
What Unites Us

Principal Type
Custom and Neue
Haas Unica Pro

Dimensions
19.7 × 27.6 in.
(50 × 70 cm)

POSTERS: TAG DER OFFENEN TÜR 2021

Concept
The building of the Basel School of Design
lives on its simple but refined play of form.
The poster is intended to reflect the simple
architecture of the school building.

Agency
Neeser & Müller

URL
neesermueller.ch

Client
Schule für
Gestaltung Basel

Principal Type
Executive

Dimensions
35.2 × 50.4 in.
(89.5 × 128 cm)

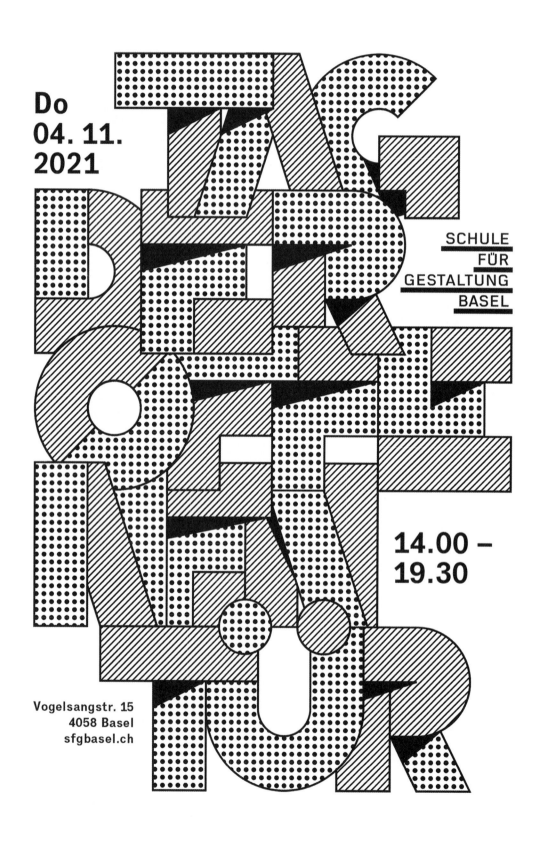

POSTERS: YOUFAB GLOBAL CREATIVE AWARDS 2021

Concept

This is a variable poster that uses a unique cellular automaton algorithm. The algorithm, in which many cells laid out in space interact with neighboring cells and change their own state over time, is a simple rule, yet it behaves similarly to the life and death and mechanisms of society.
I cut out a moment of typography and printed it with inkjet-printer. By deliberately fixing the image on paper with physical properties, I aimed to create an organic visual that evokes the workings of life and a chain of thought, rather than staying in the digital realm of expression.

Design
Natsuki Isa and
Kohki Watanabe
Tokyo

Art Direction
Natsuki Isa and
Kazushige Takebayashi

Creative Direction
Sho Hosotani
and Natsuki Sagawa

**Executive
Creative Director**
Toshiya Fukuda

**Chief Technology
Officer**
Daiki Kanaoka

Digital Artist
Takayuki Watanabe

Freelancer
1002 inc.

Photography
Akihiro Yoshida

Programmer
Junichiro Horikawa

Printing Company
SHOEI INC.

Printing Direction
Shunichi Yamashita

URL
youfab.info/2021

Design Firms
777CreativeStrategies,
Kitasenju Design,
Orange Jellies, and
SHA inc.
Toyko

Client
FabCafe and
Loftwork, Inc.

Principal Type
Custom

Dimensions
40.6 × 28.7 in.
(103 × 72.8 cm)

POSTERS: NEUBAD — JAZZ

Concept
This is a poster for a concert series at the Neubad in Lucerne. Every Wednesday, the venue turns into a space for performances of contemporary jazz music—fresh and intuitive, short but intense. There is improvisation, experimentation, and interaction—jazz unconventional and free.

Design Firm
Fons Hickmann M23
Berlin

Client
Neubad

Principal Type
Untitled and custom

Dimensions
35.2 × 50.4 in.
(89.5 × 128 cm)

COMMUNCATION DESIGN

POSTERS: FLAMENCO BIENNALE

Concept
The dynamic identity for the Flamenco Biënnale Nederland captures the spirit of this avant-garde music and dance festival. Flamenco uses a unique twelve-beat cycle. That is why, within a twelve-point grid, four points are connected. The repetition of this form makes an "F." In moving graphics, this "F" transforms in print stills from the moving graphics, which are combined to make graphic images that stand out and reflect the soul of the festival.

Design Firm
Thonik
Amsterdam

URL
thonik.nl

Client
Flamenco Biënnale

Principal Type
Flamenco F

Dimensions
46.5 × 33 in.
(118 × 83.5 cm)

Amsterdam Arnhem
Rotterdam Middelburg
Utrecht Antwerpen
Eindhoven Brussel
Den Bosch Gent

flamenco biënnale
07.11 – 28.11.21
flamencobiennale.nl

POSTERS: BAKUB 2/MAKING FROM EAST TO WEST

Concept
Art and construction have a different permanence than art that is shown in exhibition spaces. It exposes itself to the public and must confront the question of what the public is, how it is composed, and is always under special pressure to legitimize itself. We stage the acronym "BAKUB" to fill the space to the maximum and condense the layout into a typographic monument. The typographic interpretation of the acronym "BAKUB" is subject to continuous development from issue to issue. The designed systematics in the typography remain intact and form the heart of the visual appearance.

Art Direction
Céline Beyeler and Stephan Nopper
Bern

Production Company
JCM Werbedruck AG
Schlieren, Switzerland

Agency
Kornhaus Atelier

Client
Verein Basis Kunst und Bau, Bern

Principal Type
BAKUB Typeface and Monument Grotesk Regular

Dimensions
35.2 × 50.4 in.
(89.5 × 128 cm)

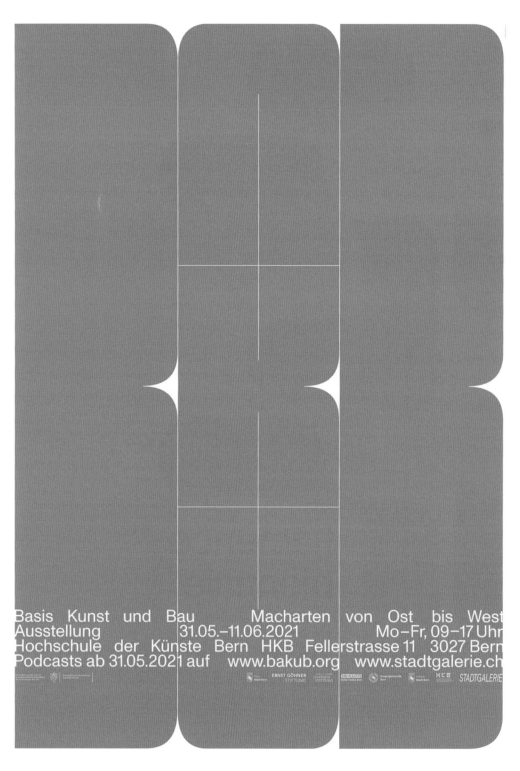

POSTERS: VKHUTEMAS.ACADEMY: POSTER-SERIES

Concept

VKHUTEMAS workshops were an amazing global phenomenon. A lot has been written about them. At the same time, it seems to be the most underestimated phenomenon in the global history of design. This style is interesting because it flourished in the USSR against the background of an emerging ideological smokescreen. It was a showcase of new Soviet design thinking, an opportunity to build freedom of creativity outside the context of what was happening in the country. The poster series pays tribute to the time and the epoch praising "the craft of mind," which creates amazing new things through the centuries.

Design
Peter Bankov
Prague

Creative Direction
Kirill Karnovich-Valua

Design Firm
Bankov Posters

Agency
RT Creative Lab
Moscow

Principal Type
VKHUTETYPE

Dimensions
23.4 × 33.1 in.
(59 × 84 cm)

POSTERS: SKEWES'S NUMBER

Concept
In the preface to Shuowen Jiezi, "Explaining Glyph and Analyzing Compound Characters," written by Xu Shen of the East Han Dynasty, Chinese characters were made from the observations of people in ancient times. Observing the phenomena of mountains, rivers, the sun and moon, and the vivid movements of fowls and animals, they were enlightened with the meanings of communication and transmission.

Design Firm
Yan-Ting Chen
Taipei City

Principal Type
Custom

Dimensions
19.7 × 27.6 in.
(50 × 70 cm)

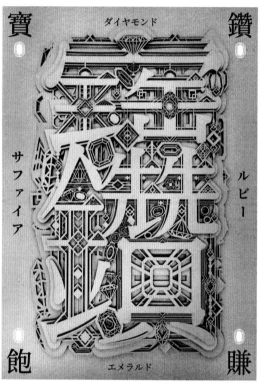

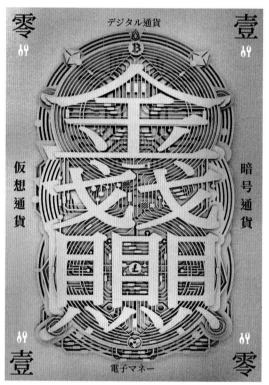

POSTERS: DAOKE ROAD FASHION ROAD

Concept
"Dao Ke Dao Fashion Road" is directed by Hong Kong theater director Mathias Woo. It is based on the concept of "Dao Ke Dao," the first sentence of the Tao Te Ching. Through fashion master Vivienne Tam, he developed the "Tao" and "Tao" tops and nine bottoms. The styles "De" and "Te" are alternately combined into ninety-nine-eighty-one styles, echoing the eighty-one chapters in the Tao Te Ching.

Art, Creative Direction, and Design
Ken Tsai Lee
Taipei

Studio
KEN TSAI LEE
DESIGN LAB

Client
Zuni Icosahedron

Principal Type
Helvetica

Dimensions
275.6 × 393.7 in.
(700 × 1,000 cm)

門票現已公開發售
Tickets Available Now
$320, $200
$100（學生Students）
節目查詢
Programme Enquiries
2566 9696

購票及詳情
Ticketing and more information
zuniseason.org.hk

道 道
The Tao of Fashion 可
道

F A S I N
F A H O
道

香港文化中心劇場
Studio Theatre,
Hong Kong Cultural
Centre

25 - 27/11
四Thu - 六Sat 8PM
27/11
六Sat 3PM

平面設計：李根在
Graphic Design: LEE Ken-tsai
© 2021 Zuni Icosahedron. All rights reserved.
進念・二十面體保留更改節目內容、表演者及座位編排的一切最終決定權
Zuni Icosahedron reserves the right to add, withdraw or substitute artists and/ or vary advertised programmes and seating arrangements.

進念・二十面體為香港文化中心場地伙伴
進念・二十面體由香港特別行政區政府資助
Zuni Icosahedron is a Venue Partner of the Hong Kong Cultural Centre
Zuni Icosahedron is financially supported by the Government of the Hong Kong Special Administrative Region

Music Olivier Cong
音樂・江逸天
Creative Direction & Director Mathias Woo
創作總監及導演・胡恩威
Fashion Design Director Vivienne Tam
服裝設計總監・譚燕玉
Mathias Woo Art Tech Theatre

POSTERS: BOOOM

Concept
This is a poster from a series for the cultural venue Kofmehl. The posters are based on a typographic visual, which is supplemented with the date of the event.

Design Firm
Studio Daniel Peter
Bern

URL
herrpeter.ch

Client
Kofmehl

Principal Type
Marfa

Dimensions
35.2 × 50.4 in.
(89.5 × 128 cm)

POSTERS: GIVE IT A SHOT

Concept

For this project, we created a visual image and identity for "Give It a Shot," the theme of BOK Festival, an annual theater festival in Macau. It was started in 2013 by the Macau nongovernmental art group, Horizon Macau Theatre Group. In the visual images, we used black, gray, and white to create "light" and "shadows," which are crucial in theater performance. The mirroring effect of the letters expresses the artistic concept of the event—"the reality" versus "the world on the performing stage."

Publisher
Todot
Macau

Type Foundry
JUN CAI

Client
Macau Experimental
Theatre

Principal Type
Raleway

Dimensions
27.6 × 39.4 in.
(70 x100 cm)

POSTERS: STONES DO REMEMBER

Concept
The communication between the text and the stone forms the main image of the poster. The poster provides an arrhythmic reading to the viewer from top to bottom. This fluidity makes the movement on the poster more visible.

Design
Erman Yilmaz
Istanbul

Twitter
@ermanyilmazcom

Client
Ordu Taşbaşı Art Space

Principal Type
Custom

Dimensions
19.7 × 27.6 in.
(50 × 70 cm)

COMMUNCATION DESIGN

POSTERS: TAPE IT EASY!

Concept
Handmade taping—then silkscreened.

Design
Niklaus Troxler°
Willisau, Switzerland

URL
troxlerart.ch

Design Firm
Niklaus Troxler Design

Client
KKLB Beromünster

Principal Type
Custom

Dimensions
35.4 × 50.4 in.
(90 × 128 cm)

POSTERS: DOOR OPEN DOOR CLOSED

Concept
The idea was to show a door that is not open but not closed, either. Since all the words in the (German) title only have up to three letters, I decided to build the door out of letters.

Design
Erich Brechbühl
Lucerne

URL
erichbrechbuhl.ch

Twitter
@erichbrechbuhl

Agency
Mixer

Client
Theater Aeternam

Principal Type
GT Maru

Dimensions
35.6 × 50.4 in.
(90.5 × 128 cm)

THEATER AETERNAM SPIELT
TÜR AUF   TÜR ZU
VON   INGRID LAUSUND
25./26. SEPT. 21   20 UHR
THEATERPAVILLON LUZERN

SPIEL FRANZISKA BACHMANN PFISTER
                CHRISTOPH FELLMANN
                    MARCO SIEBER
                   SURAMIRA VOS
REGIE   DAMIÀN DLABOHA
DRAMATURGIE CHRISTOPH FELLMANN
AUSSTATTUNG   ELKE MULDERS
STÜCKRECHTE   SUHRKAMP BERLIN
WWW.   AETERNAM.CH

POSTERS: CONCERT POSTERS

Concept
The appearance we have developed reflects
ascending and descending amplitudes.
It evokes music that is getting louder and softer. The posters
were designed in such a way that they work very well animated.
The animated vertical surfaces—getting higher and lower—
result in an even more association with volume controls.
The silkscreened posters are structured with three special
colors. A bright orange-red, a bronze tone and silver.

Creative Direction
Davide Durante,
Helen Hauert, and
Barbara Stehle

Agency
collect
Stuttgart

Client
University of
Applied Sciences
Northwestern
Switzerland

Principal Type
Euclid Circular
A Medium

Dimensions
16.5 × 23.4 in.
(42 × 59.4 cm)

POSTERS: TDC 2021 : GINZA GRAPHIC GALLERY

Concept
This is a poster designed for the
Tokyo TDC 2021 exhibition.

Design
Jianping He
Berlin

Design Studio
hesign Studio

Client
TOKYO TDC

Principal type
Helvetica

Dimensions
33.1 × 46.8 in.
(84 × 119 cm)

POSTERS: "ON GOING" ART EXHIBITION VISUAL IDENTITY

Concept

This project is a visual identity for an art exhibition of Hunan Changde Art Museum, where the main subject is shown in the form of a dynamic poster. The curation revolves around artists' geographical locations, interspersed with a chronological presentation, and focusing on the concept of "generating." In this context, for visual production, we adopted the method of program generation of geographic images combined with written texts and recorded the process of graphics being generated as an echo to the curator's idea. We used the program algorithm to iterate and fuse the overlooking satellite map and geography many times, to produce a changing graphic composition. Random mosaic plug-ins are used to form the visual form in loading.

Design Firm
Bytoby
Hangzhou, China

Client
Hunan Changde
Art Museum

Principal Type
Brwon (modified)

Dimensions
39.4 × 27.5 in.
(100 × 70 cm)

POSTERS: BYNOW X CREATER

Concept

This is a shopping mall based in Shanghai, positioned in street culture, with trendy and avant-garde intentions. Several sets of posters were designed to promote the idea. During the building of the mall, these posters were printed in large sizes of 10 meters high and 200 meters wide and hung on the front of the building.

Instagram
@tao.graphicdesign

Design
Tao Graphic
Design Studio
Shanghai

Client
Bynow x Creater

Principal Type
Guangminglu
Condensed,
Holland Regular,
Knockout HTF66, and
Octin Stencil Regular

Dimensions
656.2 × 32.8 ft.
(200 × 10 m)

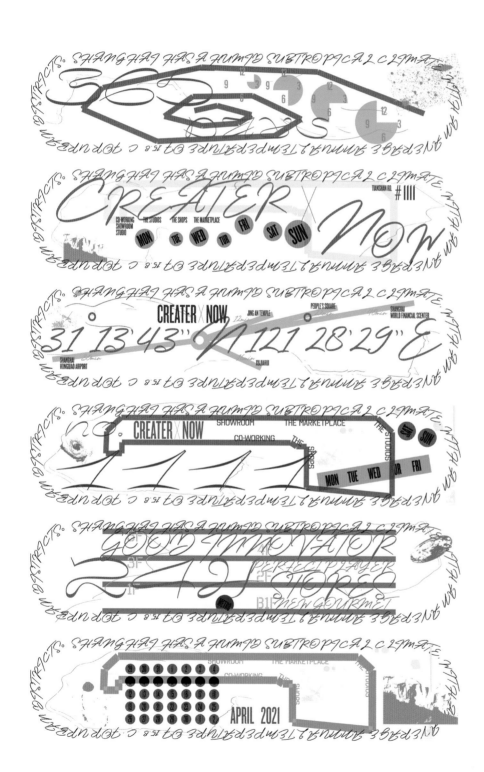

POSTERS: NEU

Concept
This is a poster (and the cover) of a new printed design magazine called Grafikmagazin. Starting a printed design magazine in 2021 at first seems a bit against the times—in a good way. To combine the idea of the old and the new in the poster, it was designed and printed using both old and new technology. The shapes in the background were printed with historic reglets and furniture from letterpress printing, while the word NEU (new) was laser-cut from a digital file.

Art Direction
Dafi Kühne
Näfels, Switzerland

URL
vimeo.com/508361827

Agency
Baby Ink Twice

Client
Grafikmagazin
Munich

Principal Type
Clarendon (metal type)

Dimensions
27.5 × 39.4 in.
(70 × 100 cm)

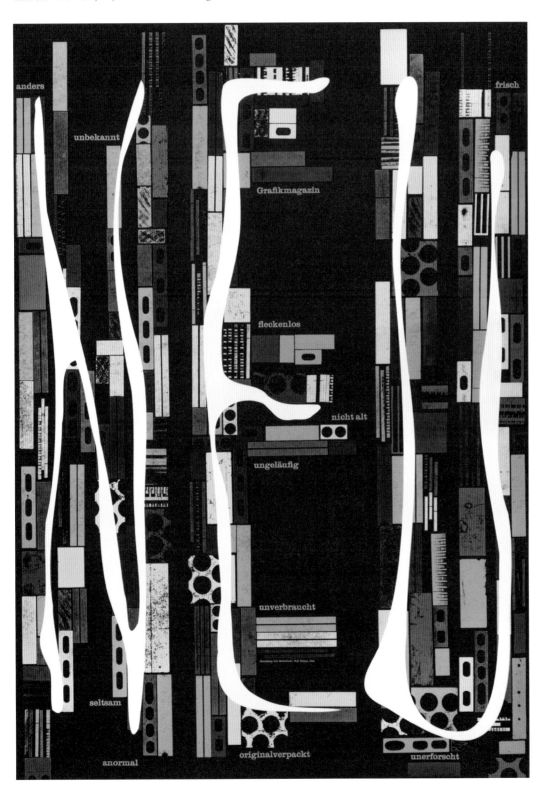

POSTERS: THE DISPLACED

Concept

This modular poster design is a tool to educate and share to a wider audience relevant data about the 82.4 million displaced people and the current migration crisis around the world. Each poster shows the two sides of the story with key facts and the updated data from the United Nations High Commissioner for Refugees about each migrant country and host destination. A time- and cost-effective piece to empower, inspire, and bring people together with more awareness around the displaced, human rights, and social causes through the positive power of relevant stories communicated with typography.

Creative Direction and Design
Miguel Vasquez
Caracas

URL
r-itual.studio

School
Prodiseño School of Visual Communication and Design

Studio
Ritual

Principal Type
ABC Gravity XX Compressed and ABC Monument Grotesk Mono

Dimensions
9.44 × 35.43 in.
(24 × 90 cm)

COMMUNCATION DESIGN

POSTERS: TE WHEKE

Concept
Atamira Dance Company is New Zealand's leading Māori contemporary dance theater creator. Te Wheke is a collaborative new work, symbolized by the eight tentacles of Te Wheke, the Octopus. We worked with the client to identify key figurative movements. Custom lettering and typography combine with dance expressions to create a sense of rhythm and movement..

Creative Direction
Lloyd Osborne° and
Shabnam Shiwan
Auckland

Photography
Petra Leary
and Toaki Okano

URL
osborneshiwan.com

Twitter
@osborneshiwan

Design Firm
Osborne Shiwan

Client
Atamira Dance
Company

Principal Type
Atamira

Dimensions
33.1 × 46.8 in.
(84.1 × 118.8 cm)

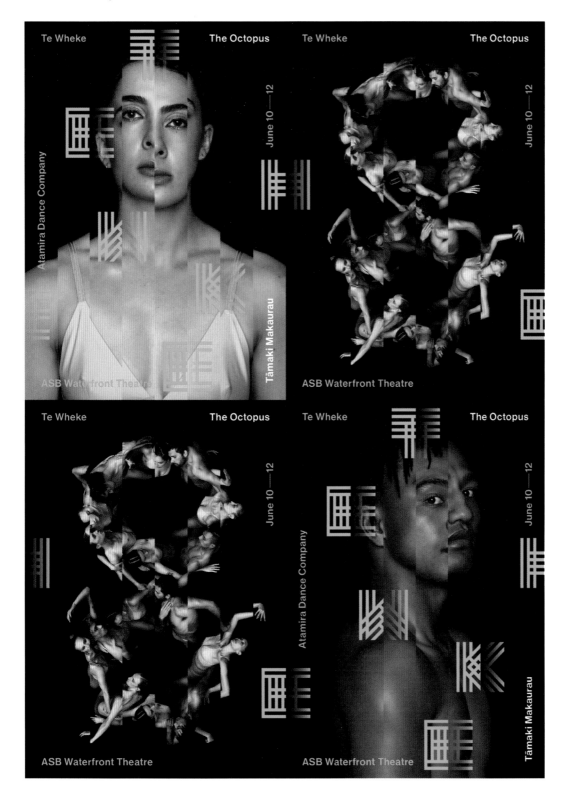

POSTERS: CALENDAR

Concept
As the Earth enters its new revolutionary cycle, people also put up a new calendar to establish plans for the year ahead and note important moments. For those who hold a job today (especially in my hometown in China), the priority of the planning list might be to reexamine the balance between work and life out of concern for our needs as human beings.

Design Firm
Bytoby
Hangzhou, China

Principal Type
Distorted Pixel

Dimensions
33.1 × 23.4 in. (84 x 59.4 cm)

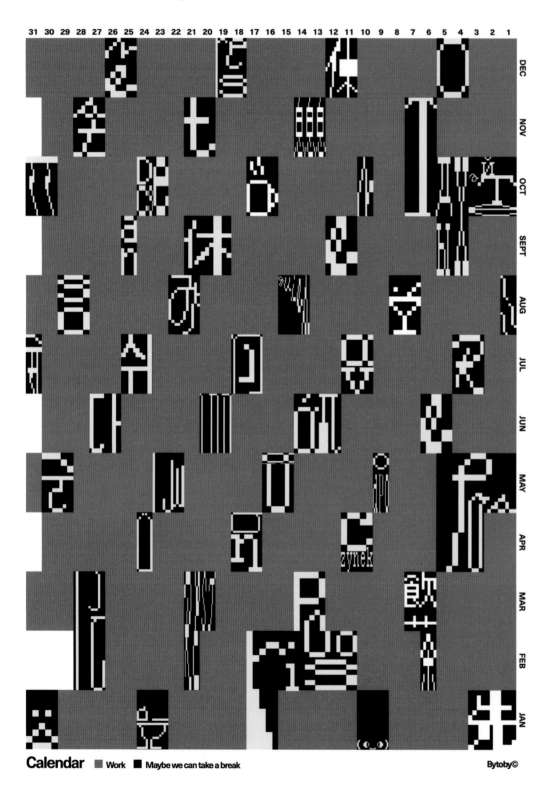

Calendar ■ Work ■ Maybe we can take a break   Bytoby©

POSTERS: 동해바다 EAST SEA

Concept
The wave was shaped by using the letters of the title, "EAST SEA," each in Korean and in English. The rippling sea wave, the wind, and the flexible movement, which may be the tailbone pattern of the fish, symbolize a new wind of creativity blowing in the East Sea that welcomes the first art biennale, and the fixed buoy on one side represents all the stereotypes of the past.

Design
Youngha Park
Seoul

URL
eiab.kr/Youngha-Park

Client
East Sea International
Art Pre-Biennale 2021

Principal Type
Lettering

Dimensions
23.4 × 33.1 in
(59.4 × 84.1 cm)

POSTERS: THE SCIENTIST'S COFFEE BEAN PRODUCTS

Concept

The Scientist is a specialty coffee brand. We put forward the concept of coding to promote coffee bean products. That is, numbers substitution for the information of origin, processing, and roast degree. Each bean forms a special code, and the poster design is based on this set of codes. We used different background colors to distinguish beans with different brewing methods, and different number colors to distinguish single origin and blend, to convey the information and stories behind the product in a rational and professional way..

Art Direction
Siguang Wu

Agency
HDU²³ Lab
Wuxi, China

Client
The Scientist Coffee

Principal Type
SourceHanSerif-
SemiBold and
Univers 55 Roman

Dimensions
22.9 × 32.4 in.
(58.2 × 82.4 cm)

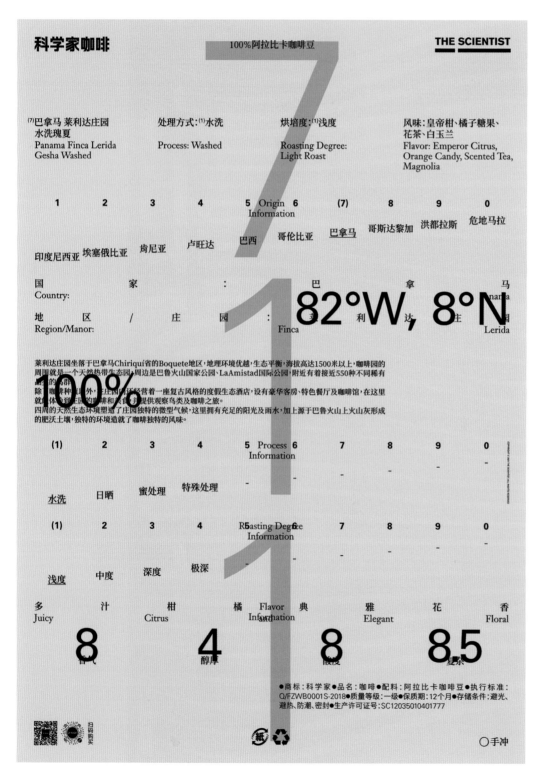

POSTERS: ZERO POSTER DESIGN EXHIBITION

Concept
This is a poster for a zero-themed exhibition—a typographic trial visualizing the invisible zero by gathering numbers.

Art Direction and Design
Shinnoske Sugisaki
Osaka

URL
shinn.co.jp

Twitter
@shinnoske_s

Design Firm
Shinnoske Design

Client
Osaka City Museum of Fine Arts

Principal Type
Frutiger

Dimensions
28.7 × 40.6 in.
(72.9 × 103 cm)

ZERO POSTER #6

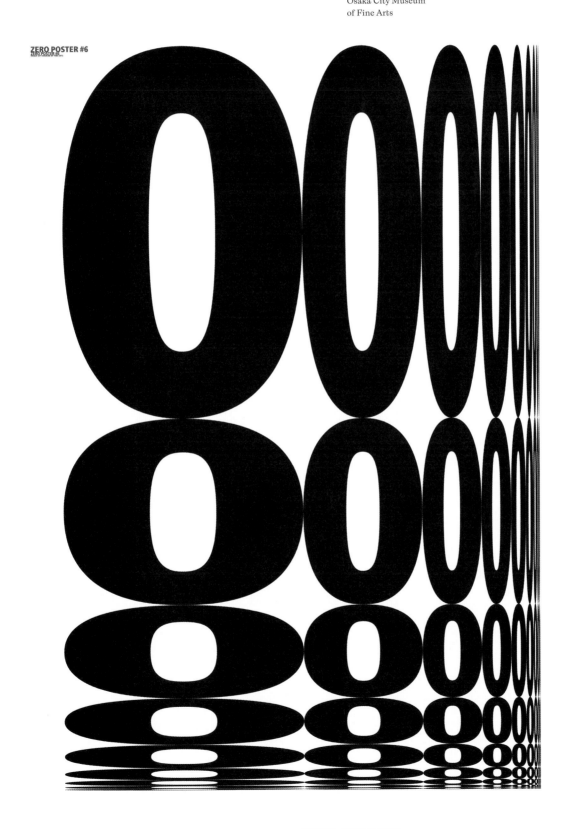

SELF PROMOTION: HOUSE OF TYPE

Concept
Beer mats are usually seen as profane everyday objects and advertising material for breweries. They keep tables clean, encourage procrastination, and help bridge boring conversations. These typographic coasters don't only look different; they deliberately celebrate diversity. None of the characters correspond to the norm. Each one has its own expression, its own intention, its own roots. Each is allowed and supposed to be different. Together, these seemingly contradictory variations form a bigger picture: the "House of Type."

Creative Direction
Sabine Schmid and
Lutz Widmaier

Art Direction and Typographer
Reiner Hofer

Junior Designer
Sarah Maria Janson

URL
swdesign.de

Design Firm
Schmid/Widmaier
Munich

Principal Type
Custom

Dimensions
3.9 × 3.9 × 1 in.
(10 × 10 × 2.5 cm)

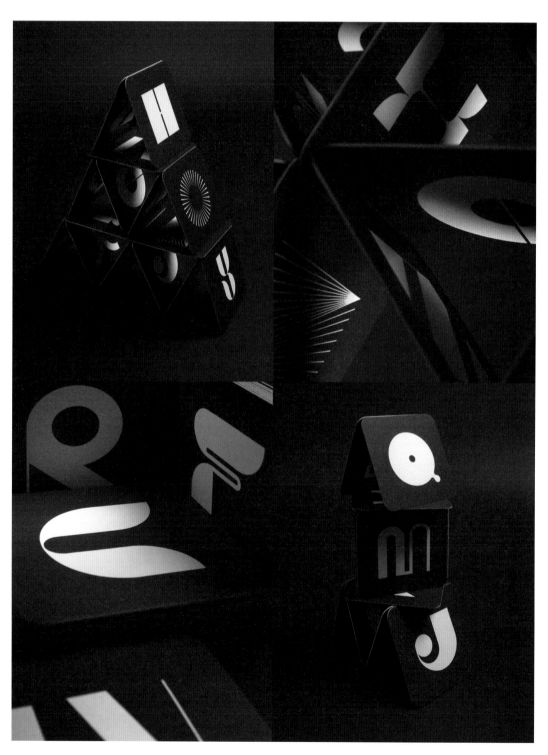

SELF PROMOTION: CANAL MAGAZINE

Concept
Canal Street has been home of the Sunday Afternoon office for five years now. It's been a source of energy and inspiration. We've channeled it all in a broadsheet newsprint that pays homage to this wonderful New York oddity that is Canal Street. We've obviously called it Canal, and this is the inaugural issue. The magazine is designed with an AR filter that allows you to bring both the front and back cover to life for those who will have the physical print.

Design
Kee Wei Chin, Beatriz Lozano, Chandni Poddar, and Xiaoyu Xue

Executive Creative Direction
Ahmed Klink and Juan Carlos Pagan

Photography
Ahmed Klink

Typographer
Beatriz Lozano

Design Firm
Sunday Afternoon New York

Publication
Canal

Principal Type
Futura Extra Bold

Dimensions
13 × 19 in. (33 × 48.3 cm)

SELF PROMOTION: COPPA STADIO

Concept

"Coppa Stadio" is the first Italian football graphic design tournament, created by Zetafonts to promote the revival of Aldo Novarese's typeface Stadio. It celebrates the memory of Italy's most loved type designer using Italy's most loved sport: football. It's a cross-medial experiment that ranges from a digital tournament held on social media to a printed specimen of the typeface in the form of a traditional Italian sports tabloid. It also includes the idea of producing a football fan scarf as part of the font promotion.

Poster Design

Matteo Bartoli, Gianluca Camillini, Francesco Caporale, Francesco Cavalli, Antonello Colaps, Alessandro Congiu, Davide Eucalipto, Federico Galvani, Nicola Giorgio, Bob Liuzzo, Alberto Mariani, Davide Pagliardini, Marco Petrucci, Francesco Paternoster, Francesca Perpetuini, Riccardo Pierassa, Marco Goran Romano, Raffaella Santamaria, Valentina Sesia, and Giovanni Stillittano

Design Firm

FRA! Design

Scarf and Poster Design

AFAB— Allfontsarebastards

Social Media Graphic Design

Sofia Bandini

Editorial Design

Isabella Ahmadzadeh

Chief Design Officer

Francesco Canovaro

Chief Marketing Officer

Debora Manetti

Social Media Manager

Manuel Alvaro

Writers

Fabrizio Gabrielli and Simone Sbarbati

Type Design

Cosimo Lorenzo Pancini

URL

zetafonts.com/blog/ coppa-stadio

Type Foundry

Zetafonts Firenze

Client

Reber R41 Treviso

Principal Type

Stadio Now

Dimensions

13.5 × 18.9 in. (34.3 × 48 cm)

SELF PROMOTION: POSTCARDS, LETTERPRESS

Concept
In today's world, even lettering is almost all digital. I wanted to draw postcards by hand, render them in vector, then print them by hand by letterpress on heavy and loose paper, so that the letters could be felt. Thanks, Demon Press, for helping me with printing.

Design
Olga Pankova
Moscow

Instagram
@olka_pankova

Production Company
Demon Press

Principal Type
Handlettered

Dimensions
4.9 × 6.9 in.
(12.5 × 17.5 cm)

STAMPS: POSTAGE STAMPS

Concept
These are stamps with the short codes of communication—a personal project. The Austrian Post offers the printing of individual stamps. This is how this series was created as a sheet of postage stamps.

Design
Gerhard Kirchschlaeger
Wels, Austria

URL
kirchschlaeger.at

Dimensions
1.4 × 1.7 in.
(3.5 × 4.2 cm)

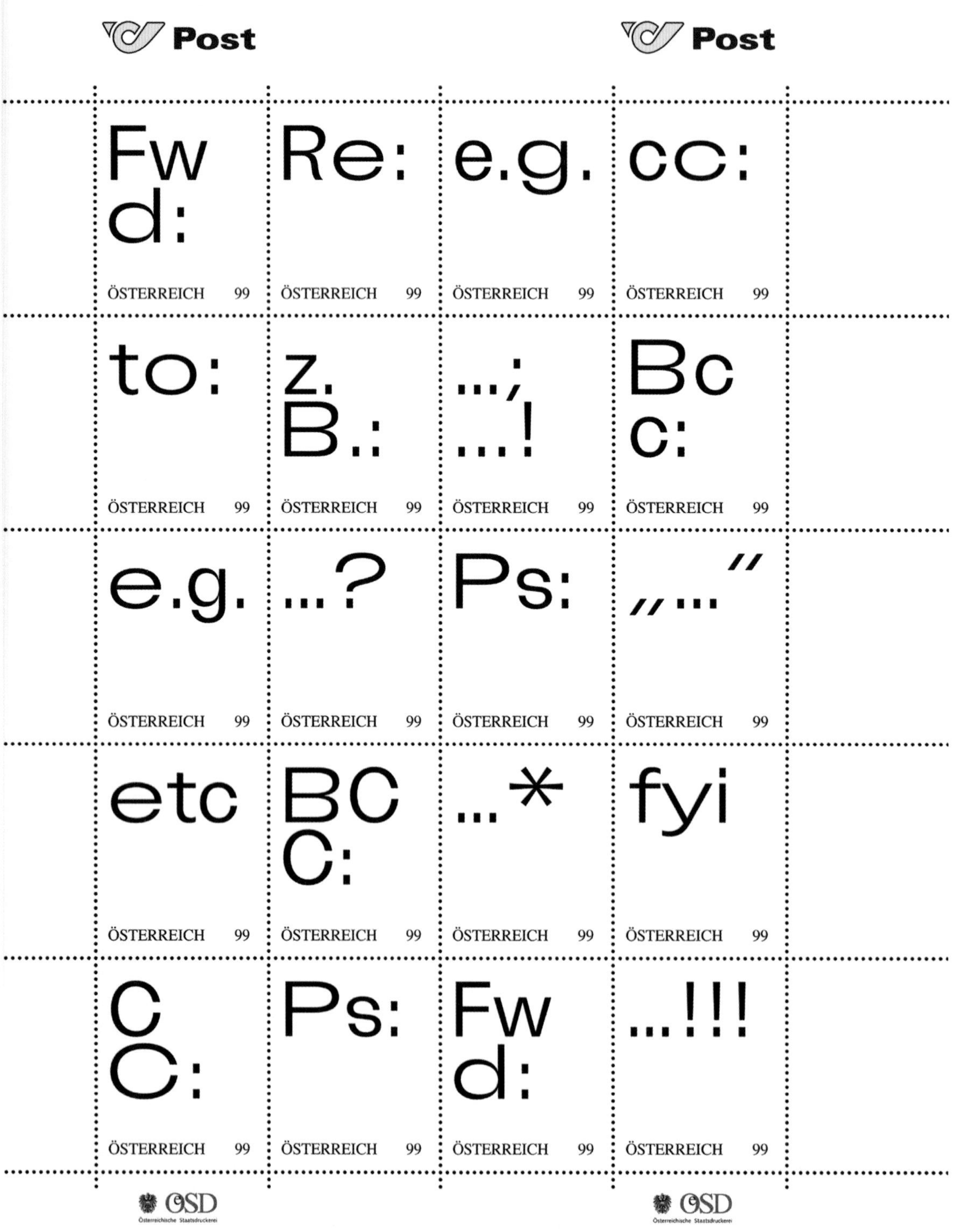

Principal type
Freizeit and Freizeit 140

STAMPS: 100 YEARS JOSEPH BEUYS

Concept
Beuys was best known for his expanded concept of art. (Everyone is an artist.) His stamps and signatures were a trademark, which he applied to almost everything—making it his and calling for people to see art everywhere. This was central to the design approach. The design also plays with the fact that the stamp design features mainly stamps, which in turn will get stamped/ franked themselves once in the post. This creates a graphic game—an ironic questioning of responsibilities and authorities. An invitation that characterizes Beuys's work: to think anew, to rethink and think beyond boundaries.

Design
Billy Kiosoglou
and Frank Philippin
Aschaffenburg,
Germany

Design Studio
Brighten the Corners

Principal Type
Akzidenz Grotesk

Dimensions
1.3 × 1.5 in.
(3.3 × 3.9 cm)

STUDENT: X MUSEUM

Concept
The interesting thing about the museum is that they are holding exhibitions in two different spaces, physical and virtual. The core value for the museum that I defined is the intersection and coexistence of two dimensions. Therefore, for the visual identity, it started from a thought experiment. How can I juxtapose the physical and virtual spaces in the same dimension? By twisting, we can see both worlds aligned together, so I created a typeface relating to the idea of twisted dimensions. The type-centric approach made the visual system instantly recognizable but also fresh and different.

Design
Jaeyou Chung

Instructor
Joseph Han

School
School of Visual Arts°
New York

Principal Type
GT America and
custom based on Giger

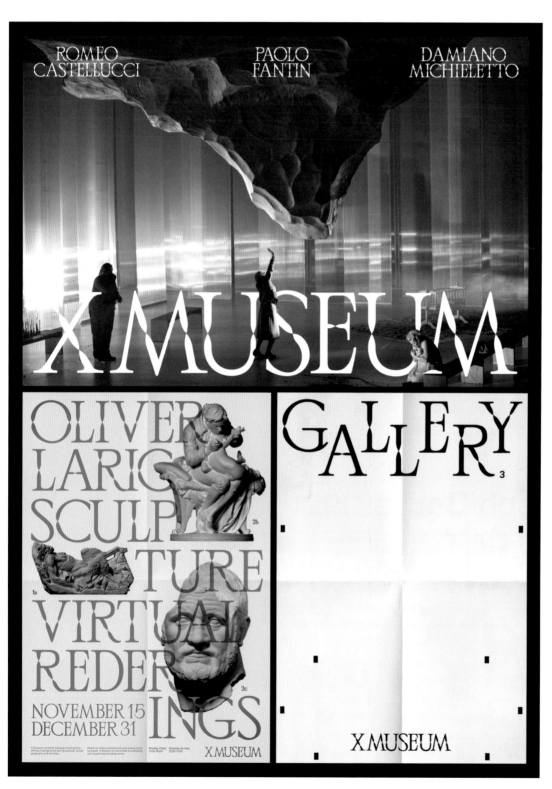

STUDENT: ARCHITECTURE BIENNALE TYPEFACE

Concept

The architectural process takes a peculiar route through space and time—beginning with an idea and its conceptual language, drawing, and ending with a built object and its experiential dimensions of mass within real space. The modularity, repetition, and the use of switching grids in this typeface capture a vivid moment of architectures making process in contemporary urban environment.

Design
Jincheng Shi

URL
charlieshi.ch

Instructor
Brad Bartlett

School
ArtCenter
College of Design
Pasadena, California

Principal Type
Klarheit Kurrent
and custom

Dimensions
24 × 36 in.
(61 × 91.4 cm)

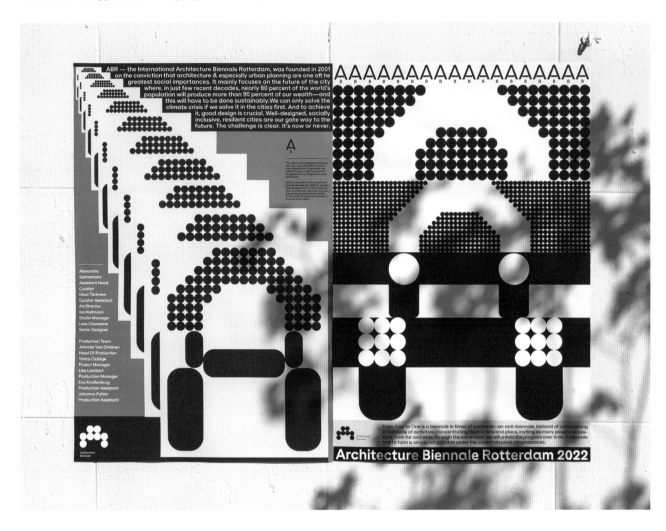

STUDENT: LIGHT MODERATE STORMY EXTREME...

Concept

Can a book layout express emotions, turning the pages create tension? Is it possible that the appearance of a text conveys the same emotional information as facial expressions or volume in the spoken word? To explore these questions, a dime novel, filled with excessive descriptions of emotions, served as dummy text for a typographic play with tension, dynamics, and contrasts. The result is a book that experiences increasingly intense outbursts of emotions in five chapters and twenty typographic experiments. This work aims to serve as an object for reflection on prevalent methods and dimensions of book design and typographic storytelling.

Design
Laura Marie Walser

Professor
Stefan Bufler

School
Hochschule Augsburg (University of Applied Sciences Augsburg) Augsburg, Germany

Principal Type
LL Bradford Regular, Bradford Mono, and Monument Grotesk Variable

Dimensions
9 × 6.6 in. (23 × 16.8 cm)

STUDENT: FREUND*INNENSCHAFT

Concept

This book uncovers and depicts friendship among women. Inspired by the concept of giving space to women's voices, I was led in conversation with my friends on their perspective on friendship. Every one of them wrote a text about Freund*innenschaft. To depict the idea of diverse voices being led together, unconventionally, both typography and image run toward the center of the book. The illustrations are inspired by medieval depictions used to accuse women of witchcraft. In contrast, the illustrations of Freund*innenschaft encourage solidarity among women.

Design
Julia Klenovsky

Writers
Lia Bach,
Celina Benedict,
Annika Fleckenstein,
Theresa Graf,
Sousou Haidar,
Julia Heinle,
Agnes Kelm,
Hannah Klenovsky,

Mona Königbauer,
Elena Landschützer,
Gai Safran Lulai,
Anna Lisa Maurus,
Jennifer Ochwat,
Michelle Pham,
Lina Reiser,
Elisabeth Sauterleute,
and Em Steinberg

Professor
Stefan Bufler

School
University of
Applied Sciences
Augsburg, Germany

Principal Type
Stempel Schneidler LT

Dimensions
7.9 × 10.2 in.
(20 × 26 cm)

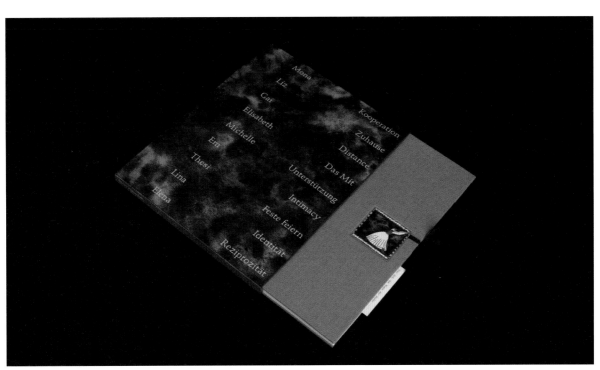

STUDENT: GEOMANIST CLUB OF UNIVERSE

Concept

The Geomanist Club of Universe is based on the study of traditional Chinese mystics, astrology, fortune-telling, learning of Feng Shui, Five Elements, and sixty-four hexagrams, communicating the aura of heaven and earth, and Yin Yang. I designed a set of exclusive visuals and a series of peripheral materials for this fictitious organization. The fonts, typography, and materials are all carefully calculated and produced in proportion to the sixty-four hexagrams of I Ching.

Design
Chuye Chen

Professor
Tao Lin

School
Shanghai University of Engineering Science
Shanghai

Principal Type
Custom

Dimensions
Various

STUDENT: THONIK AND HKNU

Concept
This is a promotional poster for the Studio Thonik (Amsterdam-based collective of designers) seminar "Why We Design," one of the events of Hankyong National University (HKNU)'s 2021 design week. Inspired by Studio Thonik's office building surrounded by black-and-white stripe patterns, which can be called their identity, I designed a typeface for the poster. The motion poster emphasizes Studio Thonik and HKNU alternately by the movements of letters and colors.

Design
Juhee Lee

Instagram
@ caution.lee

Professor
Namoo Kim

School
Hankyong National University
Anseong-si,
Gyeonggi-do,
South Korea

Principal Type
Custom

Dimensions
16.5 × 23.4 in. (42 x 59.4 cm)

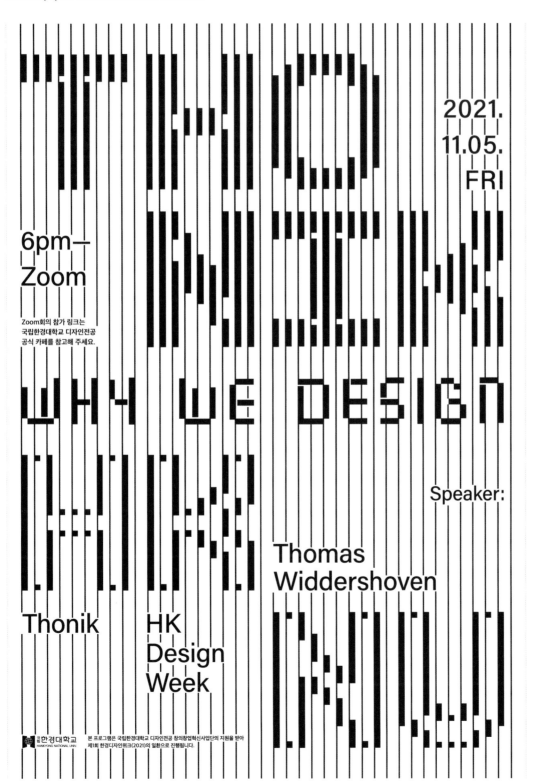

STUDENT: PLAYGROUND PROJECTS

Concept

With a custom typeface inspired by the artists' work as the capstone, the identity system celebrates playscapes by creating an open-ended playground for both the contents of the exhibition and the interaction with visitors. Utilizing new technologies, the exhibition invites the audience to explore different playing experiences in physical and virtual spaces.

Design
Gwen Geng

URL
gwengeng.xyz/
PLAYGROUND-
PROJECT

Instructor
Brad Bartlett

School
ArtCenter
College of Design
Pasadena, California

Principal Type
Neue Montreal

Dimensions
24 × 36 in.
(61 × 91.4 cm)

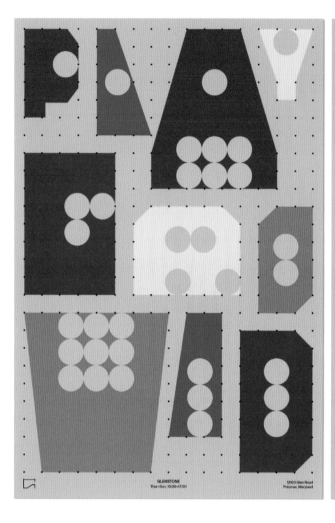

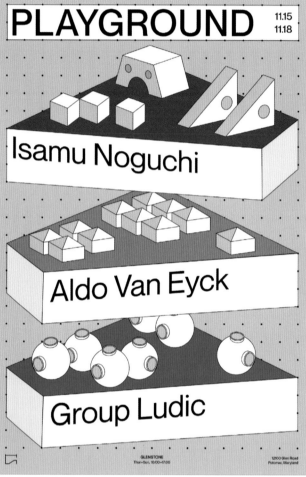

STUDENT: THE VOICE DECODE

Concept

This is a set of decoded text that needs to decipher by pronunciation. I am interested in tribal culture. Tribes with imperfect language systems will use different calls to convey their intentions. To create a double-compiled, difficult-to-decipher writing system, I applied the thoughts to font design combined with the pronunciation of English words and the splitting of strokes and radicals in Chinese characters. The font design is also visually close to the totem culture of the jungle tribe. After completing this set of decoded characters, I designed a Western font to read directly with the same visual elements.

Design
Chuye Chen

Professor
Tao Lin

School
Shanghai University of Engineering Science
Shanghai

Principal Type
Custom

Dimensions
Various

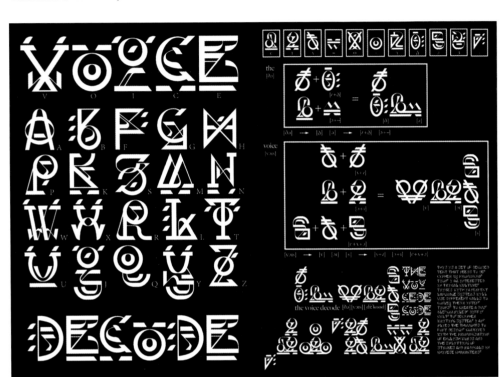

Concept

The principal method of communication consists of words conveyed by speech, writing, or gesture. According to Ferdinand de Saussure, it can be broken down into three parts: the Signifier, the Signified, and the Sign. The Signifier is the sound associated with an image of something. The Signified is the idea or concept of the thing. The Sign is the object "that combines the Signifier and the Signified into a meaningful unit."

Design
Jincheng Shi

Instructor
Brad Bartlett

School
ArtCenter College
of Art and Design
Pasadena, California

Principal Type
Monument Grotesk,
Monument Grotesk
Mono, and Sirba

Dimensions
6.4 × 7.8 in.
(16.4 × 19.9 cm)

A
BOOK
OF _____:

A book of _____ : | 1. What are the origins of language? | 2. How does language develop? | 3. What are some of the important basic facts about language? | 4. What are the forms of language? | 5. What does signifier, signified and sign mean? | 6. What do all languages share? | 7. What does morphology & phonology mean in linguistics?/ 8. Is language necessary for abstract thought? | 9. How is language related to the way we receive information? | 10. What is the relationship between language and the society? | 11. How to define language in the future? [onomatope]

A
BOOK
OF _____:

SIGN
SIGNIFIED
SIGNIFIER

I'm also including here people like Aristotle, and Plato, Hume, Locke, Freud, and Skinner. I'm also including modern day approaches to computational theory, cognitive neuroscience, evolutionary theory and cultural psychology. If you hope to make it with a theory of what people are and how people work, you have to explain and talk about language. In fact, language is sufficiently interesting that, unlike most other things I'll talk about in this class, there is an entire field fully devoted to its study, the linguistics field that

STUDENT: JOHN CAGE: 4'33"

Concept
The LP cover reflects the album's perceived silence and depicts several motifs that encapsulate the composition's genesis: an amphitheater where the piece was recorded, a subwoofer representing the amplification of sound, and a sand garden symbolizing Cage's connection to Zen Buddhism. The base color is a nod to Rauschenberg's White Painting, a series of "blank canvases" that directly inspired the creation of 4'33". The back cover exposes the hidden noise that lies beneath the composition's perceived silence. Environmental and unintended sounds act as music, emphasizing Cage's Zen worldview. 4'33" transformed sound into music and redefined the art of listening.

Design
Erin Harpur

Instructor
Cheri Gray

School
ArtCenter College
of Design
Pasadena, California

Principal Type
News Gothic
and Untitled

Dimensions
Various

STUDENT: URBAN DICTIONARY

Concept
The system uses the "U" of Urban Dictionary, the crowdsourced online dictionary of slang, as a container to hold different contents. The visual system is based on a grid built from lines and circles, as language has its own rules, but we are trying to play with and reconstruct the world of language, to have fun with it and bring in our own definitions.

Design
Yuqin Ni

Instructor
Ming Tai

School
ArtCenter
College of Design
Pasadena, California

Principal Type
Helvetica Neue LT
Pro 73 Bold Extended
and Mokoko Regular

Dimensions
24 × 36 in.
(61 × 91.4 cm)

STUDENT: MUAR

Concept
This is an identity project for the most famous museum of architecture in Moscow. I tried to emphasize the metaphor "architecture is music," so I chose rhythmic compositions as the main graphic move. I created a flexible system where graphics complement typography. To create graphics, I used Druk XX Condensed. With its help, I managed to create dense monolithic forms, which I cut and created a kind of rhythm of architecture and music at the same time.

Design
Anastasia Ibragimova

Professor
Svyat Vishnyakov

School
Bang Bang Education
Moscow

Principal Type
Druk XX Condensed
and Forma DJR

Dimensions
Various

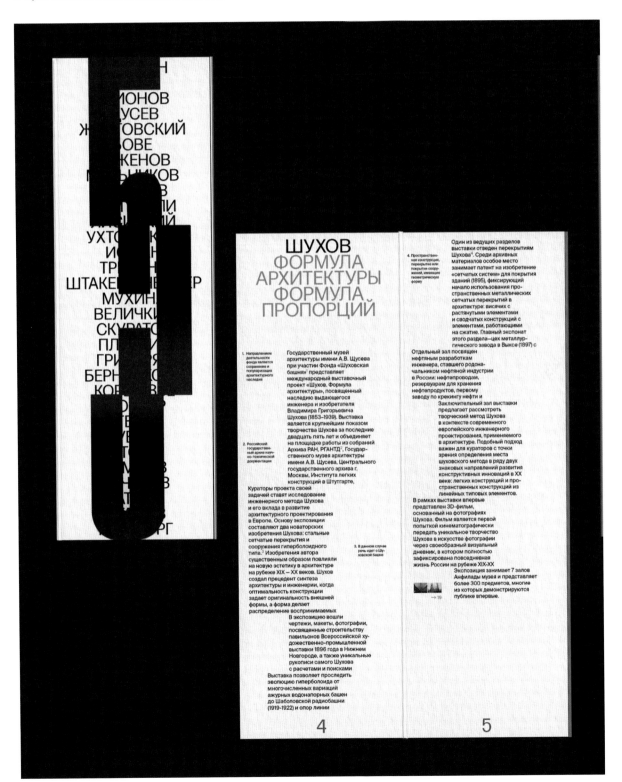

STUDENT: X MUSEUM REBRANDING

Concept

X Museum aims to connect a diversity of culture, discipline, and generations as a cultural institution. The main design system, the graphic "X," reflects the museum's core value throughout the whole identity. It represents the museum's visual identity by integrating with the primary logo and works as a functional tool that can introduce and connect various information and content throughout the whole system. Additionally, the visual system for the physical and virtual museum is divided through line style, with a solid and dashed line representing different attributes of the institution.

Design
Hyun Jung Lee

URL
iamhyun.com

Instructor
Joseph Han

School
School of Visual Arts°
New York

Principal Type
Favorit

Dimensions
Various

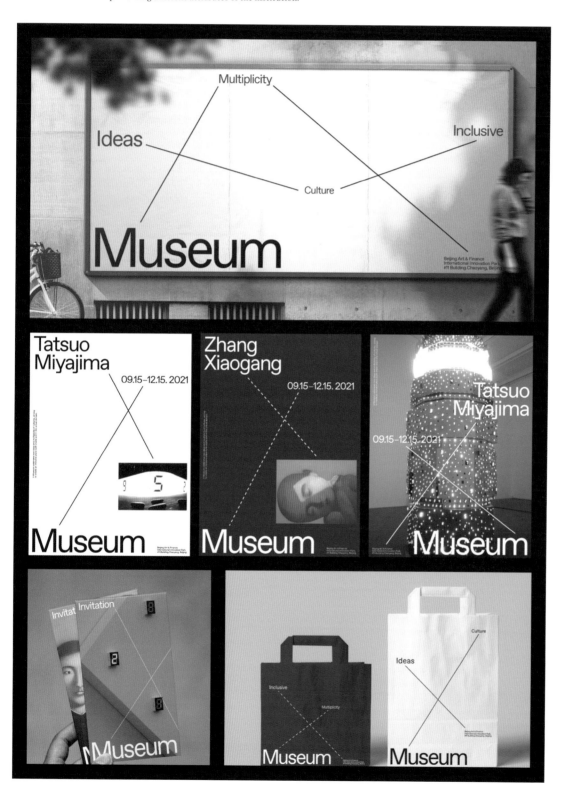

STUDENT: GROW

Concept
Grow is a new conceptual water brand designed for houseplants. The exaggeratedly stretched and curved logo conveys the fluidity of water and the strength and energy of life. The clear plastic pouch contains water, and it shows the level of acidity and the amount of magnesium and calcium, and other details about water and plants.

Design
Jaeyou Chung

Instructor
Joseph Han

School
School of Visual Arts°
New York

Principal Type
Roumald (unreleased),
Suisse Int'l Trial,
and custom

STUDENT: WORDS ON FACIAL MAKEUP

Concept
Words are used to extract the character characteristics of Chinese opera facial makeup and reshape their Chinese character facial makeup by their own name.

Design
Xingya Mao

Professor
Huanbin Liang

School
China Academy of Art
Hangzhou, China

Principal Type
Futura, Helvetica
Neue, and Helvetica
Neue UltraLight

Dimensions
27.8 × 33.5 in.
(70.6 × 85 cm)

STUDENT: BACTERIA MUSEUM BRANDING

Concept

This project is branding for Bacteria Museum. The brand identity was inspired by a reproduction process of bacteria called binary fission. A bacterium, which is a single cell, divides into two identical daughter cells in the process. My concept was to make a new creature by dividing and reassembling it. I used the alternate—a different combination of the same element—to emphasize the concept.

Design
Ji Eun Lee

URL
jieun.work/Bacteria-Museum

Instructor
Natasha Jen°

School
School of Visual Arts°
New York

Principal Type
Lausanne and custom

STUDENT: I'M PROUD OF YOU

Concept

Growing up, I struggled with insecurities and low self-esteem. Both Adler's individual psychology and Freud's psychoanalytic theory agree that childhood social experiences determine adult behavior, which inspired me to recall and analyze my own upbringing. This is a journey of self-discovery. In the book, analysis is hidden behind the story, constructing my self-talk between adulthood and childhood. Stories, parenting strategies, problems, and objects are interconnected as clues to explain the formation of my personality. My little portrait will "grow" taller as turning over the pages, which symbolizes growth itself.

Design
Yiwei Dai

Professor
Tao Lin, ClassTao

School
Tongji University
Shanghai

Principal Type
Aktiv Grotesk CNSG,
Source Han Serif, and
Times New Roman

Dimensions
4.5 × 7.4 in.
(11.5 × 18.9 cm)

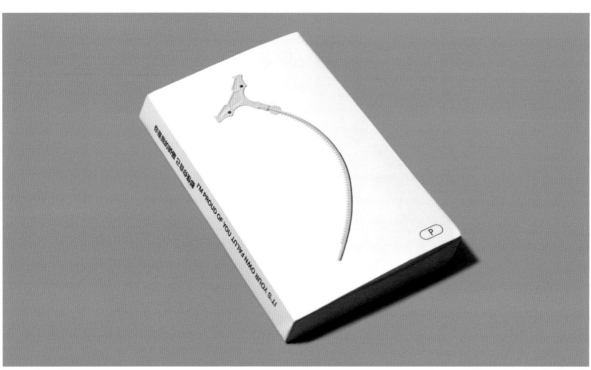

STUDENT: THE LANGUAGE'S VISUAL IDENTITY

Concept

This design research studies language (covering Latin Script) diversity as representations of visual/cultural identity through typography and how it can guide designers in understanding an equal treatment of multilingual texts. Additionally, it seeks to understand how languages are defined and are different by means of visual terms that are related to typographic parameters. Four process books visualize the identity of four languages as a pattern/black amount. A tool book defines how to set typography (i.e., the leading) in relation to the visual identity of each language. It introduces an equal and diversified (multilingual) design, expressive of cultural diversity.

Design
Marta Guidotti

Professors
Prof. Dr. Ann Bessemans, Ph.D., Carl Haase, and Dr. María Pérez Mena

School
PXL-MAD
School of Arts
Hasselt, Belgium

Principal Type
Noto Mono and Times New Roman

Dimensions
Various

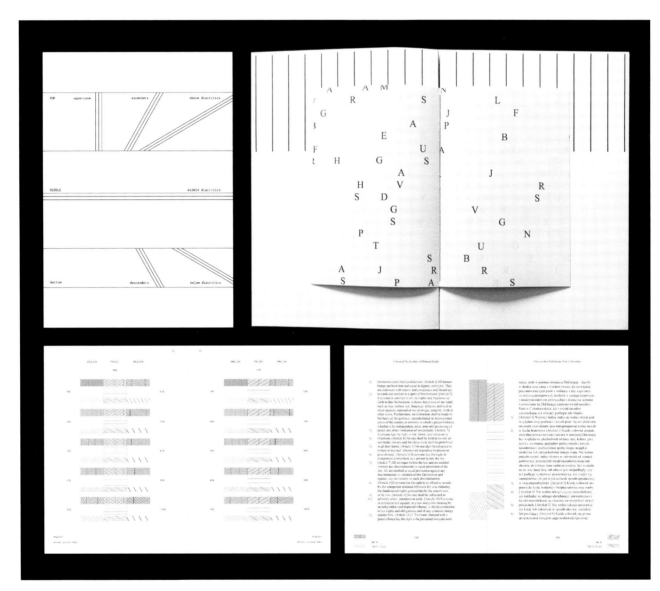

STUDENT: TADAO ANDO EXHIBITION

Concept
This is the brand identity for the architect Tadao Ando. The customized typeface was inspired by the geometric shapes within Ando's architecture, such as triangles, diamonds, and rectangles.

Design
Doah Kwon

Instructor
Pedro Mendes

School
School of Visual Arts°
New York

Principal Type
Custom

Dimensions
Various

STUDENT: ULTRAFETT TYPOGRAPHY FESTIVAL

Concept
Typographic key visuals for a digital conference take a journey through type and space. For the conference, some of the world's best typographers were invited to talks, live-action formats, and interviews with music and a lot of fun. The custom shapes and letterings are referencing the speakers' work, exploring the possibilities of three-dimensional design to increase the typographic expression.

Design
Darius Bange,
Sarah Fyrguth,
Daniel Götz,
Tilman Kunkel,
Leon Pöhler,
Maik Symann,
and Anke Warlies

Professor
Dirk Fütterer°

School
Fachhochschule
Bielefeld
Bielefeld, Germany

Principal Type
Custom

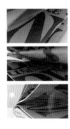

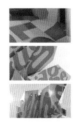

STUDENT: BACTERIA MUSEUM

Concept
Bacteria are single-celled, omnipresent microbes. This identity system is based on the two exciting traits of bacteria: their reproduction process and their rapid growth in number. They reproduce asexually by binary fission, whereby a single cell elongates and divides into two. The custom typeface is designed to capture the reproducing moment. The doubling formula helps one bacterium grow exponentially into millions. Depending on how optimized the environment is for bacteria, a single bacterium can grow to a million bacteria in just twenty minutes. The whole visual identity was designed to appreciate such attributes of bacteria.

Design
Jiin Choi

Instructor
Natasha Jen°

School
School of Visual Arts°
New York

Principal Type
JC Bacteria Mu
(custom typeface)

Dimensions
8.5 × 11 in.
(21.6 × 27.9 cm)

BACTERIA MUSEUM

BACTERIA MUSEUM

JESSICA HAN
BUSINESS SPECIALIST

261.338.7220
JESSHAN@BACTMU.COM
280 RIVER DR, NEW YORK

BACTERIA MUSEUM

BACTERIA MUSEUM

261.338.7220
BACTERIAMUSEUM.COM

280 RIVER DR, NEW YORK,
NY, 10010, UNITED STATES

STUDENT: FLORA TYPOGRAPHICA

Design
Anika Mohr

School
Muthesius University
of Fine Arts and Design
Kiel, Germany

Principal Type
Anonymous Pro

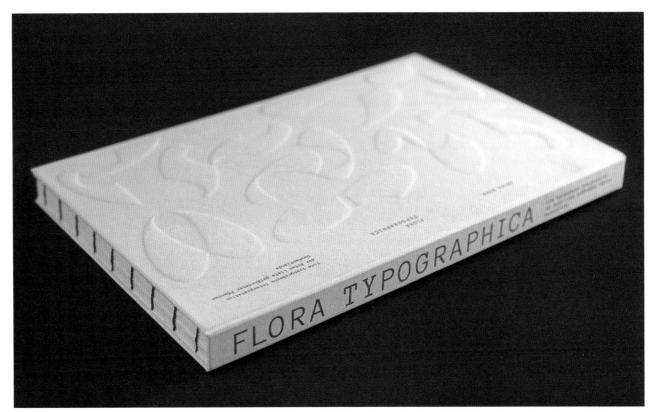

STUDENT: GLENSTONE REBRAND

Concept

Glenstone, one of the newest culture centers, harmonizes art, architecture, and nature to provide an evolving exhibiting space for influential post–World War II artworks, celebrating their historical impact on contemporary culture. Inspired by its vision of being a state of mind, the new identity system integrates the energy of architecture, the power of art, and the restorative qualities of nature to create an organic and adaptive visual interpretation of the spirited environment at Glenstone.

Design
Gwen Geng

URL
gwengeng.xyz/
GLENSTONE-2

Instructor
Brad Bartlett

School
ArtCenter
College of Design
Pasadena, California

Principal Type
Editorial New,
Lausanne, and
Neue Montreal

Dimensions
24 × 36 in.
(61 × 91.4 cm)

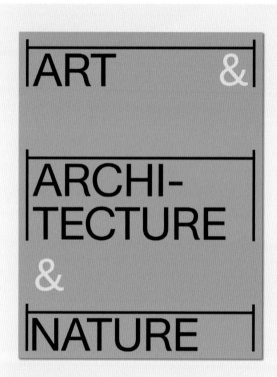

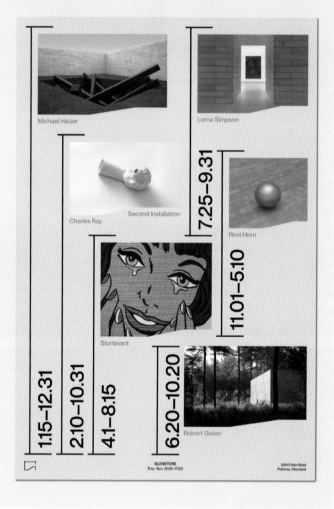

STUDENT: ARCHITECTURE BIENNIAL IDENTITY

Concept
The architectural process takes a peculiar route through space and time—beginning with an idea and its conceptual language, drawing, and ending with a built object and its experiential dimensions of mass within real space. The ABR (Architecture Biennale Rotterdam) is a cultural platform whose main objective is to bring together leading voices in design to discuss issues impacting architecture in modern-day society. In this year's edition, ABR focuses on the process of how structures are built.

Design
Jincheng Shi

Instructor
Brad Bartlett

School
ArtCenter
College of Design
Pasadena, California

Principal Type
Klarheit Kurrent
and custom

Dimensions
18 × 24 in.
(45.7 cm × 61 cm)

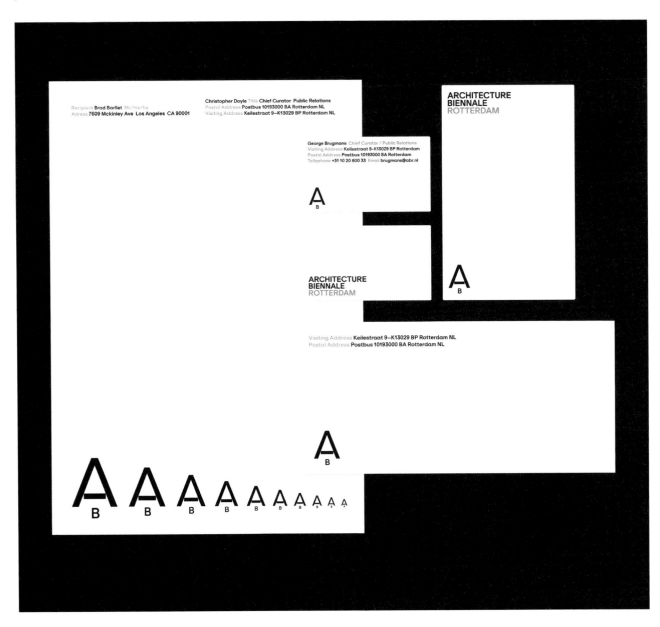

STUDENT: TYPOLA CONFERENCE BRANDING

Concept
The TypoLA project is a visual identity system for an international design conference. It pushes the design profession forward by asking provocative questions and challenging designers to think about the inclusivity and diversity in typography design. Where have all the voices gone in an industry ever dominated by white men? Typography can be a radical act in this conversation—I deconstructed the English lowercase letters "l" and "a" and rebuilt it in the shapes of different languages to let out a strong voice of the new-era typography manifesto.

Design
Chang Gao

Instructor
Stephen Serrato

School
ArtCenter
College of Design
Pasadena, California

Principal Type
Century Gothic
and Space Grotesk

Dimensions
Various

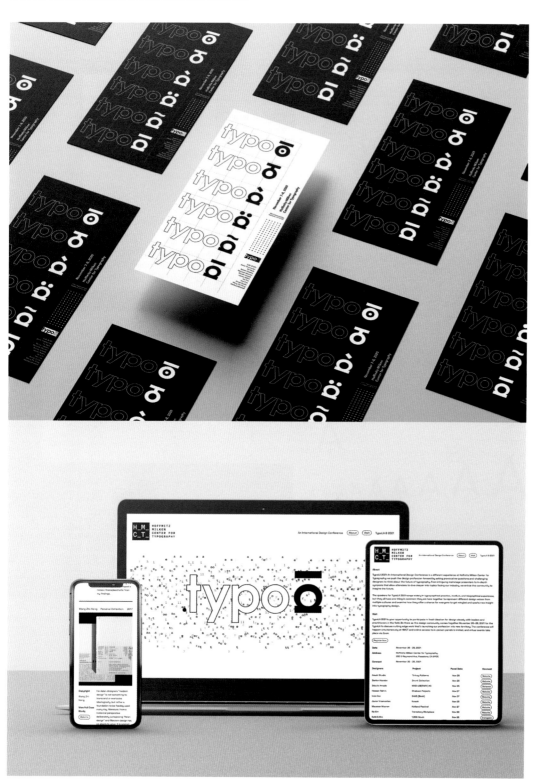

STUDENT: CHINESE CHARACTERS EXPERIMENT

Concept
This work explores the recognition limit of
Chinese characters and is a character experiment.
I exaggerated and deformed Chinese characters
without losing their original recognition.

Design
Luomin Xu

Professor
Huanbin Liang

School
China Academy of Art
Hangzhou, China

Principal Type
American Typewriter
and Fangzheng
Lanting Black Flat

Dimensions
11 × 16.5 in.
(28 × 42 cm)

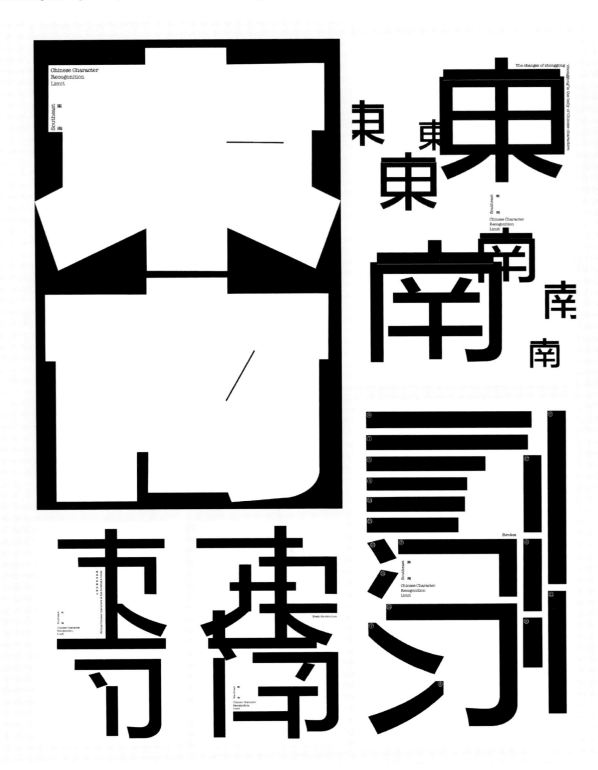

STUDENT: THE SCHOOL YARD

Concept

For our class taught by Deb Bishop, a design director at The New York Times, we were told to create a meaningful broadsheet about whatever topic we wanted. I chose bullying in the middle to high school setting. I believe this is an ongoing issue, and having two siblings in this age group made me feel closer to the subject. I called this one-off publication "The School Yard," and used expressive and experimental typography to evoke the subject of bullying. The typography being cut up and warped played on the concept of these kids' feelings.

Design
Emily Roemer

Instructor
Deb Bishop

School
School of Visual Arts°
New York

Principal Type
Gotham, Knockout, and Timmons NY

Dimensions
15 × 22.8 in.
(38.1 × 57.9 cm)

STUDENT: IDENTITY GALLERY MYTH

Concept
MYTH is a contemporary art gallery that aims to support young Russian artists. The name of the gallery stands for My Young True Heroes: In the art space, artists and curators become real heroes of contemporary art. The name of the gallery formed the basis for the corporate identity of the gallery.

Design
Alyona Puraeva

URL
behance.net/
gallery/132298109/
Identity-gallery-MYTH

Professor
Svyat Vishnyakov

Schools
Bang Bang Education
and art college named
after K.A Savitsky
Moscow and Penza

Principal Type
Bahnschrift and Louche

Dimensions
20 × 28 in.
(50 × 70 cm)

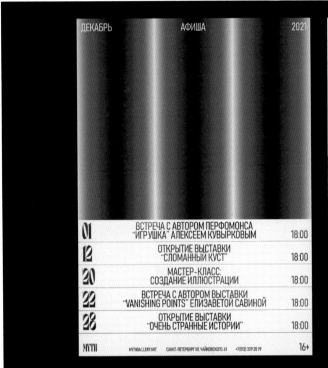
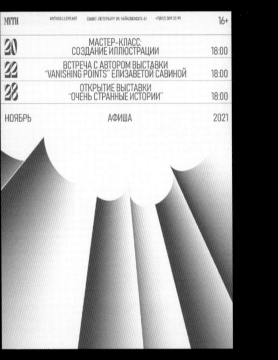

STUDENT: THIS BOOK IS A TIME MACHINE

Concept

The continuous fragmentation of time into smaller increments detaches us from the larger timescales. "This Book is a Time Machine" explores four different timescales—that of the human, technology, geology, and the timescale of the book itself. If our consideration of larger timescales impacts our current actions, perhaps we can create better futures. The nine ribbon bookmarks are nine different access points to parts of the narrative, encouraging the reader to explore the content of the book in a less linear fashion. The use of large, staggered typography represents the fragmenting of time units.

Design
Phoebe Hsu

URL
phoebehsu.design/
This-Book-is-a-
Time-Machine

Instructor
Brad Bartlett

School
ArtCenter College
of Design
Pasadena, California

Principal Type
Lyon Text and
Monument Grotesk

Dimensions
8 × 10 in.
(20.3 × 25.5 cm)

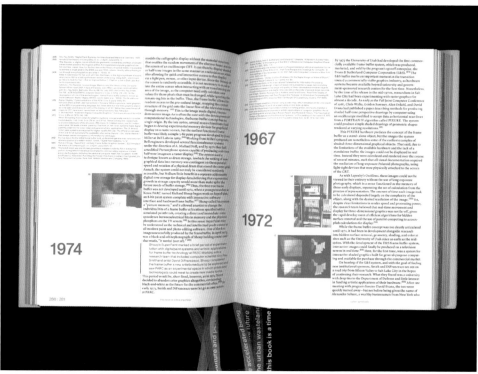

STUDENT: JAZZ MAGAZINE

Concept
I was assigned to design a zine with a typeface that I chose. GT Flexa from the Grilli Type Foundry caught my eye. Improvisation is a key theme in jazz. I felt that this concept was conveyed from the ink trap part and the syncopation created by the many weights that this typeface had to offer. GT Alpina was used as the secondary typeface because both typefaces were designed from the same foundry and have similar x-heights.

Design
Junghoon Oh

Instructor
Natasha Jen°

School
School of Visual Arts°
New York

Dimensions
8.5 × 11 in.
(21.6 × 27.9 cm)

Principal Type
GT Flexa

STUDENT: HARDLY SILENT

Concept
The use of silver metallic paper in this project reflects the silent while flourishing movie industry in the beginning of the twentieth century. The clear film pages appear quietly in the book to evoke a sense of actual film texture. Most of the book is printed in black-and-white with textured paper. The idea is that movie makers were trying all kinds of experimental ways to shoot the film on the basis of a silent medium.

Design
Jincheng Shi

URL
charlieshi.
ch/#HardlySilent

Instructor
Cheri Gray

School
ArtCenter
College of Design
Pasadena, California

Principal Type
Fabrik, Founders
Grotesk, and Serifbabe

Dimensions
6 × 12 in.
(15.2 × 30.5 cm)

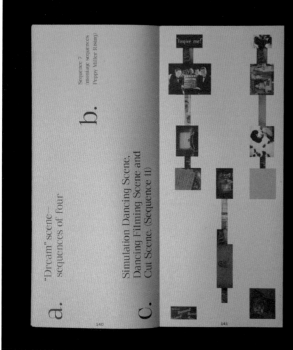

STUDENT: JUNK FOOD FESTIVAL

Concept

This festival is for those who are not afraid to add a few kilograms to their figure and for those who adore street food and fast food from different cuisines of the world. We promise you won't be able to leave without trying something delicious and not particularly healthy. The festival does not call for the constant consumption of unhealthy food, so it is held only once a year. You have endured and waited for this day for so long. Enjoy it! Yummy!

Design
Zhenya Zhuk

Tutor
Evgeny Kashirin

School
HSE Art and
Design School
Moscow

Principal Type
Arimo

Dimensions
16.5 × 23.4 in.
(42 × 59.4 cm)

STUDENT: AMMO CASE CLUB

Concept

Ammo Case Club is a club where creators from various fields gather to study the "aesthetics of violence." It is a study of the influence and correct direction of acceptance according to how violence is treated and attractive in art. Bullets collected through research were shaped to create a special typeface. The bottom of the aligned bullets represents the violent aesthetics managed by this club.

Design
Miji Kim

Instagram
@miiitball

Professor
Jakyoung Min

School
Sejong University
Seoul

Principal Type
Ammo, Authentic
Sans, and Garamond
Premier Pro

Dimensions
Various

STUDENT: IKEA BRANDING

Design
Shantanu Sharma

School
School of Visual Arts°
New York

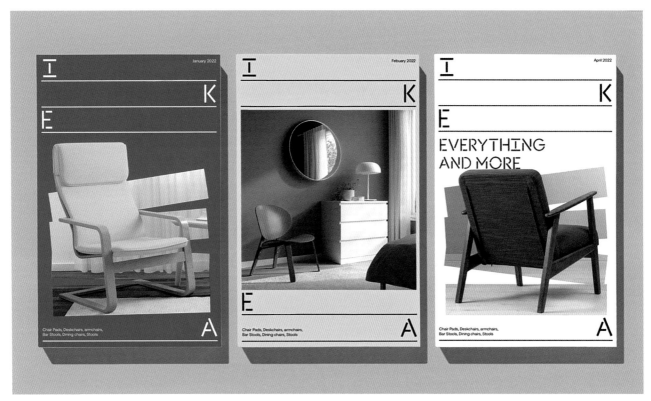

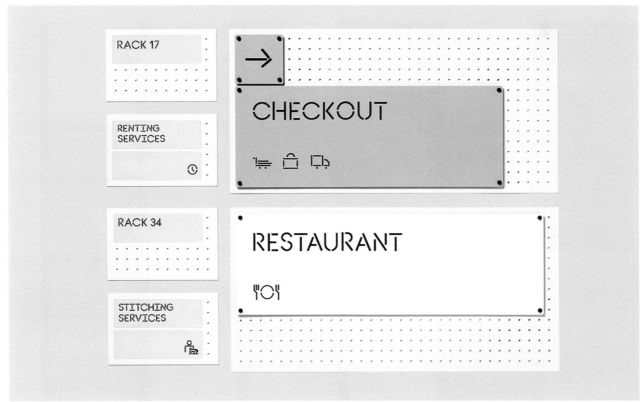

STUDENT: UNDEFINED MAGAZINE

Concept
To create a courageous voice and arouse the audience's curiosity, I used coordinates/codes as the key visual language across the system to represent each location. The design reflects its courageous voice with a confident, highly visual approach that is clean, straightforward, and inspiring.

Design
Vern Chuxuan Liu

Instructor
Tamara Maletic

School
Parsons School
of Design
New York

Principal Type
FreightDisplay Pro
and Neurial Grotesk

Dimensions
Various

Stara Zagora
Province

Bulgaria

03

*Buzludzha
Communist*

Coordinates

42° 44'8.81" N—25° 23' 37.68"E

STUDENT: ENCYCLOPEDIA OF SPACE—APOLLO

Concept
This was an academic project for the Faculty of Fine Arts of the University of Lisbon and was divided into two products: an editorial and a website. The project was created based on two sections of an encyclopedia that tells about space, more specifically about the moon and the Apollo program. My approach seeks to combine a vibrant context to the editorial together with a minimal and clean one for the website, leading to a personal experience with graphic elements and great images for the user to go deeper into space.

Design
Jade Rocha

URL
jaderocha.com

Twitter
@jaderochab

Professors
Isabel Lopes Castro and João Miguel Andrade Ferreira

School
Faculty of Fine Arts of the University of Lisbon Lisbon

Principal Type
Neue Haas Grotesk

Dimensions
5.8 × 8.3 in. (14.8 × 21 cm)

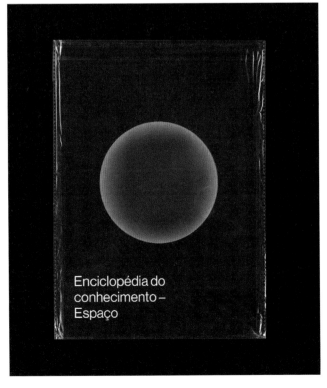

STUDENT: JUN AN(钧安)

Design
Mingyu Jia

Instagram
@mingyu_jia

Instructor
Tao Lin

School
Shanghai Institute
of Visual Arts
Shanghai

Principal Type
Fangzheng Song Keben
Xiukai (方正宋刻本秀楷),
Hanyi Qihei (汉仪旗黑),
and LL Mono

Dimensions
Each page: 4.9 × 7.1 in.
(12.5 × 18 cm)
Length: 50.1 in.
(150 cm)

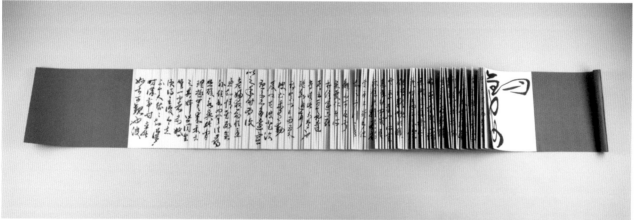

STUDENT: WORDS & WORLDS

Concept

The book is a balance of the historic and mystic using language, ancient documents, maps, data, and folklore. Acting as the narrator and interwoven between each chapter is the Tagalog ancient account of the creation of the world. It was intentional for there to be no white pages because so much of our history has been written upon them. This project aims to reclaim and relearn a history that has been kept from us.

Design
Gabrielle Pulgar

URL
gabriellepulgar.info

Instructor
Brad Bartlett

School
ArtCenter
College of Design
Pasadena, California

Principal Type
Ladybird, Lausanne, and Louize Display

Dimensions
7.5 × 10.5 in.
(19.1 × 26.7 cm)

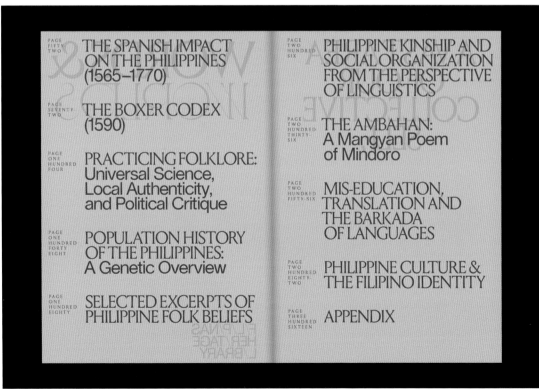

PAGE FIFTY TWO — THE SPANISH IMPACT ON THE PHILIPPINES (1565–1770)

PAGE SEVENTY-TWO — THE BOXER CODEX (1590)

PAGE ONE HUNDRED FOUR — PRACTICING FOLKLORE: Universal Science, Local Authenticity, and Political Critique

PAGE ONE HUNDRED FORTY EIGHT — POPULATION HISTORY OF THE PHILIPPINES: A Genetic Overview

PAGE ONE HUNDRED EIGHTY — SELECTED EXCERPTS OF PHILIPPINE FOLK BELIEFS

PAGE TWO HUNDRED SIX — PHILIPPINE KINSHIP AND SOCIAL ORGANIZATION FROM THE PERSPECTIVE OF LINGUISTICS

PAGE TWO HUNDRED THIRTY-SIX — THE AMBAHAN: A Mangyan Poem of Mindoro

PAGE TWO HUNDRED FIFTY-SIX — MIS-EDUCATION, TRANSLATION AND THE BARKADA OF LANGUAGES

PAGE TWO HUNDRED EIGHTY-TWO — PHILIPPINE CULTURE & THE FILIPINO IDENTITY

PAGE THREE HUNDRED SIXTEEN — APPENDIX

STUDENT: CHINA'S SHOE CAPITAL

Concept
The shoe factory is a symbol of my hometown. This project attempts to build connections between different social groups by documenting the life of marginalized groups and telling their stories. I explore and expand the narrative qualities of different materials: Shoe papers collected in shoe factories are bound into books to express the precarious fate of workers; interviews of workers are hidden behind photos, implying a lack of voice for workers.

Design
Yiwei Dai

Professor
Tao Lin, Class Tao

School
Tongji University
Shanghai

Principal Type
Source Han Serif

Dimensions
7.1 × 10.6 in.
(18 × 27 cm)

STUDENT: ANCHORAGE MUSEUM IDENTITY

Concept
Alaska has a unique location that sits on the edge of the Arctic Circle.
The new visual identity is inspired by its specific natural environments,
such as glaciers and ice cubes. In the logo, the transformation from
the right-angle corner to the rounded corner visually corresponds
to when the ice melts. Anchorage Museum aims to bring close the
relationship between people and landscape by emphasizing this
geographical characteristic. The new brand identity includes posters,
website, print collaterals, booklet, custom typeface, and applications.

Design
Grace Cai

Instructor
Brad Bartlett

School
ArtCenter
College of Design
Pasadena, California

Principal Type
Neue Montreal,
Reckless Neue,
and Custom

Dimensions
24 × 36 in.
(61 × 91.4 cm)

STUDENT: FAB

Concept

The main task in developing the exhibition's identity was to create a typographic style. The accidental font used in the design reflects one of the central messages of the exhibition—a call to reduce consumption in the fashion sector, a call for reasonable consumption. Graphically, the solution is based on a cross-type of a pair of fonts—strictly grotesque and openwork accidental font, resembling the folds of fabric.

Design
Tanya Dunaeva

Professors
Dmitry Chernogaev and Leonid Slavin

School
HSE Art and Design School Moscow

Principal Type
Custom

COMMUNCATION DESIGN

STUDENT: BREAKOUT NEWS! 删前速看

Concept

This is an era of the rapid spread of rumors. Exaggerated facts and untrue stories suggested by the stylized language created a click-bait title. Authoritative data and professional terms have attracted many devout viewers, making rumors so deceiving that they could fool the public. Therefore, we need to respond to false information by design and invite the truth into this world.

Design
Lujun Li, Yiwen Mao, and Youyou Shen

Professor
Zhou Feng

School
China Academy of Art

Principal Type
glyphworld Airland, glyphworld Animal Soul, glyphworld Desert, glyphworld Flower, glyphworld Forest, glyphworld Glacier, glyphworld Meadow, glyphworld Mountain, glyphworld Wasteland, and 方正兰亭黑

Dimensions
Various

STUDENT: EAR ROOM

Concept

Architects are accustomed to only designing visually. This project explores the interactions between sound, hearing, space, and architecture. The book's structure explores an order of magnitude from the intimate scale of the ear to the architectural scale of the environment. At the same time, it provides the reader with a framework of understanding how sound and space are deeply intertwined.

Design
Aiqi Zhang

Instructor
Brad Bartlett

School
ArtCenter
College of Design
Pasadena, California

Principal Type
Lab Grotesque
and Reckless Neue

Dimensions
7 × 10 in.
(17.8 × 25.4 cm)

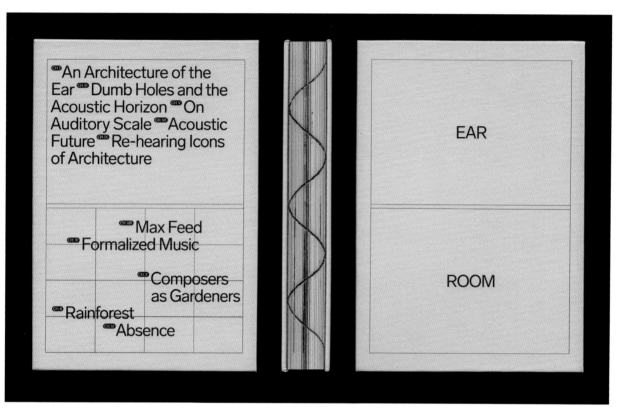

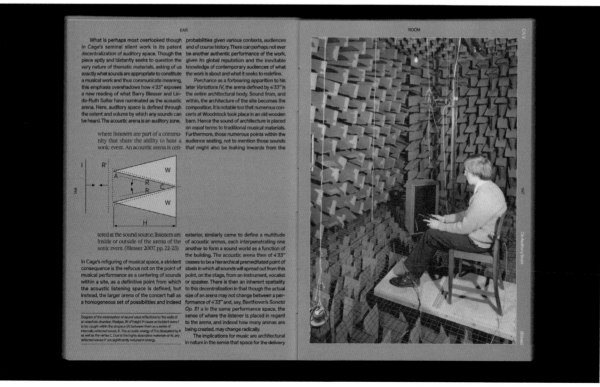

STUDENT: ONE%VINYL

Concept
Filter bubbles keep feeding nonstop streaming content based on big data. It leads to the illusion that we are the "center" of the world, making people less concerned about things outside their comfort zone. Algorithms seem to be the most efficient way of filtering information. But other than building connections based on big data, there should be other options.

Design
Ruiqi Zhou

URL
zrq.cargo.site/
ONE-VINYL-1

Instructor
Gerardo Herrera

School
ArtCenter
College of Design
Pasadena, California

Principal Type
ABC Whyte Inktrap
and Boogy Brut Poster

STUDENT: THE WIND AND MOON COLLECTION

Concept
The wind and moon described in the poetry of the Tang and Song dynasties deserve to be treasured and savored by all. The design of this book makes the Tang poems and Song lyrics more than just enlightening reading. It aims to slow down the reader's pace amid the mundane world, to pore over them word by word, and to find a sense of tranquility between the hazy lines.

Design
Minghao Lin

Professor
Caisheng Luo

School
Fujian Jiangxia University
Fuzhou, China

Principal Type
HYQuanTangShi

Dimensions
5.5 × 7.5 in.
(14 × 19 cm)

COMMUNCATION DESIGN

STUDENT: MUSEUM OF BACTERIA BRANDING

Concept

The design was inspired by the three basic morphologies of bacteria: spheres, rod-shaped, and spiral. The bacteria are constantly propagating and splitting but also generating new recombinations. I apply this process of interdependence, propagation, fragmentation, and connection to custom typeface design.

Design
Di Gu

Instructor
Natasha Jen°

School
The City College
of New York
New York

Principal Type
Intergrowth (custom)
and Objectivity

Dimensions
8.5 × 11 in.
(21.6 × 27.9 cm)

MUSEUM OF
BACTERIA

OPENING DAY
12.31.2021
02:30PM

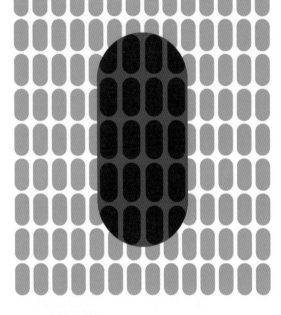

MUSEUM OF
BACTERIA

OPENING DAY
12.31.2021
02:30PM

MUSEUM OF
BACTERIA

OPENING DAY
12.31.2021
02:30PM

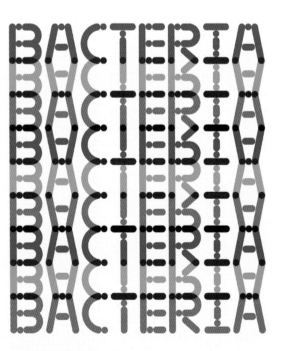

MUSEUM OF
BACTERIA

OPENING DAY
12.31.2021
02:30PM

STUDENT: BETWEEN HYPE AND HYPERREALITY

Concept

The pandemic has pushed us to be immersed in a global, interconnected galaxy of virtual worlds, avatars, and online communities, a world where the physical and virtual worlds converge. "Between Hype and Hyperreality" provides readers with a framework to understand the economy and technology of the metaverse and the hidden danger of dataveillance, while examining the unlimited potential of the spatial web.

Design
Tong Li

Instructor
Brad Bartlett

School
Art Center
College of Design
Pasadena, California

Principal Type
Akkurat-Mono
and Visuelt Pro

Dimensions
7.5 × 11 in.
(19.1 × 27.9 cm)

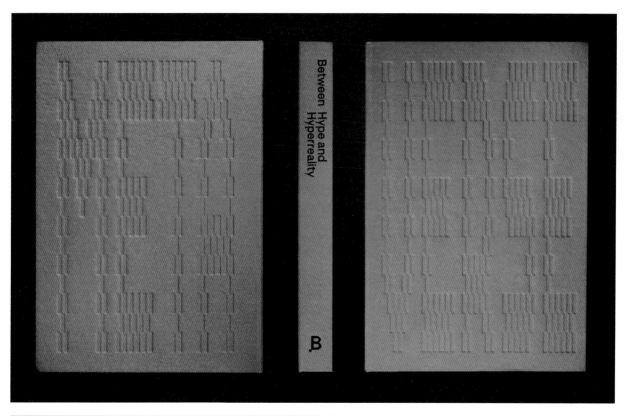

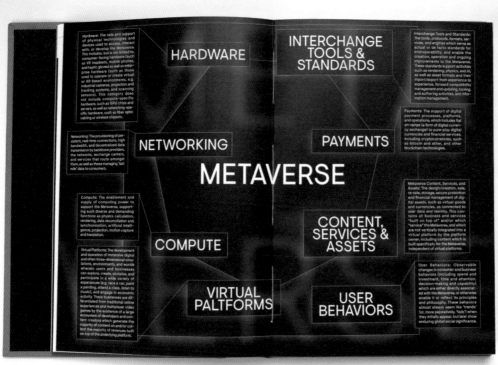

STUDENT: PROVO

Concept

Are you a robot? With the development of artificial intelligence, the answer to this question is getting more ambiguous. While AI helps improve productivity, it significantly lowers the cost of spamming. The fight against abusing technology is an everlasting campaign. Provo is one of them.

Design
Ruiqi Zhou

URL
zrq.cargo.site/provo

Instructor
Carolina Trigo

School
Art Center College
of Design
Pasadena, California

Principal Type
BallPill and
ABC Maxi Round
Mono Variable

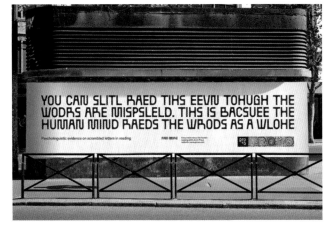

STUDENT: [ONOMATO'PE] IDENTITY TYPEFACE

Concept
This is a playful tour through the accomplishments, resilience, and creativity of our customers—Against All Odds.

Design
Jincheng Shi

URL
charlieshi.ch/
#onomato'pe

Instructors
Brad Bartlett
and Greg Lindy

School
ArtCenter
College of Design
Pasadena, California

Principal Type
Casual Grotesque

Dimensions
14 × 18 in.
(35.6 × 45.7 cm)

[onomato'pe]

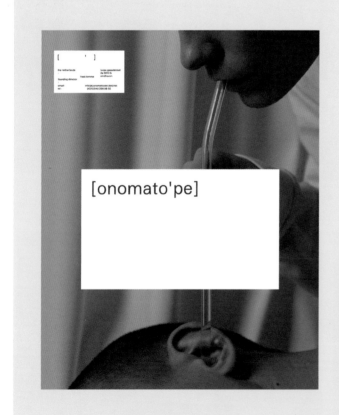

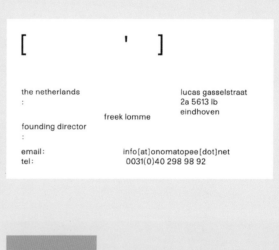

the netherlands
:
          freek lomme
founding director
:
email :   info[at]onomatopee[dot]net
tel :   0031(0)40 298 98 92

lucas gasselstraat
2a 5613 lb
eindhoven

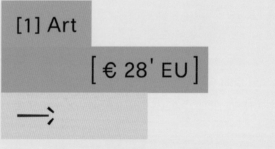

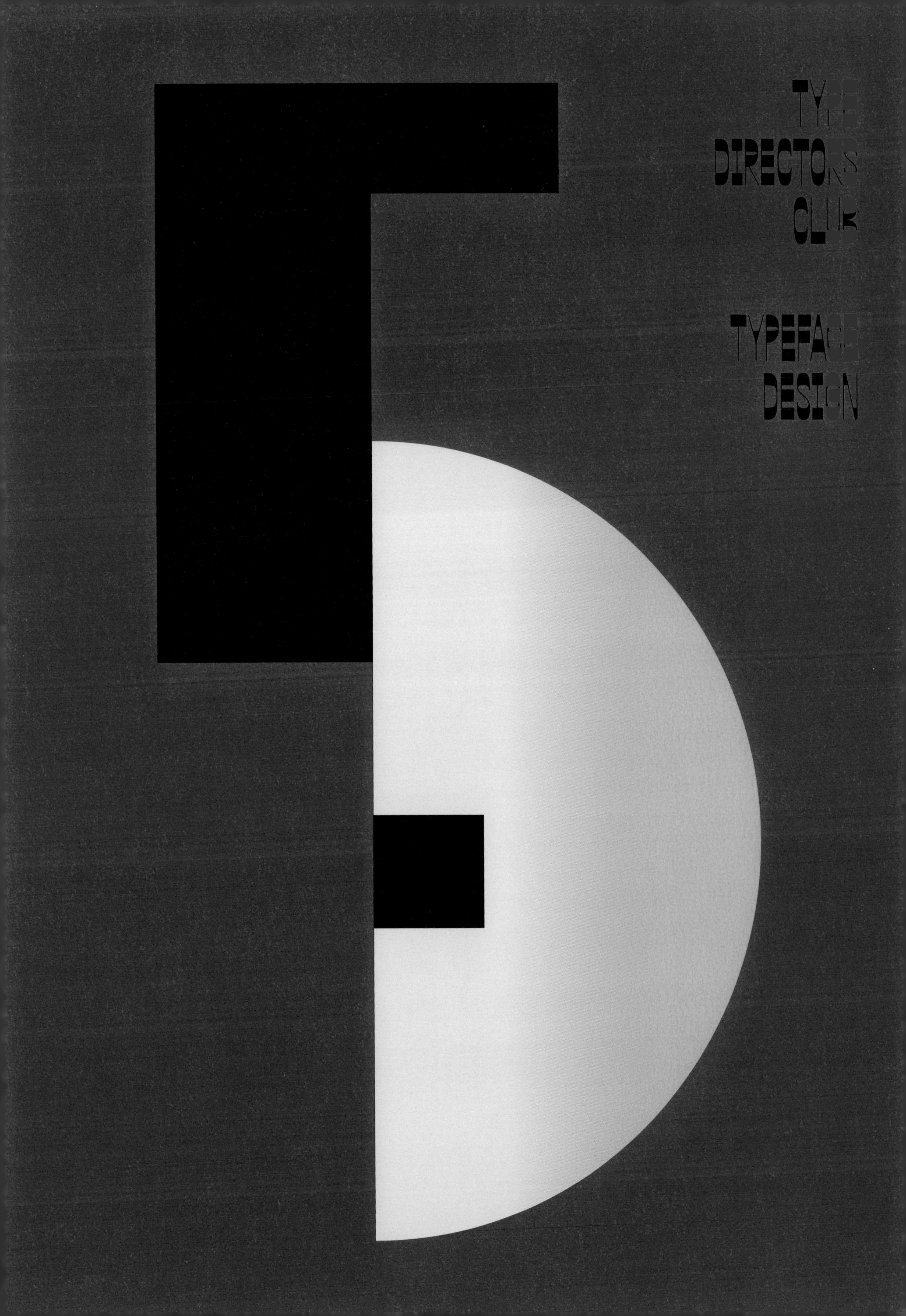
TYPE
DIRECTORS
CLUB
TYPEFACE
DESIGN

CHAIRS' STATEMENT

MEET THE JUDGES AND THEIR CHOICES

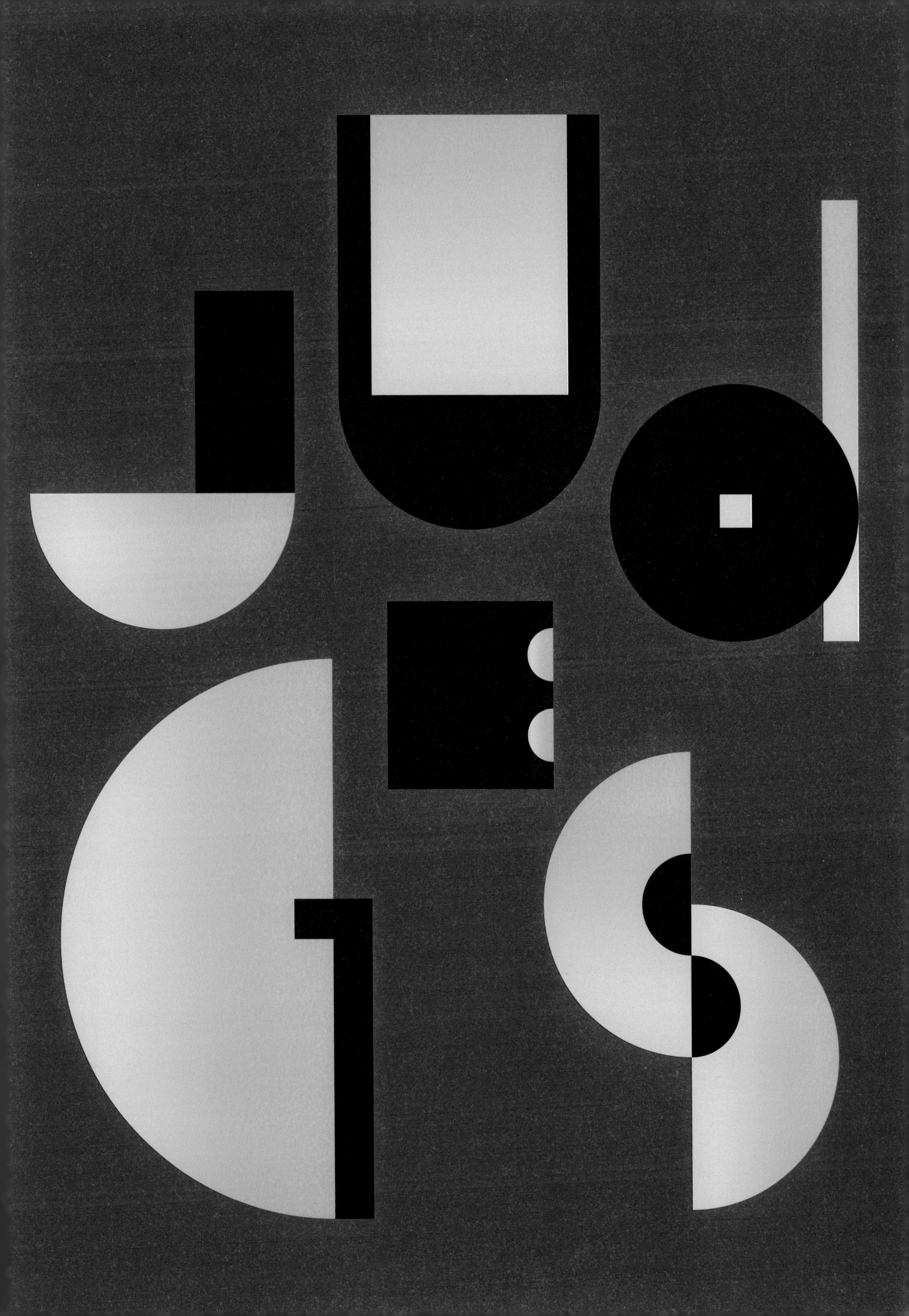

"

... THIS YEAR WE'VE ADDED ADDITIONAL VOICES INTO THE JUDGES ROOM BY BRINGING IN EXPERTS IN ARABIC, ARMENIAN, BENGALI, CHINESE, CYRILLIC, DEVANAGARI, GREEK, JAPANESE, KOREAN, LATIN, NUSHU, PERSIAN, (AND TAMILAND HAVING OUTSIDE EXPERTS CALL IN FOR JUDGING CANADIAN ABORIGINAL SYLLABICS)."

The TDC Competition regularly gets entries from over 60+ countries, with entrants speaking and writing an expanded set of languages and scripts. As part of edging toward inclusivity and representation, and giving more entrants a better chance of being adequately assessed, this year we've added additional voices into the judges room by bringing in experts in Arabic, Armenian, Bengali, Chinese, Cyrillic, Devanagari, Greek, Japanese, Korean, Latin, Nushu, Persian, and Tamil (and having outside experts call in for judging Canadian Aboriginal Syllabics). The conversations were robust and engaged, questioning what was truly excellent, and the contrast between how a script is judged by its native community versus the international gaze. Those conversations spanned between broadcast public panels, essays (Typegeist) and interviews (Typographica), judging phone-calls and shared documents. In the end—the jury selected 5 winning student pieces and 28 professional works, with a few that stole the heart of more than one judge.

NADINE CHAHINE

KSENYA SAMARSKAYA

KHAJAG APELIAN

Khajag Apelian is a lettering artist, type and graphic designer. Having grown up between Dubai and Beirut, and being raised in an Armenian family, Khajag has an affinity for different languages and writing systems, which he has applied to the development of typefaces in many scripts, including Arabic, Armenian, and Latin. He designed Arek, a typeface that was awarded the Grand Prize at Granshan 2010 Type Design Competition, and was among the winners of Letter.2, the 2nd international type design competition organized by the Association Typographique Internationale (ATypI). He currently operates under the name debakir Armenian for printed type, and is in constant collaboration with different type foundries and design studios like, Commercial Type, Bold Monday, Typotheque and Morcos Key. He has worked with various international brands including IBM, Apple, Samsung and Disney ME. Khajag also teaches design courses at the American University of Beirut.

debakir.com
⬡ khajag

"THIS TYPEFACE ADDS A FRESH OUTLOOK TO THE ARABIC TYPE DESIGN SCENE; THROUGH ITS RESEARCH, VISUAL MANIFESTATION, AND THE PROGRESSIVE DESIGN APPROACH IT TAKES."
— BORNA AND KHAJAG

BORNA IZADPANAH

Borna Izadpanah is a Lecturer in Typography at the University of Reading, UK, from where he was also awarded a PhD, and an MA in Typeface Design. His doctoral research explored the history of the early typographic representation of the Persian language. Borna has received numerous prestigious awards for his research and typeface design, including the Grand Prize and the First Prize in Arabic Text Typeface in the Granshan Type Design Competition, a TDC Certificate of Typographic Excellence, and the Symposia Iranica Prize for the best paper in Art History.

⬡ BornaIz
⬡ UniofReading

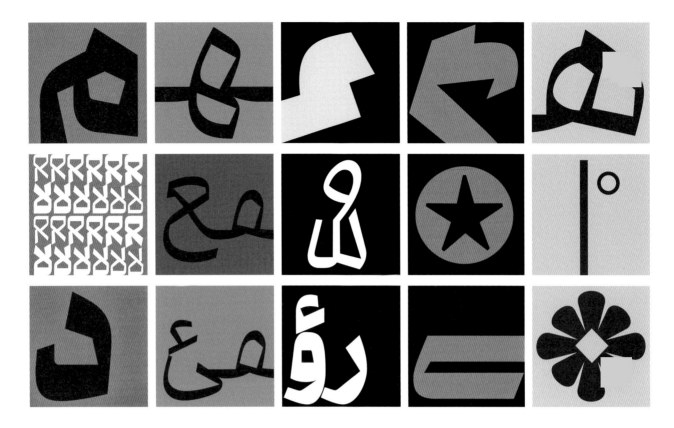

العمارة هي فن وعلم تصميم وتخطيط والمباني

العمارة هي فن وعلم تصميم وتخطيط والمباني

العمارة هي فن وعلم تصميم وتخطيط والمباني

العمارة هي فن وعلم تصميم وتخطيط والمباني

العمارة هي فن وعلم تصميم وتخطيط والمباني

العمارة هي فن وعلم تصميم وتخطيط والمباني

العمارة هي فن وعلم تصميم وتخطيط والمباني

The TMOCA typeface is one of the most outstanding winners of the TDC68 competition.. Although it is based on the Naskh style and demonstrates its designer's understanding of the script rules, it is not constrained by conventional forms. Instead, it creatively explores new avenues to achieve visual harmony with the architecture of TMOCA.

The introduction of the cuts is unexpected, and this is where the innovation comes in. As a reader the overall texture looks very familiar as it is based on the contemporary Naskh typographic sensibilities; however, a closer look highlights its elaborate and well-crafted details. The contrast between the smooth outer outlines of the letters and the sharp and abrupt forms of the inner outlines give it an elegant peculiarity that is almost architectural.

Tehran Museum of Contemporary Art

Type Design
Damoon Khanjanzadeh
Toronto

Client
Tehran Museum of
Contemporary Art

Concept
In 2021, I was commissioned by the Tehran Museum of Contemporary Art to design an original typeface for their rebranding, and I had about a month to complete it. To achieve this, I undertook a series of experiments to deconstruct conventional forms of the Naskh style without making the distortions immediately noticeable. Although the TMOCA typeface does not faithfully follow conventional forms and proportions, two important factors were taken into consideration in its design: Persian writing conventions and Iranian geometric patterns. My aim was to keep the structure of the typeface based on the established conventions while giving it a progressive and contemporary feel by designing details and patterns that are inspired by the particularities of TMOCA's renowned architecture.

KOSTAS BASTSOKAS

Kostas Bastsokas is a Greek typeface designer and typographer. During his freelance career he specialised in graphic design, illustration, web design, packaging, and animation; he finally chose to pursue his passion with typography. Kostas holds an MA in Typeface Design from the University of Reading and enjoys innovative explorations in Latin, Greek, Cyrillic, and Arabic type design. He spends his time designing original typefaces, expanding script support of existing ones, and offering consultation for designers and type foundries. He is also one part Foundry5.

kostasbastsokas.com
⧉ kosbarts

> "...IT'S NOT JUST YOUR OLD FELLOW NEO-GROTESQUE! NORBERT SMILES, LAUGHS, MOCKS — WE SEE A LOT OF HUMOR IN ITS CURVES."
> — DARIA AND KOSTAS

DARIA PETROVA

After graduating from the TypeMedia course in 2016, Daria spends her days working at Swiss Typefaces and her nights drawing odd typefaces.

dariapetrova.com
⧉ typodaria

What sets Norbert apart from its worthy competitors is its refreshingly anti-utilitarian approach to literally everything. Starting with family planning: nothing is interpolated. Only extremes are present, so those who seek a workhorse should look elsewhere. And the extremes push the limits of what would be considered reasonable – a little wider or narrower and it would have been a farce, but they're clearly too much for most situations.

Don't you grin at this 'Breit' g, or those 'Mager' commas? And then instead of atoning for being so irreverent, Norbert slants in both directions. To quote Norbert himself: 'If everyone likes it, it's mediocre' — a useful mantra. Norbert makes a mockery of everything. And indeed it is so well executed that it puts everything else to shame.

NORBERT
Type Design
Philipp Neumeyer
Berlin

URL
typemates.com

Twitter
@TypeMatesFonts

Type Foundry
TypeMates

Members of the Type Family
Norbert Schmal-Mager
and Norbert Schmal-MagerKontra

Concept
A collection of somehow familiar extremes with a deliberate absence of a "Regular" width. Related, not interpolated. Norbert is not as naive as Philipp Neumeyer expected. A collection of extremes, Norbert reflects on how the bundled-together styles of early hot metal type families were enriched by their contradictions and looks ahead. The result is an unaffected Grotesque and everything you never needed.

KIMYA GANDHI

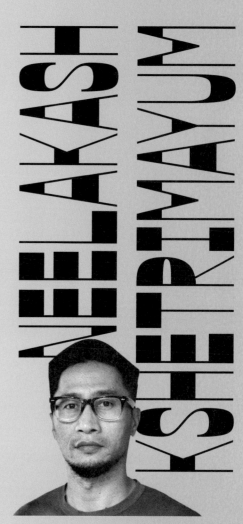

Kimya Gandhi is a type designer from Mumbai, currently living in Berlin. Specialising in designing Devanagari typefaces, Kimya draws her inspiration from India's rich and diverse visual landscape and hopes to create new and innovative designs for Indic scripts. Kimya is a partner at the type foundry Mota Italic where she along with Rob Keller designs custom and retail typefaces for clients from various parts of the world. When not drawing typefaces she spends her time teaching, or conducting workshops on typography and type design at various design institutes. Other than letters, she likes cooking, plants and the colour black.

motaitalic.com
🅾 kimyagandhi

NEELAKASH KSHETRIMAYUM

Neelakash Kshetrimayum is a type and graphic designer from Manipur, India. He graduated from the National Institute of Design in India, and holds an MA in Typeface Design from the University of Reading, UK, where he was awarded the Monotype Studentship. He has worked with Adobe, Google, Tiro Typeworks, and Dalton Maag on several Indic script projects.

neelakash.webflow.io
🅾 NKshetrimayum

ANAGHA NARAYANAN

Anagha Narayanan studied design at DJ Academy of Design in India and has interned at Black[Foundry] in Paris. Throughout her childhood art and design has been the single connecting thread. As someone whose father owned an offset printing press, her interest in type and all things related started early on. In 2018, Anagha joined Universal Thirst type foundry where she has been able to contribute to a diverse range of projects and scripts. She is currently working on her first typeface release Ilai.

🅾 anaghanarayanan

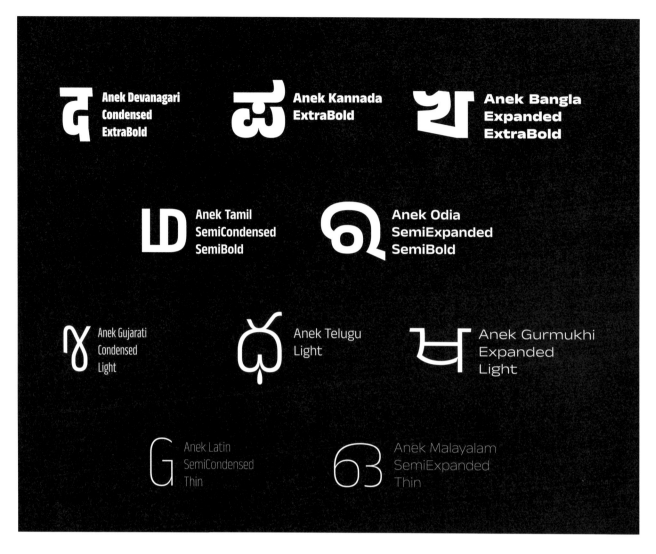

Designing a multi-script type family that includes scripts from different writing traditions is not an easy task, and ANEK makes this mammoth of a task seem effortless. The design displays rich experimentation in forms while remaining true to each script's indigenous writing traditions.

The wide array of weights and widths redefines what can be accomplished with Indian scripts. The resulting type family is fresh, rich in character, and relevant for India's increasing typographic needs.

— **Anagha , Kimya, and Neelakash**

ANEK Multiscript Variable Indic

Type Design
Omkar Bhoir,
Girish Dalvi,
Noopur Datye,
Mrunmayee Ghaisas,
Yesha Goshar,
Sarang Kulkarni,
Kailash Malviya,
Vaishanvi Murthy,
Aadarsh Rajan,
Sulekha Rajkumar,

Mahesh Sahu, and
Maithilli Shingre
Mumbai

Twitter
@EkTypeFoundry

Type Foundry
Ek Type

Client
Google Fonts

Concept
This is a contemporary, multi-script, variable type-family designed for large sizes and short texts. Characterized by distinct visual features, balanced structures, and rhythmic textures, this family of nine Indic scripts and Latin has multiple weights and widths. While its shared aesthetics are drawn from a collaboratively decided pool of visual features, the design of each script amalgamates influences from its own typographic culture as well as the perspectives of individual designers. A well-informed, conscientious, and refreshing interpretation of scripts traditions from India, this family offers a versatile system that can meet the demands of a wide range of applications.

KARA GORDON

Kara Gordon is a type designer at Commercial Type working out of Brooklyn, NY. Before joining Commercial Type in 2018, she worked as a publication designer at The Atlanticand Point Five Design. She holds a BFA from Washington University in St. Louis in communication design and English, and was a part of the inaugural 2015 class at Type@Paris.

karagordon.com
kayessgordon

> "SUCH STRIKING DISPLAY TYPES SEEM AT ODDS IN THE SAME FAMILY, AND HOW ZIDIĆ MANAGES TO BRIDGE THIS GAP WITH THREE SUBDUED TEXT STYLES IS IMPRESSIVE."
> — KARA AND MINJOO

MINJOO HAM

Minjoo Ham is a type designer from South Korea. With Mark Frömberg Minjoo Ham founded Hypertype in 2020 in Berlin. She completed the TypeMedia master course at the Royal Academy of Art (KABK) in The Hague, Netherlands, concentrating on research and type design of a Latin and Hangul double-script. With her interest in the relation between Latin Characters and Hangeul, Ham has been running multi-lingual projects with multinational companies.

minjooham.com
minjooham_

CHIAROSCURO
caliginous ailurophile
information
Gregariousness
Incandescent
BRZO & POLAKO
unexplainable mellifluous

Aside from being well-crafted, we were delighted by the experimental nature and bravery of Zalfia. A wide palette ranging from classic to renegade interpretations of the flat brush, Neva Zidić plays with proportions and personality. This is most obvious in the two display styles, each marching to the beat of its own drum: one is an ornate condensed with cursive elements, the other is brittle and squarish.

Such striking display types seem at odds in the same family, and how Zidić manages to bridge this gap with three subdued text styles is impressive. The italic's severe upward strokes speak most clearly to the sharp cuts of the displays, while the soft and warm upright text styles are the reasonable, nurturing members of the family. With five distinct voices, this oddball family would be so much fun to play with in an editorial design project.

Zalfia

Design
Neva Zidić
Zagreb, Croatia

Instructors
Erik van Blokland,
Paul van der Laan,
and Peter Verheul

School
Master TypeMedia,
Royal Academy of Art
The Hague

Concept
The first idea for the project was translating the concept of introvert and extrovert personalities into letters, visualizing their opposing element and the space between them.

With the introduction of the flat brush as the main tool for experimenting and sketching, the topic broadened to an exploration of many contrasting personalities through letters. By manipulating different parameters when writing with the brush, a wide range of feelings and emotions were achieved, and the idea was to have them inside one type family. Translating this vibrancy of the brush strokes into digital drawings was at the same time the most challenging part. Zalfia now consists of two distinct display styles, which determined the family's features, and three text styles, intended to better function at smaller sizes.

LISA HUANG

Chinese by origin, Lisa Huang 黄丽莎 was born and grew up in France. After studying in graphic design in Paris, she continued a specialization in type design with renowned programs such as Type@Cooper in New York City and Type and Media in The Hague. Since 2018, she is a type designer specialized in Latin and Chinese scripts, currently based in Nantes, France. Lisa's interest in type and graphic design relies strongly in multi-cultural works, especially those mixing Latin / French and Chinese cultures.

lisahuang.work
⟳ hellolisahuang

"BEAUTIFUL WRITING WAS (AND STILL IS TODAY) CONSIDERED AS ONE OF THE HIGHEST QUALITY ONE PERSON COULD HAVE, AS A MIRROR OF ONE'S SOUL."
— LISA HUANG

乾隆行书

念孝贤
三秋别忽尔
一晌莫酸然
追忆居中阃
深宜称孝贤
平生难尽述
百岁妄希延
夏日冬之夜
远期只廿年

乐善堂全集是弘历在藩邸时期诗文作品的集结
集中显示了年轻皇子弘历浸透着正统儒家的理念
闲适恬淡的弘历心境其中乐善堂全集付梓行世最早

兔目当年李氏槐
槎老干倚春阶何
当绿叶生齐日高
枕羲皇梦亦佳三
秋别忽尔一晌莫
酸然追忆居中阃
深宜称孝贤平生
难尽述百岁妄希
延夏日冬之夜远
期只廿年冻酥岸
觉看波漾春到物
知听雁还今日悦
心真恰当窗凭积
素慰开颜铁岭老

With Chinese script being a writing system strongly related to the pointed brush, the same tool used for several millennia, it is almost more "natural" to see handwritten style Chinese rather than the mechanical shapes we are more used to see with Latin typefaces, thus my preference and awe each time I see a great handwritten Chinese typeface!

Beautiful writing was (and still is today) considered as one of the highest quality one person could have, as a mirror of one's soul. The Emperor, being the most important human on Earth during the many dynasties of China, had to give the example. Qianlong Xinshu by FounderType keeps the high calligraphic quality from the Emperor's writings, making it a typeface to be used in situations where human touch is welcome, a typeface that brings life into Chinese lively characters. Even today, some three centuries after the Emperor's reign.

FZ QianLongXingShu

Type Design
Tong Lin

Type Foundry
FounderType
Beijing

Concept
Qianlong, the Qing Dynasty emperor, whose calligraphy art has a certain special status in Chinese cultural history. Qianlong's calligraphy is mellow, dignified, and elegant. It has a gentle and smooth structure with an elegant atmosphere. The brush stroke is restrained and balanced. When designing this Qianlong script typeface, we collected a large number of his calligraphy and took a large number of his inscription pictures. In the one-and-a-half-year designing process, we divided the strokes one by one, extracted different parts from the whole, carefully interpreted the transformation from traditional Chinese characters to simplified Chinese characters, and kept finessing many times. We adjusted horizontal, vertical, and oblique strokes, so as to complement each other and create a brush form in line with modern aesthetics.

MARTIN MAJOOR

Martin Majoor has been designing type since the mid-1980s. During his study at the School of Fine Arts in Arnhem (1980-1986), he shortly worked in a student placement at URW in Hamburg. It was there, in 1984, he was able to work with Ikarus, the first digital typedesign system

Since 1997 Majoor works as a graphic designer and type designer in both The Netherlands (Arnhem) and in Poland (Warsaw).

martinmajoor.com
martinmajoor

> " RESONAY IS A HIT RIGHT AWAY! IT DEFINITELY DESERVES A CHANCE TO BE SEEN AND TO BE USED BY THE ENTHUSIASTIC TYPE LOVERS AROUND THE GLOBE. WE JUST CAN'T STOP LOOKING AT IT!"
> — MARTIN AND ULRIKE

ULRIKE RAUSCH

In 2009 Berlin-based type designer Ulrike Rausch founded her own type foundry called LiebeFonts, providing high-quality typefaces with a charming personality and obsessive attention to detail. Her growing portfolio of handwriting fonts has been used in publications, advertisements, and websites all around the world. She also creates custom typefaces for clients.

When Ulrike is not busy with her next font release, she enjoys teaching at art schools and giving type design workshops in her studio. Together with letterer and writer Chris Campe, she wrote the book "Making Fonts!", a comprehensive guide to type design and font production.

liebefonts.com
LiebeFonts

Resonay is a typeface that stands out immediately! Andrej Dieneš who is responsible for this gem must have a huge passion for type design. The joy of designing this typeface is clearly showing off and the sheer quality stands out, there is no hiding from its nifty details.

Apart from the gorgeous five conventional weights (called 'Solid'), there is a 'Base' display version that — combined with a sophisticated layers font —creates a fascinating world of elegant but unconventional shapes.

The italic is a beauty at itself, roman and italic complement each other perfectly. The numerous ligatures and swash characters reveal a great sensitivity. There are stylistic alternates for various characters and the possibilities that OpenType offers have been optimally exploited.

Resonay

Type Design
Andrej Dieneš
Bratislava, Slovakia

URLs
adtypo.com
typemates.com

Type Foundry
TypeMates

Members of the Type Family
Resonay, Resonay Base Thin, Resonay Base Light, Resonay Base Regular, Resonay Base Medium, Resonay Base Bold, Resonay Cover Thin, Resonay Cover Light, Resonay Cover Regular, Resonay Cover Medium, Resonay Cover Bold, Resonay Solid Thin, Resonay Solid

Light, Resonay Solid Regular, Resonay Solid Medium, Resonay Solid Bold, Resonay Base Thin Italic, Resonay Base Light Italic, Resonay Base Regular Italic, Resonay Base Medium Italic, Resonay Base Bold Italic, Resonay Cover Thin Italic, Resonay Cover Light Italic, Resonay Cover Regular Italic, Resonay Cover Medium Italic, Resonay Cover Bold Italic, Resonay Solid Thin Italic, Resonay Solid Light Italic, Resonay Solid Regular Italic, Resonay Solid Medium Italic, Resonay Solid Bold Italic

Concept
Resonay's a vivacious layer font that takes classical lettering somewhere new. Combining elegant details

from stone carving with the flow of calligraphy, a sharp attitude with exuberant bézier curves, Resonay is suitable for logotypes and refined display setting. Enriched with swashes, titling alternates and a broad range of decorative ligatures, Resonay brings expression and poetry to headlines.

Attentive to setting titles in a classical fashion, Resonay has wide small caps and a set of nested capitals. For other typefaces, 200 lowercase ligatures may be enough, but with handsome initial and final swashes for its upper and lowercase letters, Resonay goes further. The uppercase italic is swashy by default.

MAMOUN SAKKAL

Dr. Mamoun Sakkal is founder and principal of Sakkal Design in Bothell, Washington. After a career as an artist and architect, his firm has focused on Arabic calligraphy and typography since the 1990s. Clients include National Geographic, Microsoft, Linotype, and Adobe, among others. Sakkal Design was commissioned to design the corporate Arabic typefaces for Dubai's Burj Khalifa and Armani Hotel, and several of his Arabic fonts are now widely used as Microsoft Windows system fonts.

He has received several awards for calligraphy, graphics, and type design, including four awards of excellence from the Type Directors Club of New York and one from IRCICA in Istanbul.

sakkal.com
mamoun@sakkal.com

"THIS IS A LIGHT-HEARTED, INNOVATIVE DESIGN THAT INTRODUCES ATTRACTIVE TYPOGRAPHIC FORMS THAT ARE WELL WITHIN THE VISUAL PALETTE OF ARABIC SCRIPT."
— MAMOUN SAKKAL

Mithaq

Type Design
Yara Khoury Nammour
Beirut, Lebanon

Design Firm
AlMohtaraf Design House
Jeddah, Saudi Arabia

Client
Architecture and Design
Commission, Ministry
of Culture (KSA)

Concept
Mithaq is a custom-designed Arabic geometric display typeface that investigates the level of abstraction letterforms can reach within a typeface. Inspired by the triangular Lahj openings of mud houses typical of Najdi architecture in the Kingdom of Saudi Arabia, the typeface is based on basic elementary shapes. It seeks to modernize, unify and standardize letters into an idealistic form that combines function and form while challenging its own legibility. The letters also seek to reflect the visual heritage of the area, particularly early inscribed Hijazi script; they are clean and concrete, as if cut from stone. The strokes are very brisk and uniform in width. The counter spaces within the one letter and the inter-letter spacing maintain the geometric aspect with an emphasis on the triangular form.

There has been an extra ordinary production of Arabic typefaces in recent years, most of which is rehashing of existing familiar designs. Mithaq typeface is a fresh take on the geometric treatment of the alphabet. Although the letter and word shapes are abstracted and simplified, the design is not a simplistic solution and many typographic refinements make it a pleasure to see and read.

This is a light-hearted, innovative design that introduces attractive typographic forms that are well within the visual palette of Arabic script. The typeface succeeds in avoiding two pitfalls of similar geometric typefaces, namely the difficulty of reading (illegibility) and alien, eccentric letter and word forms. It is a venture into new realms of typographic expression conceived thoughtfully and executed skillfully. In Arabic we call this kind of design: the simple recalcitrant السهل لممتنع

KAZUHIRO YAMADA

Kazuhiro Yamada is the founder of Nipponia, a Tokyo-based design studio. He holds a BA from Tama Art University where he studied visual communication design. After graduation, he worked as a book designer in the office of Yukimasa Matsuda, a famous graphic designer in Japan. He was a senior type designer at Monotype from 2014 to 2017, designing Japanese typefaces. He launched Nipponia in 2017 and became independent from Monotype.

nipponia.in
⊙ ymdkzhr

"DIGITIZING BRUSH STROKES IS NOT AN EASY TASK, AS IT INVOLVES DECIPHERING THE UNEVEN LINE QUALITY, BALANCING BLACK AND WHITE (FIGURE AND GROUND), AND NOT LOSING THE CHARM OF THE ORIGINAL REFERENCE."
— KASU

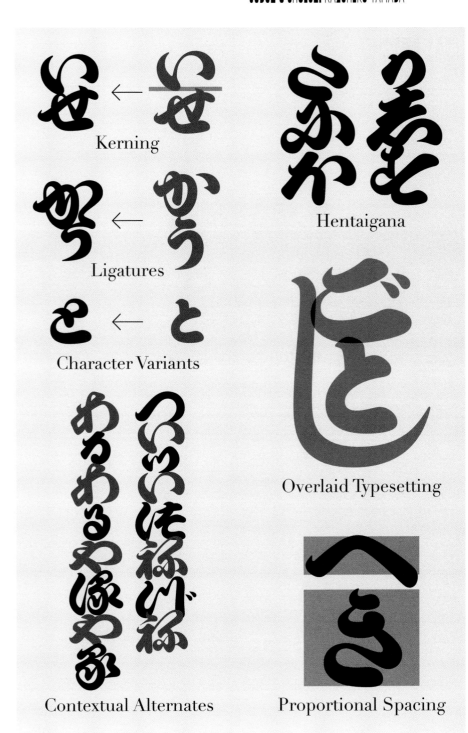

Kerning

Ligatures

Character Variants

Contextual Alternates

Hentaigana

Overlaid Typesetting

Proportional Spacing

The greatest challenge for Japanese typeface designers today is to recover the original beauty of the Japanese script that was once lost with the introduction of the Western type system. Uwabami is an attempt to revive the brush strokes used in very limited situations during the Edo period (seventeenth through nineteenth centuries).The bold, undulating strokes, derived from the strength of the brush script from which they are derived, are free from typographical constraints and amplify the pleasure of writing (or typesetting).

Digitizing brush strokes is not an easy task, as it involves deciphering the uneven line quality, balancing black and white (figure and ground), and not losing the charm of the original reference. Uwabami has cleared all these issues, and it shows the designer's knowledge of brush strokes and design ability. It is a good example of how learning the context from history can lead us to the next level.

Uwabami

Type Design and Foundry
Hisashi Iwai
Tokyo

Concept
About 150 years ago, well before the introduction of modern typography to Japan, publications used woodblock printing. Originally, Japanese characters could be overlaid with each other, but the technology of movable type made this expression impossible.

With the advent of new technology such as photo/digital typesetting, Japanese texts have been freed from many technological constraints of setting metal type. However, it seems that it still follows the same system without enough consideration.

Uwabami replicates the appearance of the handwriting used in librettos of traditional Japanese narrative music, which is known for its extremely tight letter spacing. It recognizes the existence of an invisible shackle that today's Japanese text unwittingly wears and tries to unleash itself from such constraints.

TYPEFACES: SHINBAKUSAI REISHO

Concept

A Japanese typeface, Shinbakusai Reisho is a modern revival of the calligraphic clerical script (reisho in Japanese) tthat once graced the imperial collection of enamelled porcelain (yousai in Japanese) from the flourishing age of the Qing Dynasty (1644-1912) of China. In contrast to other reisho styles in the imperial collection, this typeface harmoniously blends yet juxtaposes soften-curves and sharpened-tips in key designated stokes. These distinguishing aesthetic attributes have also been further applied to Japanese hiragana and katakana for usage in Japan..

Type Design

Han-yi Shaw

Type Foundry

HYS Design
Redmond, Washington

金陵　帝王の州
江南　佳麗の地

天の川瀬ごとに　幣をたてまつる
心は君を幸く来ませと
鳳凰台の上にて　長安望み
五色の宮袍　水に照らして寒し
彩筆十年にして　翰墨を留し
銀河一夜にして　闌干に臥す

一千多導書本河線あげとみわクテマラ
三南夜山心来灯翰遠いこなむをゲトミリラ
五杏天島情案照考里うごにめんケナムルリ
七又女川成嘉独聞銀えさぬもアコニメレル
九可妹幣我歌留臥長おしねやイサヌモロワ
也君始帝於晩台自靜かすのゆウシネヤワヲ
人和学年抱母発佳響がせはよエスノユヲン
上喜安尋挙水登興飛きそひらオセハヨン
京国宮幸新永私限鳳ぎたふりカソヒ
令地密庭日汪筆色凰くちへるガタフ
勢報寒彩明瀬絢袍麗ぐつほれキチへ
十墨対愛望蘭緒語隷けてまろギツホ
永あア

Concept

Jinhua Mincho is inspired by the charms and nuances of a woodblock print from the Republican Era. Its slightly short look comes with relaxed counter and gentle, defined strokes full of articulated details. The overall quality Jinhua Mincho aims to offer is a classic, cordial feeling without the old-time, clichéd overtones that a woodblock usually carries. It is simple, unpretentious, yet incisive and powerful. If set horizontally, the well-leveled font slows down the reading, giving it a calm and paced rhythm; a vertical arrangement would render the text columns compact, elegant, and well-tproportioned.

Type Design and Direction
Tianmeng Xue
Hangzhou, China

Type Foundry
Mallikātype

36pt 古典平和溫潤舒放

24pt 錦華明朝體 Jinhua-Mincho

14pt The character 樂 means happiness or music.

36pt 竹影青明草木淡雅

24pt 国東風影清，城西雨光寒。

12pt 解析：此句描写诗人记忆之景，清净空灵，如在眼前。

108pt 永

36pt 24pt 心灵的实践——《印度散文》50年刊目集

108pt 愛

14pt

你是從詩三百篇中，
襄裳涉水而來。
髭彼兩髦，
一身古遠的芹香。
越陌度阡到我身邊躺下，
到我身邊躺下，
已是楚辞蒼茫了。

TYPEFACES: FZ GUOMEIJINDAO

Concept

FZ GuoMeiJinDao was jointly developed by FounderType and the China Academy of Art. This font takes the old letterhead of the China Academy of Art as the style source and inspiration, to carry forward and convey the spirit in the new era. Strokes are standardized and unified, giving people a sense of pleasing to the eyes.

Type Design

Huasha Chen,
Lixiao Chen,
Bingquan Guo,
Xu Han,
Yanqing Li,
Huanbin Liang,
Yanzhao Lin,
Jiayu Lu,
Xiduo Luo,
Yin Qiu,
Zhiqiang Xing,
Lingli Zhang,
Ranyi Zhong,
and Liang Zhou

Type Foundry

FounderType
Beijing

Client

China Academy of Art
Hangzhou

行健

上古结绳以治后世圣人易之以书契百官以治万民以察盖取诸夬中生有积点成线山水化为符号万物聚于笔端天地人在汉字初文中交汇弥漫着旷古悠远的力与美人的思

居敬

过时空穿透暗暗生发出不息日的文明说文日书者如也存储

沟通延伸串联汉字的流转使用幻化出万千形体古往今来的设计者怀着匠心劳作在不知不觉间完成对观

会通

沟通延伸串联汉字的流转使用幻化出万千形体古往今来的设计者怀着匠心劳作在不知不觉间完成对观

以汉字的精美教化移风俗神九十多年前西子湖畔在新文

履远

化的激越浪潮中国立艺术院创立带着奋发的气息以介绍西洋艺术整理中国艺术调和现中西艺术创造时代艺术为志业欲化沧桑世为乐土我们的学院正是这样中国艺术的

天地玄黄寒来暑往云腾致雨露结为霜金生丽水玉出昆冈剑号巨阙珠称夜光果珍李柰菜重芥姜海咸河淡鳞潜羽翔龙师火帝鸟官人皇始制文字乃服衣裳推位让国有虞陶唐吊民伐罪周发殷汤坐朝问道垂拱平章爱育黎首臣伏戎羌遐迩壹体率宾归王鸣凤在竹白驹食场化被草木赖及万方盖此身发四大五常恭惟鞠养岂敢毁伤女慕贞洁男效才良知过必改得能莫忘

张阳冈姜皇列调昆芥人陶吕出重官虞律玉菜鸟有辰律果珍李垂宿火柰菜拱律宿龙师宾及

介绍西洋艺术整理中国艺术调和中西艺术创造时代艺术

中国美术学院

学院精神的时代宣言

中国艺术的先锋之旅

美术教育的核心现场

画彩仙灵
浮渭据泾
好爵自縻
心动神疲
造次弗离
入奉母仪
礼别尊卑
摄职从政
慎终宜令
渊澄取映
临深履薄
资父事君
祸因恶积
德建名立
墨悲丝染
闾谈彼短

技进乎道

TYPEFACES: KLAKET

Concept

This is a Ruqah Arabic typeface inspired by the Egyptian visual culture, especially the film posters. Ruqah is a regular handwriting typeface and generally less expressive among the major calligraphy styles, but the film posters made me realize its potential for display use. I made a heavy monolinear style using the hidden ingredient: the Iranian film posters. The accompanying Latin was designed as a slab serif that stands on its own as an equally fun display face.

Creative Direction
Toshi Omargari
London

URL
tosche.net

Twitter
@tosche_e

Type Foundry
Omega Type Foundry

TYPEFACES: SF ARABIC

Concept

The goal was to expand the coverage of San Francisco, the system font for Apple platforms, to include the Arabic script with a voice that is neutral, rational, and approachable. We optimized and refined mixed script typesetting, enabling Arabic to seamlessly integrate with Latin, Greek, and Cyrillic scripts. We also created a broad, flexible design space with variation axes for weight, contrast, and tracking for versatility across hardware and software.

Type Design

Apple Design Team
Cupertino, California

TYPEFACES: YOUTUBE SANS ARABIC

Concept

The Arabic font family presented here is the companion of a clear and joyful Latin sans serif that also includes a rounded version for kids. It is a low-contrast typeface, intended to appear on screens, at sizes 18pt and above. The family remains true to the ductus and proportions of Arabic script while introducing forms of playfulness, abstraction, and geometry that characterize the Latin version. The goal was to cover all languages that actively use the Arabic script, as well as their design specificities, to ensure all communities are represented.

Type Design
Lara Captan and YouTube Art Department
Amsterdam and San Bruno, California

Art Direction
Robyn Lee and Amy Yip

Creative Direction
Chris Bettig

Producer
Ash Qualischefski

Engineer
Kelsey Mayfield

Font Consultant
David Berlow°
Martha's Vineyard

Font Engineer
Khaled Hosny
Cairo

Program Manager
Dave Crossland
New York

Members of the Type Family
YouTube Sans Arabic: Hairline, ExtraLight, Light, Regular, Medium, SemiBold, Bold, ExtraBold, Black, ExtraBlack
YouTube Rounded Arabic: Regular, Medium, Bold
Styles: Static + Variable (YouTube Sans AR, YouTube Rounded AR)
Grades: YouTube Sans AR, YouTube Sans Overlay AR, YouTube Sans Dark AR

317

TYPEFACES: AMAALA ARABIC

Concept

This is a custom typeface for a luxury resort. It is a multiscript (Arabic, Latin, and Cyrillic), Sans, Serif, Display, and Text family that could be used in signage and print publications and web. This submission is for only the Arabic part of the family.

Type Design
Bahman Eslami (Arabic)
Ilya Naumoff (Latin)

Type Foundries
GlyphSets (Arabic)
Interval Type (Latin)
The Hague and Paris

Twitter
@glyphsets

Agency
Landor Paris

**Members of the
Type Family**
Amaala Closed Eye:
Light, Regular, Medium,
Bold, Extrabold
Amaala Open Eye:
Light, Regular, Medium,
Bold, Extrabold
Amaala a Sans: Light,
Regular, Medium, Bold

Amaala Display

في ثلاثة مواقع في قلب البحر الأحمر

Amaala Sans

الاستجمام والرياضة

Amaala Display

استكشف المخططات الرئيسية

Amaala Display

وجهة لا مثيل لها

Amaala Sans

وبفضل تصاميمها التي تستخدم

Amaala Text

وتتميز ببيئتها النقية

Concept
This is a transitional Arabic typeface, designed for branding, that connects traditional aspects of Arabic letterforms to the new-age approaches.

Type Design
Hirbod Lotfian
Amiens, France

Consultant
Nastaran Kechechian
Amiens, France

Twitter
@hirbodlotfian

Client
Charisma Capital
Market Services
Tehran

**Members of the
Type Family**
Charisma (Light,
Regular, Bold,
ExtraBold, Black)

TYPEFACES: OCEANIC

Concept
Oceanic draws inspiration from the eighteenth and nineteenth-century fat faces with upright contrast like Bodoni, Canon, or Scotch Romans and adds odd and quirky details, such as the letters c or e that look like prehistoric oceanic creatures, as well as capital R and K that are designed to stand out and make you feel a little uncomfortable. Display is at the core of the family, with its vibrant personality and quirks. The text family is sober, has reduced contrast, and is slightly more condensed, designed to work for small sizes and running text. Oceanic brings neutrality, elegance, and personality to design projects without drawing too much attention and becoming boring too fast..

Type Design
Ilya Naumoff

Type Foundry
Interval Type
Paris

URL
intervaltype.com

Members of the Type Family
Oceanic, Oceanic Text (Bold, Extrabold, Light, Regular, Medium, and Poster)

Oceanic · Text & Display · Latin, Cyrillic · Light, Regular, Medium, Bold, Extrabold, Poster

Лайт
Регуляр
Медиум
Болд
Экстра
Постер

Oceanic Text → A quick brown fox jumps over the lazy dog ←

A

Display и текст

Oceanic — from the depths of the Mariana Trench

Creative Direction
Toshi Omagari
London

Type Foundry
Omega Type

ΨΩΡΙΑΡΙΚΟΥ

QUADRANT

Крановщице

Себер Запад

Rhythm & Blues

Κεραμικός

01558 Großenhain

DIAL M FOR MUSTARD

3,66 m × 1,83 m = 6,6978 m²

TYPEFACES: THE EPICENE COLLECTION

Type Design
Noe Blanco,
Dave Foster,
and Klim Type Foundry
Barcelona, Sydney,
and Wellington

Type Foundry
Klim Type Foundry

TYPEFACES: MARGIT

Senior Type Designer
Miriam Surányi
Vienna

Foundry
Schriftlabor Foundry

TYPEFACES: THE MANUKA COLLECTION

Type Design
Noe Blanco,
Dave Foster, and
Klim Type Foundry
Barcelona, Sydney,
and Wellington

Type Foundry
Klim Type Foundry

TYPEFACE DESIGN

TYPEFACES: KRISTAL

Type Design
Barbara Bigosińska,
Eyal Holtzman,
Myrthe Stel,
Paul van der Laan,
and Peter van Rosmalen
The Hague

Type Foundry
Bold Monday

TYPEFACES: GOLDICH

Type Design
Jasper de Waard
Amsterdam

Type Foundry
Bold Monday
Eindhoven,
The Netherlands

Goldich, designed by Jasper de Waard for Bold Monday

Fotografie EMPIRISK

OBEŠANJI Raziskujoč

Expecting BENELUX

ADQUIRE Plastenka

Stoplight MARSCH

WEIMAR Ineffektiv

visit goldich.xyz

Type Design
Xiaoyu Liu and Yu Liu
Beijing

Type Foundry
Hanyi Fonts

TYPEFACES: RVS BASIC

Type Foundry
3Type
Shanghai

Professors
Peter Biľak,
Fred Smeijers,
Erik van Blokland,
Paul van der Laan,
and Peter Verheul

Type Foundry
Interval Type
Paris

Lovestruck
Wellwishers
Miscellanea
Discomfited
Disruptively
Subdivisions

Sires
Relic
Fatty

Englisch   Light, Regular, Medium, Bold, Extrabold, Black   Englisch

Quantisation
Acknowledge
Regurgitated
Reintegration
Chairpersons
Infinitesimally

TYPEFACES: QING MOCAI LISHU

Concept

A Traditional Chinese typeface, Qing Mocai Lishu is a modern revival of the calligraphic clerical script (lishu in Chinese) that once graced the imperial collection of enamelled porcelain (yangcai in Chinese, or "foreign porcelain") from the flourishing age of the Qing Dynasty (1644-1912) of China.. In contrast to other lishu styles in the imperial collection, this typeface harmoniously blends yet juxtaposes soften-curves and sharpened-tips in key designated stokes

Type Design

Han-yi Shaw

Type Foundry

HYS Design
Redmond, Washington

一九也人上京令利勢
十千南杏又可君你喜妹
國報地墨又天女山島
始安宮密寒導小尋幸庭
川帝州幣干年我扁抱
彩愛心情成望本案照
新日明晚書望江河語
條歌母水永江筆瀬語
王留台登私約自臺興
緒線翰考聞臥自里金
舉色袍語警蘭遠隸
銀長響陵鳳凰飛麗隸

金陵帝王州
江南佳麗地
登鳳凰臺
鳳凰臺上望長安
五色宮袍照水寒
彩筆十年留翰墨
銀河一夜臥闌干

金陵帝王州
江南佳麗地

登鳳凰臺

鳳凰臺上望長安

五色宮袍照水寒

彩筆十年留翰墨

銀河一夜臥闌干

TYPEFACES: NOVEMBER TAMIL

Type Design
Peter Bil'ak and
Aadarsh Rajan
The Hague
and Pune, India

Type Foundry
Typotheque

மொழி	மொழி	மொழி
மொழி	மொழி	மொழி
மொழி	மொழி	மொழி
மொழி	மொழி	மொழி
மொழி	மொழி	மொழி
மொழி	மொழி	மொழி
மொழி	மொழி	மொழி
மொழி	மொழி	மொழி
மொழி	மொழி	மொழி
NOVEMBER TAMIL COMPRESSED	NOVEMBER TAMIL CONDENSED	NOVEMBER TAMIL NORMAL

Type Design
Peter Bil'ak
and Kevin King
The Hague and Toronto

Type Foundry
Typotheque

Lava Syllabics / ᐸᕐ ᖃᓂᐅᔮᖅᐸᐃᑦ

A contrast Syllabics typeface family with a
secondary style for greater modes of expression

ᑕᑐᓘ&ᐅᕼ

ᒥ ᑕᑉ ᐅᖃᖅ·ᐊᑯᐸ ᓇᐴᖏ ᐁᔪᓂᑲᕆᓂᑯᐸᑐ ᒪᑲᕝᕖˣ

ᐟᓂᐊᕝᐨᖁ

'ᐅᐁ·ᐞᐁ· ᕐ" ᐅ ᐟᐍᕐᐠ. ᐅᔐ ᐊᐃᕿᐁ·ᐥ

ᑎᕀᕐᐨ−ᑌ ᖝ"ᕘ

ᒥᔦᕦᕜ, ᐃᕐᑐ, ᑭ'ᔾᐊᒥ, ᒥᒥᐊᒼ, ᑲᓇᑐᖅᕛ, ᐃᒧᕈᐊᖅᕛ ᐊᓰ: ᐛᕝ−

ᐊᕤ·ᐃᕦᕐᕟ

typotheque.com/syllabics

TYPEFACES: SF SYMBOLS 3

Type Design
Apple Design Team
Cupertino, California

**Type Design
and Foundry**
Typotheque

Consultants
Khajag Apelian
and Gor Jihanian
Yerevan, Armenia,
and Denver

Greta Sans Armenian / Գրետա Սան Հայերեն

a complete type system for online and offline communication
ամբողջական համակարգ՝ առցանց և անցանց հաղորդակցության համար

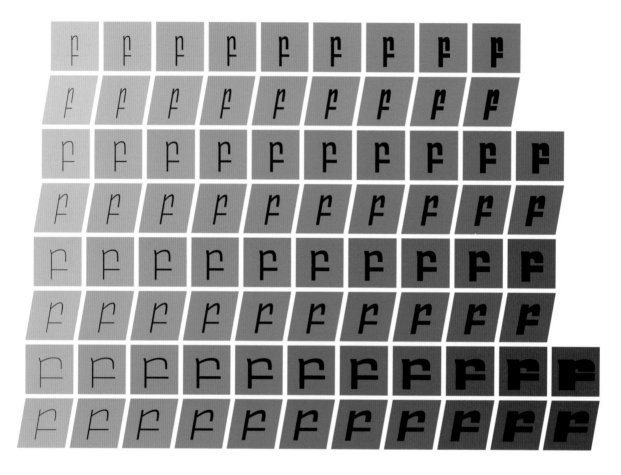

typotheque.com

Concept
Tanrie is a type family that revisits twentieth-century
American book jackets to explore how particular lettering
traits can be distilled across a typeface. It draws inspiration
from the idiosyncratic qualities of lettered pieces across the
works of W. A. Dwiggins, George Salter, and Philip Grushkin.
Currently, the family includes four styles: Headline, Headline
Italic, Text Regular, and Text Bold. This variety provides a
toolkit that can be used in a number of applications, such as
logotypes or editorial layouts, both together and separately.

Design
Ryan Hutson
San Carlos, California

Instructors
Graham Bradley,
James Edmondson,
and Lynne Yun

School
Type West at
Letterform Archive

Type Family
Headline, Headline
Italic, Text Regular,
and Text Bold

Tanrie Headline & Headline Italic

W.A. Dwiggins to Rudolph Ruzicka:
A Letter about Designing Type, 1940
Dear RR: The way I work at present is to draw an
alphabet 10 times 12 point size, with a pen or brush,
the letters carefully finished. *I start with the lower-case,*
and let its characters settle the style of the capitals.

Tanrie Text Regular & Text Bold

Ten times twelve point is a convenient size to work; and I
have a diminishing glass that reduces the letters to something like
twelve point size when I put the drawing on the floor and squint at
it through the glass held belt high. **This gives a rough idea of
what the reduction does to curves and things.**

Design
Aditya Prasetya
Wiraatmaja
Jakarta

School
Type@Cooper
New York City

Instructors
Zrinka Buljubašić,
Hannes Famira,
and Gen Ramírez

Pane

Regular & Bold

Uppercase

ABCDEFGHIJKLMNOPQRSTU
VWXYZ

Lowercase

abcdefghijklmnopqrstuvwxyz

Symbols

@#%^&*©®$¢£€¥ƒ¶§/\¦¦
+−=÷×±<>~¤¬≈

Punctuation

.,:;·!¡?¿()[]{}""''"'«»_-—

Figures

0011223344556677889 9

Uppercase Accents

ÆĄÁÂÃÄÅÀĀĂĆĈČÇĎÐÈÉÊ
ËĘĒĔĖĘĜĞĠĢĤĦÌÍÎÏĨĪĬĮİĴĶĹĻ
ĽĿÑŃŅŇŊÑNÞÒÓŐÔÒŎÖÕŌ
ŒØŔŖŘŚŜŞŠŞŢŤŦŢÙÚÛÜŨŪ
ŬŮŰŲŴŴŴŴŶŸÝŶŶŽŹŻŽ

Lowercase Accents

æąàáâãäåāăăａæćĉĉčçďđèéêëē
ĕéęěēĝğġġĥħīīĭįıìíîïĭĵıjȷĵķļľŀńņň
nŋṅnðòóőôòŏöõōōøǿœŕŗřśŝşšş
ßţťŧũūŭůűüųŵẁŵẅŷỳźżžž

TYPEFACES: NAUSEA

Design
Frederick Wiltshire
London

Professor
Gerry Leonidas

School
University of Reading
Reading

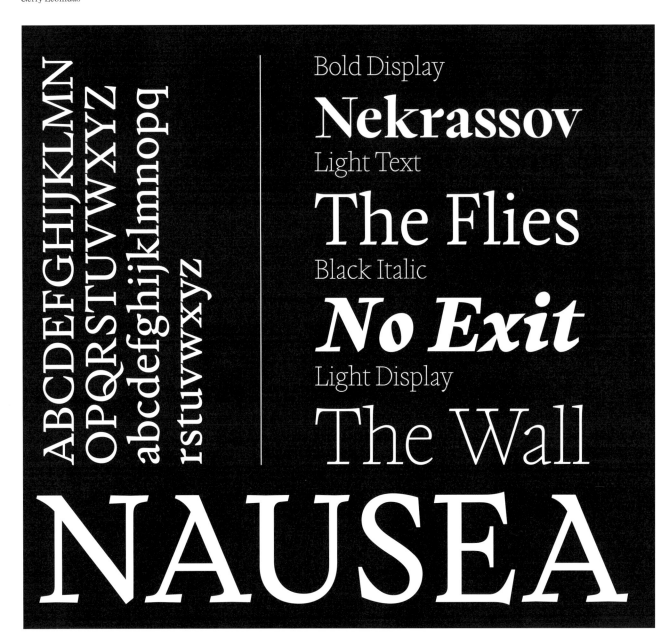

TYPEFACES: HUAN YUAN CALLIGRAPHY

Design
Chang Liu

School
Shandong University
Jinan, China

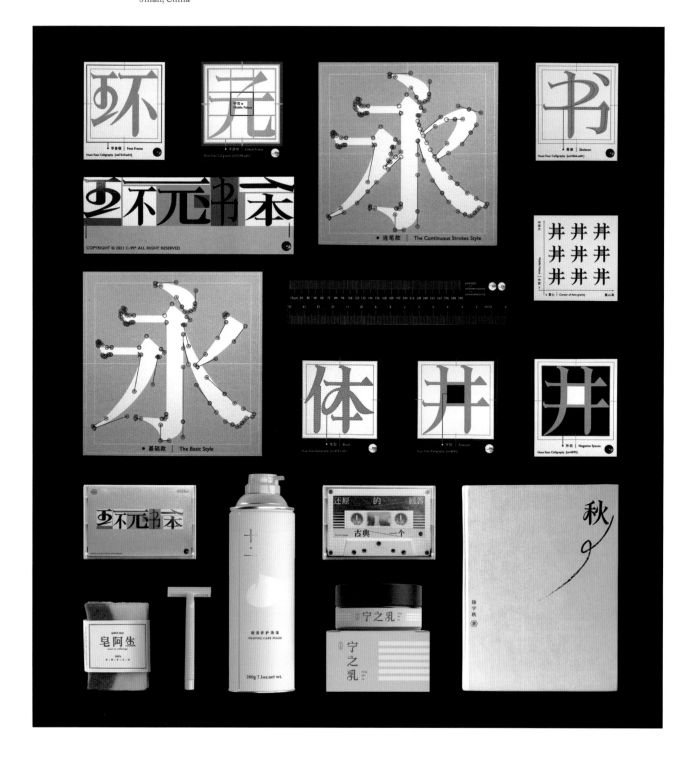

ASCENDERS

JUDGES
Gail Anderson
Aditya Bayu
Eleni Beveratou
Erik Brandt
Anthony Bryant
Fer Cozzi
Cem Eskinazi
JP Haynie and Davis Ngarupe
Jessica Hische
Tien-Min Liao
Eric Q. Liu
Dafne Martinez
Gabriel Martínez Meave
Abbott Miller
Miguel Reyes
Alex Trochut
Albert Trulls
Liu Zhao

ASCENDERS 3
Andrej Barčák and Andrej Čanecký
(Andrej & Andrej)
David Barnett
Scott Biersack
Ryan Bugden
Chris Caldwell
Asal Farshchi
Dan Ferreira and Kun Lam
(Indego Design)
Kimya Gandhi
Han Gao
Roxane Gataud
Matthijs Herzberg
Au Chon Hin (Untitled Macao)
Marko Hrastovec
Wei Huang
Mark van Leeuwen
Alistair McCready
Valerio Monopoli
Gemma O'Brien
Shivani Parasnis
Claudia Rubín
Alexander Slobzheninov
Tina Smith
Benjamin Tuttle
Mat Voyce
Kurt Woerpel

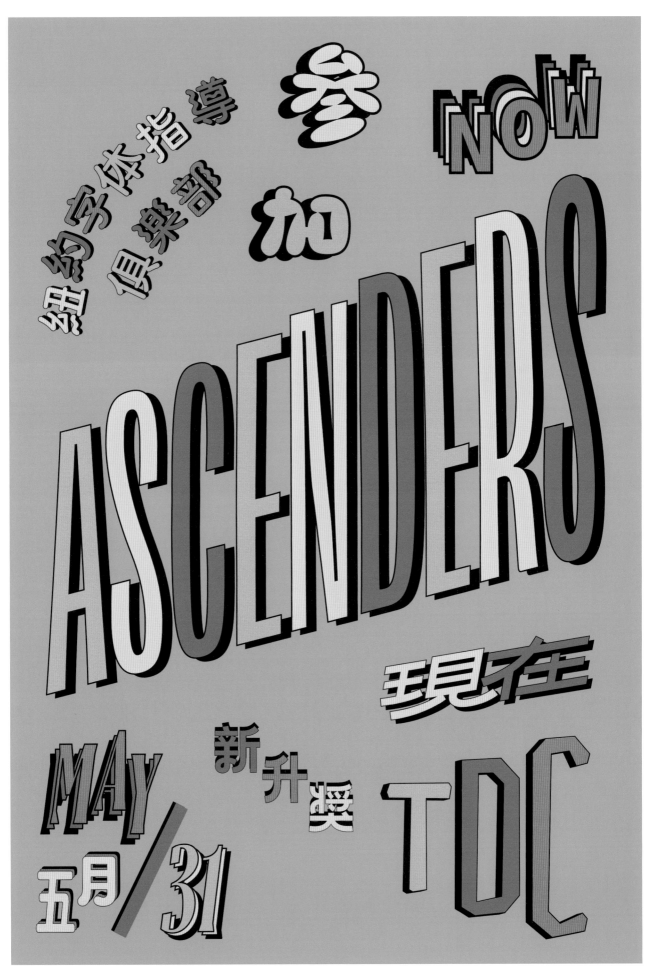

Concept and design by Zipeng Zhu

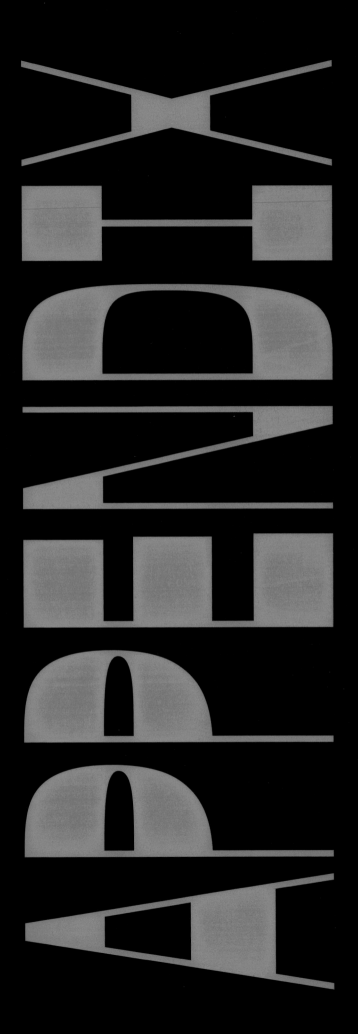

APPENDIX

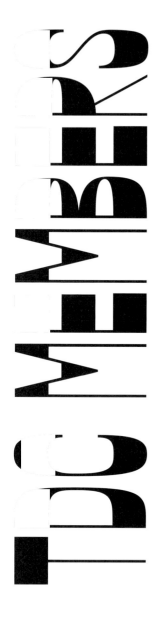

A

Logan Acton 2021
Seth Akkerman 2008
Roman Albertini 2021
Paul Albertson 2021s
Marta Cerda Alimbau 2020
Ximena Amaya 2021s
Lisa Amoroso 2015
Jack Anderson 1996lll
Ana Andreeva 2016s
Christopher Andreola 2003
Allyson Andryshak 2021
Colette Angel 2021s
Ben Anthony 2021
Ann Antoshak 2020
Hugo Aranha 2017
Agyei Archer 2020
Judith Aronson 2021
Potch Auacherdkul 2018s
Bob Aufuldish 2006
Yomar Augusto 2013

B

Joosten Baarts 2021s
Frances Baca 2020
Eun Jung Bahng 2020s
Peter Bain 1986lll
Andreu Balius 2021
Lindsay Barnett 2017
Antonio Mondragón Becker 2020
Pernicias Bedow 2021
Christoph Beier 2018
Patricia Belen 2020
Misha Beletsky 2007
Sakinah Bell 2021s
Carlos Beltran 2020
Felix Beltran 1988lll
Nima Ben Ayed 2020
Jaamal Benjamin 2019s
Anna Berkenbusch 1989lll
Ana Gomez Bernaus 2014
Brendan Bernicker 2022lc
John D. Berry 1996lll
Peter Bertolami 1969lll
Teresa Bettinardi 2020
Michael Bierut 2010
Klaus Bietz 1993
Murathan Biliktü 2022s
Abe Bingham 2015
David Bingham 2020
Henrik Birkvig 1996
Heribert Birnbach 2007
Roger Black 1980lll
Jennifer Blanco 2017{
Susan Block 1989lll
Peggy Bloomer 2019
Halvor Bodin 2012
Vlad Boerean 2019
Matteo Bologna 2003
Scott Boms 2012
Derrick Mensah Bonsu 2021s
Lily Boyce 2018lc
Annabel Brandon 2018
Isabelle Brawley 2020lc
John Breakey 2006
Melinda Breen 2022
Daniel Brevick 2018
Jax Brill 2020
Marisa Ten Brink 2017
September Broadhead 2020
Ed Brodsky 1980lll
Claire Brown 2019
Craig Brown 2004
Helen Bruno 2021
Paul Buckley 2007

Ryan Bugden 2015s
Michael Bundscherer 2007
Nicholas Burroughs 2017

C

Susana Cadena 2016
Wenchao Cai 2021s
Ronn Campisi 1988ll
Paul Carlos 2008
Edman Carrillo 2021
Scott Carslake 2001
Matthew Carter 1988lll
Catherine Casalino 2020
Mariana Castellanos 2020
Ana Valeria Castillos 2021s
Ken Cato 1988lll
Jackson Cavanaugh 2010
Eduard Cehovin 2003
Luc Chaissac 2021
Joniclare Chan 2022s
Akshita Chandra 2020lc
Chi Hao Chang 2021s
WenChia Chang 2020s
Frank Chavanon 2014
Len Cheeseman 1993lll
David Cheung Jr. 1998
Patricia Childers 2013
Todd Childers 2011
Janice Cho 2021
Hanju Chou 2019lc
H.Y. Ingrid Chou 2017
Ellen Christensen 2020
Sarah Christus 2020lc
Calen Chung 2020s
Stanley Church 1997lll
Scott Citron 2007
John Clark 2014
Rob Clarke 2015
Graham Clifford 1998
Doug Clouse 2009
Ed Colker 1983lll
Brett Collins 2021
Nancy Sharon Collins 2006
Rixin Cong 2022lc
John Connolly 2022
Cherise Conrick 2009
Nick Cooke 2001
Jonathan Correira 2017
Madeleine Corson 1996lll
Daphnee Cote 2021s
James Craig 2004
Andreas Croonenbroeck 2006
Ray Cruz 1999lll
John Curry 2009
Rick Cusick 1989lll

D

Si Daniels 2020
Susan Darbyshire 1987lll
Simon Daubermann 2015
Douglas Davis 2022
Mark Davis 2020
Michael Day 2022
Josanne De Natale 1986lll
Vonetta De Vonish 2020lc
Christopher DeCaro 2017
Lynda Decker 2020
Anthony deFigio 2020
Sébastien Delobel 2021
Liz DeLuna 2005
Constantin Demner 2018
Wenqiao Deng 2018s
Xiyu Deng 2020
Mark Denton 2001
Cara Di Edwardo 2009

Biagio Di Stefano 2017
Fernando Diaz 2016
Lisa Diercks 2018
Chank Diesel 2005
Claude Dieterich A. 1984lll
Kirsten Dietz 2000
Joseph DiGioia 1999
Yiyua Ding 2020
Heather-Mariah Dixon 2022
Petra Docekalova 2021lc
Eric Doctor 2018
Joyce Domingo 2021s
Xiaoyi Dong 2019s
Ross Donnan 2017
Maria Doreuli 2022
Eva Dranaz 2018
Zhihua Duan 2021
Sara Duell 2021
Denis Dulude 2004
James Dundon 2017s
Patrick Durgin-Bruce 2016
Mark Duszkiewicz 2017
Simon Dwelly 1998

E

Kyle Eberle 2021
Dianne Bahram Zadeh Ebrahimi 2021s
Yvonne Eder 2020s
Koray Ekremoglu 2019
Garry Emery 1993lll
Manija Emran 2021
Marc Engenhart 2006
Carrie Epps-Carey 2020s
Konstantin Eremenko 2017
Pauline Esguerra 2021s
Joseph Michael Essex 1978lll
Manuel Estrada 2019
Yasmina Garcia Estudillo 2022
Florence Everett 1989lll
Michelle Evola 2017

F

David Farey 1993lll
Aron Fay 2019
Lily Feinberg 2014
Rafael Ferreira 2020s
Jonathan Ferrer 2022s
Louise Fili 2004
Anne Fink 2013
Kristine Fitzgerald 1990lll
Alanna Flowers 2021
Jacob Ford 2022
Marisa Fornaro 2021
Louise Fortin 2007
Karlo Francisco 2018s
Tristan Free 2020s
Carol Freed 1987lll
Christina Freyss 2017
Dinah Fried 2018
Dirk Fütterer 2008

G

Evan Gaffney 2009
Louis Gagnon 2002
Maria Galante 2016
John Gambell 2017
Kimya Gandhi 2022
Jeremy Garcia 2020
Jeffrey Garofalo 2020s
Giuliano Garonzi 2020
Avalon Garrick 2021s
Christof Gassner 1990lll

David Gatti 1981lll
Verena Gerlach 2020
Isaac Gertman 2021
Samya Ghosh 2021
Amit Gilboa 2022s
Jack Glacken 2020
Lou Glassheim 1947l
Howard Glener 1977lll
Valerie Gnaedig 2021
Kristin Goble 2022s
Abby Goldstein 2010
Deborah Gonet 2005
Jason Gong 2021s
Derwyn Goodall 2017
Zan Goodman 2018
Kara Gordon 2022
Yuliana Gorkorov 2018
Jonathan Gouthier 2009
Justin Graefer 2016
Diana Graham 1984lll
Amit Greenberg 2017s
Joan Greenfield 2006
Becky Greubel 2021
James Grieshaber 2018
Katie Griffin 2020s
Lena Gruschka 2020
Artur Marek Gulbickl 2011
Nora Gummert-Hauser 2005
Meng Guo 2020
Noa Guy 2017
Peter Gyllan 1997lll

H

Andy Hadel 2010
Muhammed Abdel Hadi 2021s
Allan Haley 1978lll
Debra Hall 1996
Tosh Hall 2017
Carrie Hamilton 2015
Drew Hamlin 2021
Lisa Hamm 2015
Yanwen Hang 2019s
Pernille Sys Hansen 2020
Abigail Hanson 2022
Egil Haraldsen 2000
Jesse Harding 2021s
Jon Hartman 2019
Knut Hartmann 1985lll
Brooke Hawkins 2021
Luke Hayman 2006
Bonnie Hazelton 1975ll
Jonas Hecksher 2012
Eric Heiman 2002
Elizabeth Heinzen 2020
Anja Patricia Helm 2008
Brendan Hemp 2020
Oliver Henn 2009
Eleazar Hernandez 2022
Andrea Herstowski 2020s
Klaus Hesse 1995lll
Cassie Hester 2021
Jason Heuer 2011
Fons M. Hickmann 1996
Bill Hilson 2007
Kit Hinrichs 2002
Masaaki Hirano 2021
Reid Hitt 2017
Fritz Hofrichter 1980lll
Alyce Hoggan 1987lll
James Hondros 2021
Kevin Horvath 1987lll
Pamela Howard 2019
Paul Howell 2017
John Howrey 2022
Debra Morton Hoyt 2016
Christian Hruschka 2005
Bin Hu 2021

Hannah Huang 2020s
Andrea Hubbard 2020
John Hudson 2004
Aimee Hughes 2008
Katherine Hughes 2021
Thomas Hull 2019
Keith C. Humphrey 2008
Ginelle Hustrulid 2021

I

Robert Innis 2021
Sabah Iqbal 2020
Todd Irwin 2016
Danika Isdahl 2021
Yuko Ishizaki 2009
Alexander Isley 2012
Yusuke Ito 2020

J

Donald Jackson 1978ll
Torsten Jahnke 2002
Mark Jamra 1999
Janneke Janssen 2019s
Charles Jeffcoat 2021
Natasha Jen 2022
Tim Jetis 2022
Thomas Jockin 2016
Luciano Johnson 2018
Matthew Johnson 2019
Giovanni Jubert 2004

K

John Kallio 1996lll
Boril Karaivanov 2014
Richard Kegler 2017
Jeff Kellem 2020
David Kelley 2017
Scott Kellum 2019
Russell Kerr 2018s
Jonathan Key 2021
Farah Khan 2020
Thoma Kikis 2020
Gowan Kim 2021s
Peter Kimmins 2019
Rick King 1993
Dmitry Kirsanov 2013
Amanda Klein 2011
Arne Alexander Klett 2005
Keith Knueven 2020
Akira Kobayashi 1999lll
Mokoena Kobell 2020
Boris Kochan 2002
Anmari Koltchev 2020s
Irina Koryagina 2018
Yuliya Kosheeva 2020s
Nikola Kostic 2019
Thomas Kowallik 2022
Johannes Kramer 2020
Markus Kraus 1997
Stephanie Kreber 2001
Ingo Krepinsky 2013
Bernhard J. Kress 1963lll
Prem Krsihnamurthy 2021
Karin Krochmal 2020
Stefan Krömer 2013
John Kudos 2010
Christian Kunnert 1997
Melissa Kuperminc 2020s
Amber Kusmenko 2021
Joshua Kwassman 2019lc

L

Brandon Labbe 2019
Ginger LaBella 2013
Raymond F. Laccetti 1987lll
Caspar Lam 2017
Melchoir Lamy 2021
Horacio Lardés 2019
Jay Lathigra 2022
Quang Huy Le 2021s
Cindy Lee 2020lc
Diane Lee 2020
Eric Lee 2020s
Gracia Lee 2021
David Lemon 1995lll
Brian Lemus 2015
Kevin Leonard 2021
Olaf Leu 1966lll
Jean-Bapiste Levée 2019
Aaron Levin 2015
Edward Levine 2021
Tom Lewek 2018
Chaosheng Li 2019
Lisha Liao 2020s
Jasper Lim 2017s
Karla Faria Lima 2019
Guosheng Lin 2021
Jessica Lin 2017s
Armin Lindauer 2007
Sven Lindhorst-Emme 2015
Shadrack Lindo 2018
Alison Lindquist 2020
Domenic Lippa 2004
Wally Littman 1960lll
Xiaoxing Liu 2018
Richard Ljoenes 2014
Diana Lodi 2022
Margeaux Loeb 2018
Uwe Loesch 1996
Christie Logan 2021s
Oliver Lohrengel 2004
Utku Lomlu 2016
Kirsten Long 2019
Xin Long 2017
Christian Loos 2019
Elaine Lopez 2022
Tatiana Lopez 2020s
Brandon Lori 2021
Frank Lotterman 2016
Diana Luistro 2021
Claire Lukacs 2014
Gregg Lukasiewicz 1990lll
Abraham Lule 2017
Ken Lunde 2011
Ching-Fa Lung 2019s
Ellen Lupton 2021

M

Iain Macmillan 2018
Saki Mafundikwa 2021
Ruggero Magri 2020s
Jenny Makarchik 2019
Avril Makula 2010
Nicholas Marabella 2020s
Caleb Marcus 2022
Crystal Marquez 2020
Bobby C. Martin, Jr. 2011
Emilee Martin 2019s
Frank Martinez 2013
Jakob Maser 2006
Abraham Mast 2020s
Sol Matas 2022
Tammie Matthews 2020s
Pedro Mattos 2021
Scott Matz 2011
Ted Mauseth 2001

Andreas Maxbauer 1995lll
Elizabeth May 2017lc
Trevett McCandliss 2016
Mark McCormick 2010
Rod McDonald 1995
Daniel McManus 2018
Marc A. Meadows 1996lll
Veeksha Mehndiratta 2020lc
Amanda Mei 2021s
Maurice Meilleur 2020
Uwe Melichar 2000
Gloria Mendoza 2021
Hope Meng 2020
Trevor Messersmith 2017
Rachael Miller 2020s
John Milligan 1978ll
Michael Miranda 1984ll
Raven Mo 2020lc
Mary Moffett 2017
Rachel Mondragon 2017
Sakol Mongkolkasetarin 1995
Charrel Montalbo 2018
Jessica Moon 2017
Jaymes Moore 2019
Richard Earl Moore 1982lll
William Moran 2021
Wael Morcos 2013
Minoru Morita 1975lll
Jimmy Moss 2019
Gillian Mothersill 2017
Lars Müller 1997
Joachim Müller-Lancé 1995
Gary Munch 1997
Camille Murphy 2013
Kaisha Murzamadiyeva 2021s
Jerry King Musser 1988lll

N

Natalie Nardello 2020s
Masahiro Naruse 2018
Helmut Ness 1999lll
Joe Newton 2009
Michelle Ng 2019
Vincent Ng 2004
Yuko Nishida 2020
Charles Nix 2000
Dirk Nolte 2012
Alexa Nosal 1987lll
Peter Nowell 2019

O

Gemma O'Brien 2022
Megan Oldfield 2022
lLloyd Osborne 2017
Andy Outis 2018
Robert Overholtzer 1994lll
Aimee Overly 2017
Lisa Overton 2017

P

Michael Pacey 2001lll
Juan Carlos Pagan 2015
Jason Pamental 2018
Kyla Paolucci 2021
Amy Papaelias 2008
Chaeyron Park 2020lc
Inn Sun Park 2021
YuJune Park 2017
Amy Parker 2016
Jonathan Parker 2020
Jim Parkinson 1994
Michael Parson 2016

Donald Partyka 2009
Neil Patel 2011
Sachi Patil 2021lc
Gudrun Pawelke 1996lll
Denis Pelli 2022
Marc Peter 2018
Lindsey Peterson 2021
Max Phillips 2000
Stefano Picco 2010
Massimo Pitis 2017
Benjamin Plimpton 2021
Joep Pohlen 2006
Niberca Polo 2022
Maria Pombo 2022s
Albert-Jan Pool 2000lll
Jean François Porchez 2013
Jason Powers 2017
Patricia Preikschat 2021
Colleen Preston 2020lc
Anna Prince 2021lc
Ellie Prisbrey 2021s
James Propp 1997lll
Jean-François Proulx 2020
Cesar Puertas 2020
John Pugsley 2020
Sean Puzzo 2020s

Haonan Qi 2020s
Yingbo Qiao 2020
Tianyi Qin 2022s
Nicholas Qyll 2003s

Jochen Raedeker 2000
Jesse Ragan 2009
Erwin Raith 1967lll
Bjorn Ramberg 2016
Jason Ramirez 2016
Steven Rank 2011
Nicole Ravenscroft 2022
Matthew Rechs 2014
Nicole Regan 2022
Christian Reiner 2020s
Maarten Renckens 2018s
Graham Rendoth 2020
Douglas Riccardi 2010
Tamye Riggs 2016
Daniel Riley 2021
Michael Riley 2021
Amanda Rios 2020
Oliver Rios 2022
Phillip Ritzenberg 1997lll
Blake Robertson 2016
Nic Roca 2018
Cory Rockliff 2018lc
Yasmin Rodriguez 2021
Salvador Romero 1993lll
Manuela Roncon 2019
Jen Roos 2019
Kurt Roscoe 1993lll
John Roshell 2020
Erkki Ruuhinen 1986lll
Carol-Anne Ryce-Paul 2020
Michael Rylander 1993

Jan Sabach 2018
Tala Safie 2017s
Mamoun Sakkal 2004
Richard Salcer 2021
Kallista Salim 2021s
Ilja Sallacz 1999

Ina Saltz 1996
Ksenya Samarskaya 2018
Rodrigo Sanchez 1996{
Ádan Santos 2021
Nathan Savage 2001
Hakan Savasogan 2020
Khaled Sawaf 2021lc
DC Scarpelli 2020
Hanno Schabacker 2008
Isabell Schart 2020
Paula Scher 2010
Hermann J. Schlieper 1987lll
Pascale Schmid 2020lc
Holger Schmidhuber 1999
Klaus Schmidt 1959lll
Krista Schmidt 2020
Bertram Schmidt-Friderichs 1989lll
Thomas Schmitz 2009
Elmar Schnaare 2011
Guido Schneider 2003
Werner Schneider 1987lll
Anna-Lisa Schoenecker 2021
Markus Schroeppel 2003
Eileen Hedy Schultz 1985lll
Shoshana Schultz 2020s
Eckehart Schumacher-Gebler 1985lll
Robert Schumann 2007
Tré Seals 2017
Ringo R. Seeber 2016
Lee Selsick 2020
Christopher Sergio 2011
Thomas Serres 2004
Kara Sexton 2021s
Michelle Shain 2012
Ellen Shapiro 2017
Paul Shaw 1987lll
Benjamin Shaykin 2014
Nick Sherman 2009
Lynne Shlonsky 2020
Philip Shore Jr. 1992lll
Carl Shura 2019
Gregory Shutters 2019
Scott Simmons 1994
Mark Simonson 2012
Dominque Singer 2012
Elizabeth Carey Smith 2010
Ralph Smith 2016
Ben Smyth 2020
Natalie Snodgrass 2019
Gregg Snyder 2020
Lynn Sohn 2020s
Jan Solpera 1985lll
Kris Sowersby 2018
ZiZi Spak 2020
Christina Speed 2017
Erik Spiekermann 1988lll
Adriane Stark 2017
Rolf Staudt 1984lll
Olaf Stein 1996lll
Soniya Stella 2021s
Audrey Stensrud 2020s
Charles Stewart 1992lll
Roland Stieger 2009
Clifford Stoltze 2003
Nina Stössinger 2015
DJ Stout 2010
Ilene Strizver 1988lll
Emily Suber 2020
Dawang Sun 2018
Qian Sun 2017
Zempaku Suzuki 1992
Molly Swisher 2021Lc
Paul Sych 2009

Yukichi Takada 1995
Yoshimaru Takahashi 1996lll
Jerry Tamburro 2020
Katsumi Tamura 2003
Trisha Wen Yuan Tan 2011
Matthew Tapia 2018
Pat Taylor 1985lll
Shaun Taylor 2015
Kevin Teh 2020
Marcel Teine 2003
Bansri Thakkar 2021lc
Eric Thoelke 2010
Jayla Thompson-Bey 2021s
Bina Thorsen 2021s
Jason Tiernan 2021
Eric Tilley 1995
Laura Tolkow 1996
Stephen Tortorici 2021
Andrey Tovcigrechko 2020
Kayla Tran 2020s
Jeremy Tribby 2017
Klaus Trommer 2012
Niklaus Troxler 2000
Adam Trunk 2019
Irene Tsay 2020s
Ling Tsui 2016
Minao Tsukada 2000
Viviane Tubiana 2020
Natascha Tümpel 2002s
François Turcotte 1999
Benjamin Tuttle 2018

Andreas Uebele 2002
Ryota Umemura 2018
Cağdas Ilke Ünal 2018

Diego Vainesman 1991lll
Oscar Valdez 2017
Victoria Valenzuela 2019
Patrick Vallée 1999
John Van Hamersveld 2021
Jarik van Sluijs 2020
Jeffrey Vanlerberghe 2005
Zara Vasquez-Evens 2022
Pano Vassiiou 2020
Bruno Vera 2020s
Hagen Verleger 2016s
Leo Vicenti 2020s
Christa Vinciquerra 2017s
Franci Virgill 2021
Svenja von Doehlen 2020
Danila Vorobiev 2013
Matija Vujovic 2019

Frank Wagner 1994lll
Oliver Wagner 2001
Allan R. Wahler 1998
Jurek Wajdowicz 1980lll
Sergio Waksman 1996lll
Clark Walecki 2020s
Zakk Waleko 2020
Garth Walker 1992lll
Renjia Wang 2021s
Yiqi Wang 2020s
Emily Wardwell 2017
Graham Weber 2016s
Harald Weber 1999lll

Maggie Weidner 2021s
Yoni Weiss 2021
Craig Welsh 2010
Yalan Wen 2022lc
Amelia Whittington 2022lc
Lutz Widmaier 2018
Christopher Wiehl 2003
Richard Wilde 1993lll
Edith Williams 2020
James Williams 1988lll
Steve Williams 2005
Delve Withrington 1997
David Wolske 2017
Gloria Wong 2019s
Fred Woodward 1995lll
Chris Wu 2021

X

Yuchen Xie 2020s

Y

Zeynep Yildirim 2020
Lori Young 2021
Garson Yu 2005

Z

Weixi Zeng 2019s
Shuo Zhang 2018
Xinyl Zhao 2021s
Maxim Zhukov 1996lll
Holger Ziemann 2020
Roy Zucca 1969lll

Corporate Members
Adobe 2014
AEGraphics 2021
Bleacher Report 2019
École de Visuelle
Communications 2011
Disney 2022
Font Bureau 2015
Lobster Phone 2020
School of Visual Arts,
New York 2007
SXM Media 2020

Charter member
ll Honorary member
lll Life members
s Student member (uppercase)
lc Lowercase student member
Membership as of June 27, 2022

In Memoriam
Hermann Schmidt 1983lll
Hanjörg Stulle 1987ll

GENERAL INDEX

130 students of the Design Dept. at Burg Giebichenstein, Fall 2018/19: 43
1002 inc.: 57, 211
3Type: 328
35A: 168
360i New York: 58
777CreativeStrategies: 57, 211

A

@anaghanarayanan: 300
@antoniostudioa:24
@anilaykan: 28
@at_cb: 67
@BlackbirdRevolt: 96
@BornaIz: 296
@brightpolkadot: 50
@caution.lee: 245
@debakir: 296
@designbyaodot.com:199
@devethanvalladares:195
@EkTypeFoundry: 301
@erichbrechbuhl: 222
@ermanyilmaz.com: 220
@garbettdesign: 184
@glyphsets: 318
@HagenVerleger: 73
@harley_johnston: 123
@heartgutsgrit: 172, 174
@hirbodlotfian: 319
@imburrow :84
@instaggramlich:34
@jaderochab: 275
@jannimaroscheck: 77
@JethTorres: 126
@kayessgordon:302
@kellenbergerwhite: 36
@kevincantrell: 62
@kosbarts:298
@laurascofield: 44
@leandrosenna: 129
@LiebeFonts: 306
@mamgobozi: 46
@martinmajoor: 306
@Mehdisaeedistudio: 42
@miitball: 272
@mingyu_jia: 276
@minjooham: 302
@NKshetrimayum: 300
@olka_pandova: 237
@osborneshiwan: 229
@shinnoske_s: 233
@StudioBanggu: 47, 65, 127
@rynbgdn: 41, 45
@plea.studio: 49
@senna_leandro: 129
@tao.graphicdesign: 226
@tenisvermelho: 129
@tosche_e: 315
@TypeMatesFonts: 299
@typodaria: 298
@typotheque: 67
@UniofReading: 276
@verenamack: 39
@wakwatshuma: 46
@ymdkzhr: 310
@ymdkzhr: 310
A Tea Store: 199
A.A. Trabucco-Campos: 108, 193
Abary, Dan: 100
ABC Dinamo: 72, 116
Acheimastos, Spyros: 183
ACRM: 183
adc1994.zjgsu.edu.cn: 133
adtypo.com: 307
AFAB – Allfontsarebastards: 236
Agence Souffle: 143

Aguiló Mora, Roberto: 49
Ahmadzadeh, Isabella: 236
Alberty, Thomas: 113
Alcalá, Antonio: 24, 25
Ali.Hamza: 59, 93, 118
Ali Forney Center: 59, 93, 118
All-Russian Decorative
Art Museum: 157
Allen, Haley Kattner: 172, 174
Allergy Studio: 132
AlMohtaraf Design House: 309
Altenbrandt, Catrin: 25, 29
Alvaro, Manuel: 236
Alves, Sergio: 197
AlYafei, Nada: 121
AlYousuf, Eman: 121
Amaala Arabic: 318
American University
of Sharjah: 121
Andreadis, Stefanos: 103
ANEK Multiscript: 301
anenocena.com: 33
Ani, Hala Al: 121
Anika, Pehl: 124
ANÔNIMA — A Galeria
Herself: 145
Ansbach Theater: 71
Apelian, Khajag: 296, 297, 334
Apeloig, Philippe: 26, 27
Apple Design Team:
31, 102, 316, 333
Architecture and Design
Commission, Ministry of
Culture (KSA): 309
ArtCenter College of Design:
241, 246, 248, 249, 250, 262,
263, 264, 268, 270, 277, 279,
282, 283, 286, 287, 288
Arte Musica: 144
artexperiments.withgoogle.
com/withplasticair: 104
Association des architectes
paysagistes du Québec, AAPQ: 178
Atamira Dance Company: 229
Atelier Carvalho Bernau: 67
Atelier d'Alves: 197
Attardo, Steve: 79
Atwood, Emily: 148, 163
Aykan, Anil: 28, 29

B

babyinktwice: 234
Baby Ink Twice: 35, 227
Bach, Lia: 243
Bai, Tian: 170
baklazanas.com/veshch: 147
Bandini, Sofia: 236
Bang Bang Education: 251, 267
Bange, Darius: 259
Bank™: 83
Bankov, Peter: 27, 215
Bankov Posters: 27, 215
barnbrook.com:28
Bartlett, Brad: 159, 214,
241, 246, 248, 262, 263, 268,
277, 279, 282, 286, 288
Bartoli, Matteo: 236
Baseman, Gary: 109
Bastsokas, Kostas: 298, 299
Basiq Design:236
Bates, Nigel: 114
Beaudouin, Patrick:90
behance.net/gallery/132298109/
Identity-gallery-MYTH: 267
behance.net/gallery/133659055/
Lipa-art-collection-
Identity-System: 169

behance.net/StudioSaber: 128
Bell, Lucas: 187
Bellamy, Andrew: 175
Ben's Best: 198
Benedict, Celina: 243
Benelux Boekbinders: 67
Berkeley Rep: 148
Berlow, David: 317
Bernau, Kai: 67
Bessemans, Ann: 257
Bestard, Joan Canyelles: 49
Bettig, Chris: 317
Bewry, Lyam: 151, 177, 179
Beyeler, Céline: 214
Bhoir, Omkar: 301
Bian, Shuyao: 69
Bichler, Gail: 51, 109, 111, 112
Bierut, Michael: 55
Biesinger, Raymond: 111
Bift: 85
Bigosińska, Barbara: 325
Biľak, Peter: 67, 328, 331, 332
Birman, Ilya: 120
Bishop, Deb: 109, 111, 266
BITE Studio: 154, 176, 200
Bitton, Julie: 187
Blackbird Revolt: 96
blackbirdrevolt.com: 96
Blanchard, Ben: 203
Blanco, Noe: 322, 324
bleed.com/historisk-
museum: 156, 185
Bleed Design Studio: 156, 185
Blokland, Dr. Frank E: 16
Blöink, Carolin: 72
Blow, Paul: 109, 111
Bo, Tian: 150, 201
Bold Monday: 325, 326
Bradley, Graham: 335
Brad Bartlett Design: 159
bradbartlettdesign.com: 159
Brechbühl, Erich: 222
Brighten the Corners: 239
brightpolkadot.com: 50
Bruch—Idee&Form: 155
BRUTUS: 164, 181
Bufler, Stefan: 242, 243
Bugden, Ryan: 41, 45
Bulckens, Koen: 73
Buljubašić, Zrinka: 336
Bullock, Kurt: 169
Bureau Sepaen: 121
Burg Giebichenstein
Kunsthochschule Halle: 43
burg-halle.de/typoarchiv: 43
Burg Printing Workshop: 43
Burickson, Abraham: 137
büro uebele visuelle
kommunikation: 124, 157
Burrow: 84
BY-ENJOY DESIGN: 91, 188
by-enjoy.com/branding/
formuleCAFE.html 188
Bynow x Creater: 226
Byrne, David: 187
Bytoby: 225, 230

C

Cai, Grace: 279
Caldas, Giordano: 186
Camillini, Gianluca: 236
Canal Magazine: 115, 125, 235
Canovaro, Francesco: 236
Cantrell, Kevin: 62
Canyelles Bestard, Joan: 49
Caobu Public Library: 205
Caporale, Francesco: 236

Captan, Lara:317
Carlisle, John: 62
Carnegie Hall:,172, 174
Carnegie Hall Marketing and
Creative Services: 172, 174
Carter, Carissa: 90
Carter, Nic: 114
Carter, Nina: 174
Carvalho, Susana: 67
carvalho-bernau.com: 67
Casali, Valentina: 135
Castro, Isabel Lopes: 275
Cavalli, Francesco: 236
Cdcromo: 110
Center for Book Arts: 75
centerforbookarts.org/book-shop/
catalogs/summer-reading: 75
Centre Design: 205
Chahine, Nadine: 294, 295
Champions Design: 172, 174
championsdesign.com 172, 174
Chan, Wing: 154, 176, 200
Chandran, Ashwin: 99
Chang, Rex: 166
Charisma Capital
Market Services: 319
Charisma Typeface: 319
charlieshi.ch: 241
charlieshi.ch/#HardlySilent: 270
charlieshi.ch/#onomato'pe: 288
Chase, Patrick: 59, 93, 118
Cheang, Wakka: 194
Chen, Andy: 100
Chen, Chuye: 29, 244, 247
Chen, Huasha: 314
Chen, Janice: 59, 93, 118
Chen, Lixiao: 314
Chen, Nan: 81
Chen, Yan-Ting: 216
Chen, Yiqiang: 182
Chen, Yu: 95
Cheng, Ting Fang: 101, 104
Chengdesign: 191
Chengdu Art Museum: 182
Cher, Liora: 175
Chernogaev, Dmitry: 280
Chin, Kee Wei: 115, 125, 235
China Academy of Art: 133,
171, 254, 265, 281, 314
China Shadow Play Museum
(中国皮影博物馆): 161
Choi, Jiin: 260
Choksi, Mishant: 111
Chung, Jaeyou: 240, 253, 289
Cifu, Claudia: 116
Cindymode: 131
The City College of New York: 285
Clarke, Greg: 111
Clarke, Rob: 180
ClassTao: 256
Clifford, Graham: 30, 31
Code Switch: 209
codeswitchdesign.com: 209
Colaps, Antonello: 236
Cole Phillips, Jennifer: 137
Collect: 71, 223
Collins, Jack: 198
Communication University
of Zhejiang: 56
Congiu, Alessandro: 236
Connectivity Standards
Alliance: 175
Cottier, Nigel: 66
Cotton, Talia: 101, 104
Cournoyer, Mathieu: 208
Cox, Phillip: 101, 104
Crafts Museum of Caa: 171
CREATIAS ESTUDIO: 189

creatias.es: 189
Crépeau-Viau, Justine: 208
Crossland, Dave: 317
Curi, Sebastian: 155
Curtis, Matt: 51

D
D'Ellena, Michele: 110
daanrietbergen.com:130
Dai, Yiwei: 256, 278
Dake, Kelsey: 109
Dalvi, Girish: 301
Damien & The Love Guru: 73
Daniel Frumhoff
Design: 90, 92, 137
Daniel Wiesmann Büro
für Gestaltung: 72
danielfrumhoff.com/projects/
architectural-type-studies: 90, 137
Daniels, Katie: 187
danielwiesmann.de: 72
dariapetrova.com: 298
Darnell, Adrienne: 58
Daskalakis, Manos: 106
Dasso, Carla:187
Datye, Noopur: 301
Davison, Raphael: 172, 174
de Lange, Paul: 73
De Montaigu, Alexis: 59, 93, 118
de Waard, Jasper: 326
De Wit, Gunther: 73
debakir.com: 296
Dehlr, Kate:111
Delago, Ken: 111
Demon Press:237
Denzer, Ben: 75
DePumpo, Megan: 153
Design by AO:199
Design Department at
Burg Giebichenstein, Fall
2018/19 (130 students): 43
Design Studio Baklazanas:147
designbyao.com: 199
Didini, Fernanda: 109
Dieneš, Andrej: 307
DiGiovanni, Jenna: 186
Dino Burger: 166
Dommann, Monika: 82
Döring, Sophia: 37
Doshi, Tishani: 67
Drimalas, Dora: 203
Dunaeva, Tanya: 280
Duncan, Rob: 151, 177, 179
Durante, Davide: 71, 223
Dutch Design Week: 149
Drukkerij Tielen: 67

E
East Sea International Art
Pre-Biennale 2021: 231
Éditions Denoël:78
Edmondson, James: 335
eiab.kr/Youngha-Park: 231
Ek Type: 301
Emilia, Piia: 116
Emran, Manija: 22,23
Englisch 329
Enright, Michelle: 203
EPFL Pavilions: 152
erichbrechbuhl.ch: 222
Erner, Jule: 72
Eronen, Tiina: 116
Eslami, Bahman: 318
Etchison, Jeremy: 203
Eucalipto, Davide: 236

Eulji Medical Center: 158
Eulji University: 158
Everill, Addsyn: 62

F
FabCafe: 57, 211
Fachhochschule Bielefeld: 259
Faculty of Fine Arts of the
University of Lisbon: 275
Faith:119
faith.ca: 119
Falloon, Claire: 186
Famira, Hannes: 336
Farbanalyse: 72
Fawcett, Cole: 119
Fedor, Dexter: 187
Feng, Zhou: 281
FERGUS: 143
Fernande, Luis: 197
Ferrari, Emanuele: 119
Ferreira, Daniel: 194, 196
Ferreira, João Miguel
Andrade: 275
FEW magazine: 116
few-mag.com 116
Filippou, Efthimis: 183
Fillie, Joanna: 187
Firebelly Design: 153
Flamenco Biënnale: 213
Fleckenstein, Annika: 243
Flynn, Katharine: 59, 93, 118S
fmrizzotti.it/
Fons Hickmann M23: 110
Folk: 167
Foster, Dave: 322, 324
FounderType: 305, 314
Fox TV Portugal: 173
FRA! Design: 236
Frankies Burger Bar: 189
Freeman, Sean: 58
Freitas, Catarina: 164, 181
French, Renee: 109
Frere-Jones Type: 172, 174
FRONT: 98
Frumhoff, Daniel: 90, 92, 137
f(u)=formule CAFÉ: 188
Fujian Jiangxia University: 284
Fukuda, Toshiya: 57, 211
Fuller, Jarrett: 121
Fütterer, Dirk: 259
Fyrguth, Sarah: 259
FZ Guomeijindao: 314
FZ QianLongXingShu: 305

G
Gagnon, Louis: 252
Gallart, Esther: 80
Gallegos, Ben: 50, 51
Gambineri, Giacomo: 115
Gandhi, Kimya: 339
Garcia, Anna Sera: 98, 99
Garcia, Sandra: 307,
311, 317, 330, 331
Gary, Richard: 217
Gaudet, Marie-France: 226
Gelchenko, Bogdana: 281
Gelli, Fred: 179, 202
Georgiev, Teo: 186
gggrafik: 236
Giampietro, Rob: 98
Gibson, Phil: 171
Giné, Alba: 80
giuliabardelli.com: 106
Goes, Lilia: 100

Golledge, Lachlan: 111
Goncharova, Varvara: 104
Gooch, Courtney: 301
Google: 98, 99
Goucher, Kara: 105
Grab: 349
Graff, Sondra: 42, 43
Gramlich, Goetz: 236
GrandArmy: 50, 51, 178, 212
Grandgenett , Ben: 52,
53, 58, 59, 117, 118, 131
Grandjean, Cybele: 81
Grantham, Matt: 221
Graves, Jeanne: 126
Graw, Renata: 89
Gray, Cheri: 271, 286
Greenwich: 204
Grimshaw, Adam: 217
Grumer, Daniel: 343
Guangzhou Academy of
Fine Arts: 152, 245
Guccini, Andrea: 106
Gwangju Design Biennale: 228

H
Haas, Christina: 83
Haase, Carl: 257
Hadar, Yotam: 117
Hagen Verleger • Typography,
Book Design, Research:73
hagenverleger.com:73
Hai, Liang: 67
Haidar, Sousou: 243
Hale, Taylor W.: 172, 174
Half of the Mountain
Art Space: 91
Hallstein, Bernard: 172, 174
Ham, Minjoo: 302, 303
Hamdy, Mahmoud: 70
Hammann, Christian: 187
Han, Byunghoon: 187
Han, Grace: 63
Han, Joseph: 240, 252, 253
Han, Xu: 314
Hang, Yanwen: 139
Hangzhou Muke Cultural
Creativity: 56
Hankyong National
University:245
Hanyi Fonts: 327
Hanyi Yihexianjing: 327
Hanzi Club: 133
Happy Brand: 182
Harley Johnston Design:123
Harmsen, Lars: 70, 77
Harpur, Erin: 249
Harsanyi, Anna: 140
Hartstone, Lauren: 187
hassanrahim.com: 40, 41
Hauert, Helen: 71, 223
Havas New York: 59, 93, 118
HDU23 Lab: 232
He, Jianping: 224
He, Yuxuan (何宇轩): 88
He, Zhihua: 142
Heasty, David: 79
Hébert, Julien: 143, 178
Heigl, Josef:155
Heinle, Julia: 243
Helmhaus: 35
Heo, Yulim:175
Herrera, Gerardo: 283
herrpeter.ch: 218
hesign Studio 68, 88, 224
hesign.cn: 88
Hesse, Katharina: 72

Hilbert, Laura: 25
Hilton, Kyle: 109
Himmel, Carolin: 124, 157
Hin, Au Chon: 166
Historisk museum: 156, 185
Hochschule Augsburg
(University of Applied
Sciences Augsburg): 242
Hochschule für Gestaltung
Offenbach: 25
Hofer, Reiner: 234
hohachina.com: 192
Holeman, Erica: 90
Holtzman, Eyal: 325
Hongdai, Ling: 150, 201
Honkanen, Helmi: 116
Horikawa, Junichiro: 57, 211
Hosny, Khaled: 317
Hosotani, Sho: 57, 211
Hotel Blü: 155
HSE Art and Design
School: 271, 280
Hsieh, Jan: 131
Hsu, Phoebe: 268
Huan Yuan Calligraphy: 338
Huang, Jin: 76
Huang, Jingyi: 205
Huang, Lisa: 304, 305
Huang, Xiaoshuang: 182
Hubei Fine Arts
Publishing House: 81
Hubei Han Embroidery
Association: 95
Huber, Kirstin:163
Huber, Marina: 37
Hubertus: 74, 82, 141
Hunan Changde Art Museum: 225
Hunt, Louis: 70
Hunter, Andrew: 58
Hutson, Ryan: 335
Hybrid Design: 203
HYS Design: 312, 330

I

iamhyun.com: 252
Ibragimova, Anastasia: 251
Ibrahim, Riem: 121
IDOLONSTUDIO: 84
Ina Bauer
Kommunikationsdesign: 165
indego design: 194, 196
indegodesign.com: 194, 196
Infante, Lauren: 187
Interbrand: 175
International Center
of Photography: 55
Interval Type: 318, 320, 329
intervaltype.com: 320
Isa, Natsuki: 57, 211
Isometric Studio:100
isometricstudio.com: 100
Iwai, Hisashi:311
Izadpanah, Borna: 296, 297

J

jaderocha.com: 275
JCM Werbedruck AG: 214
Jakob, David: 116
Jager, Shannon: 164, 181
Jämseniu, Hanna: 116
Jannis Maroscheck: 77
Janošćík, Václav: 73
Janson, Sarah Maria: 234
Janssen, Janneke: 97
Javanmard, Saber: 128

Jawaid, Waqas: 100
Jen, Annie: 51
Jen, Natasha: 255, 260, 269, 285
jethtorres.com: 126
Ji, Seung Yeon: 158, 272
Jia, Mingyu: 276
jieun.work/Bacteria-Museum: 255
Jihanian, Gor: 334
Jilin HOHA Advertising
Co., Ltd: 192
Jinhua Mincho: 313
Jongen, René: 130
Josef Spinner Großbuchbinderei
GmbH: 72
JUN CAI: 219
Jung, Emma: 122

K

Kahl, Julia: 70, 77
Kamholz, David: 67
Kamola, Jadwiga: 83
Kanaoka, Daiki: 57, 211
karagordon.com: 302, 303
Karnis, Loukas: 105
Karnovich-Valua, Kirill: 27, 215S
Kashirin, Evgeny: 271
Kechechian, Nastaran: 319
Kedia, Akshat: 99
Keith, Gideon: 168S
Kellenberger, Eva: 36, 37
kellenberger-white.com: 36, 37
Kelm, Agnes: 243
KEN TSAI LEE DESIGN LAB: 217
Kennally, Brenda Ann: 111
Kerr, Frith: 38, 39
Kevin Cantrell Studio: 62
kevincantrell.com: 62
kfdesign.co.il: 136
Khaitan, Ananya: 80, 99
Khanjanzadeh, Damoon: 297
Khoj: 99
Khür, Jan: 156, 185
Kim, Miji: 272
Kim, Namoo: 245
King, Diana: 111
King, Kevin: 332
Kinon, Jennifer: 172, 174
Kiosoglou, Billy: 239
Kirchschlaeger, Gerhard: 238
kirchschlaeger.at: 238
Kitasenju Design: 57, 211
KKLB Beromünster: 221
Klaket: 315
Kleespies, Josefine: 72
Klenovsky, Hannah: 243
Klenovsky, Julia: 243
Klim Type Foundry: 90, 322, 324
Klink, Ahmed: 115, 125, 235
Knoth & Renner: 152
Kobayashi, Akira: 6-11
Kobi Franco Design: 136
Kofmehl: 218
Kokkonen, Arttu: 116
Königbauer, Mona: 243
Kornhaus Atelier: 214
kostabastsokas.com: 298
Kramer, Domi: 169
Kristal: 325
Kshetrimayum,
Neelakash: 300, 301
Kühne, Dafi: 35, 227
Kulkarni, Sarang: 301
Kumar, Bharat: 59, 93, 118
Kumi Studio: 169
Kunkel, Tilman: 259
Kwon, Doah: 258
Kyoyo: 191

L

Lacaz, Thiago: 61
Lai, Brian: 59, 93, 118
Lam, Ieong Kun: 194, 196
Lamm & Kirch: 152
Lamonde, Bryan-K. 143, 178, 208
Lanctot, Raymond: 78
Landor Paris: 318
Landry, Kristina: 143
Landschützer, Elena: 243
Langton, Conor: 109
Lao, Oliver: 196
Lapo Latini, Niccolò: 119
laurahilbert.de: 25
laurascofield.com: 44
Lava Syllabics:332
Lavergne, Laureline: 49
Leadbeater, Joe: 114
Leary, Petra: 229
Lee, Daisy DalHae: 47, 65, 127
Lee, Eddy: 175
Lee, Juhee: 245
Lee, Hyun Jung: 252
Lee, Ji Eun: 255
Lee, Ken Tsai: 217
Lee, Mikyung: 109
Lee, Robyn: 317
Leino, Unni: 116
Lempiäinen, Eveliina: 116
Lempiäinen, Piia: 116
Leong, Keika: 194
Leonidas, Gerry: 337
letterformvariations.
com/book: 66
Levine, Jodi: 109
Li, Charlotte: 175
Li, Kyle: 140
Li, Qiushuo: 138
Li, Tong: 286
Li, Xiang: 69
Li, Yanqing: 314
Lia, Svein Haakon: 156, 185
Liang, Huanbin:254, 265, 314
Liangxiang （良相设计）: 161
liebefonts.com: 306
Lim, JIn: 187
Lin, Minghao: 284
Lin, Tao: 29, 244, 247, 256, 276, 278
Lin, Yanzhao: 314
Lindy, Greg: 388
Lineto Type Foundry:92
linkedin.com/in/maria-
vilaverde-95197486: 107
Lípa Art Collection: 169
lisahuang.work: 304
Liu, Chang: 338
Liu, Cherry: 172, 174
Liu, Lobbin: 87
Liu, Sissi: 87
Liu, Vern Chuxuan: 274
Liu, Xiaoyu: 327
Liu, Xijiang: 182
Liu, Yu: 327
Liuzzo, Bob: 236
Liveright: 79
Lixenfeld, Elmar: 72
Loeffler, Max: 109
Loes, Maria 100
Loftwork Inc: 57, 211.
Lok, Koroh: 196
Losacco, Nick: 208
Lotfian, Hirbod: 319
Loucks, Rachel: 175
Louie, Travis: 109
Lozano, Beatriz: 94, 115, 125, 235
Lu, Jiayu: 314

Lubeznik Center for the Arts: 153
lubeznikcenter.org: 153
Lucey, Dan: 59, 93, 118
Lulai, Gai Safran: 243
Luo, Caisheng: 284
Luo, Xiduo: 314
Lupi, Giorgia: 101, 104
Lupton, Ellen: 135
Luyi, Chen: 150
Lychkovskiy, Mikhail: 64

M

M-N Associates: 154, 176, 200
m-n.associates: 154, 200
Mabaum, Dirk: 83
Mack, Verena: 29
Macau Experimental Theatre: 219
Made Music Studio: 187
Magloire, Tara: 101
MAH – Musee d'Art
et d'Histoire: 141
Mai, Lan: 154, 176, 200
Majoor, Martin: 306, 307
Make:, 184
Maletic, Tamara: 274
Malli, Karthik: 67
Mallikātype: 313
Malone, Nick: 59, 93, 118
Maltby, Oliver: 175
Malviya, Kailash: 301
mamgobozidesign.com: 46
Mandlik, Claudia: 198
Manetti, Debora: 236
Manufatura: 98
Mao, Mao:190
Mao, Xingya: 254
Mao, Yiwen: 281
Margit: 323
Mariani, Alberto: 236
Maroscheck, Jannis: 77
maroscheck.de: 77
Martin, Jr., Bobby C: 172, 174
Martinez, Paul: 59, 93, 118
martinmajoor.com:306
Maryland Institute
College of Art: 137
Masa: 202
Masbaum, Dirk:, 83
Master TypeMedia, Royal
Academy of Art The Hague: 303
Matias, Carlos: 59, 93, 118
Matousek, Abby: 55
Matter of Sorts: 116
Mauru, Anna Lisa: 243
May, Susan: 55
Maya, Lili: 137
Mayer-Stoltz, Jana: 72
Mayfield, Kelsey: 317
McCaughley, Michael: 172, 174
McEvoy, Blaine: 175
McNaught, Jon:111
McNeil, Paul: 66
mehdisaeedi.com: 44
Melandinou, Anastasia: 183
Mena, María Pérez: 257
Mendes, Pedro: 258
Mendes Manente, Marcos: 98
Meng, Hannah: 100
Meredith, Mia: 109, 111S
Micaliuc, Anatolie: 120
Migliaccio, Sal: 59, 93, 118
Miller, Andrew: 175
Miller, Will: 153
Min, Jakyoung: 272
minjooham.com: 302
MINT BRAND DESIGN: 86, 162
Misiak, Marian: 70, 121

Mister Gatto: 236
Mithaq: 309
Mixer: 222
MNP: 103, 183
Mohr, Anika: 261
Monaghan, Keirnan: 109
Mora, Roberto Aguiló: 49
Morin, François: 143
Morinaga, Rafael: 186
Mortensen, John Kenn: 109
motaitalic.com: 300
Movement Research: 117
MPL: 79
Mucho: 151, 177, 179
Muesa, Kira: 116
Muldrow, Kristmar: 160, 167S
Mundy, Alicia: 114
Murphy, Delta: 55
Murthy, Vaishanvi: 301
Museum für Kunst und
Gewerbe Hamburg 204
Muthesius University of
Fine Arts and Design: 261

Nammour, Yara Khoury: 309
Nan Chen: 81
Nanjing Han Qing Tang Design: 76
Narayanan, Anagha: 300, 301
National Women's
History Museum: 163
Naughty Roll: 194
Nausea: 337
neelakash.webflow.io: 300
Neeser & Müller: 106, 210
neesermueller.ch: 106, 210
Nesi, Emily: 186
Neubad: 212
Neue Gestaltung GmbH: 37, 86
Neue Musik Rümlingen: 106
Neufquatre Editions Paris:170
Neumeyer, Philipp: 299
Nevada Museum of Art: 159
Neville, Engy: 175
New Orleans Tourism: 58
New York Magazine: 59, 93, 113, 118
Newman, Brett: 203
Newton, Joe: 22-23
Ng, Hiuman: 151, 179
Ng, Joo Leng Lucien: 47, 65, 127
Nguyen, Anh: 154, 176, 200
Nguyen, Duy: 154, 176, 200
Nguyen, Quan: 154, 176, 200
Ni, Yuqin: 250
Nichols, Ben: 187
Nießler, Adrian: 25, 29
Niklaus Troxler Design: 221
Nishi, Tatsuya: 207
Nishigraph: 207
Nøkleby, Christoffer: 156, 185
Nolte, Gertrud: 77
Nopper, Stephan: 214
Norbert: 299
Nordrum, Halvor: 156, 185
Northeast, Christian: 109
Noordzij, Gerrit: 12-17
Novel: 80, 99
November Trail: 331
Novikov, Artur: 64
Nueva Balear: 49
Nyman, Tino: 116
Nys, Alexandre: 175

Oatly: 100

Oceanic: 320
Ochwat, Jennifer: 243
Odzinieks, Nina: 37, 86
Oetker-Kast, Julia: 187
Offhand Type: 169
Offset Projects: 80
Oh, Junghoon: 269
OhnoType Foundry: 90
Okano, Toaki: 229
Okkonen, Sofia: 116
Olan, Anita: 187
Olecki, Pam: 187
Oledzka, Natalia: 186
Oler, Anna: 79
Olsthoorn, Joshua: 106
Omagari, Toshi: 315, 321
Omega Type Foundry: 315, 321
Omnibus 79
Omotesando: 123
Opara, Eddie: 198
Orange Jellies: 57, 211
Ordu Taşbaşı Art Space: 220
Osaka City Museum
of Fine Art: 233
Osborne, Lloyd: 229
Osborne Shiwan: 229
osborneshiwan.com:229
Osorio, Felipe: 202
Ou Zhuopeng, Jordan: 205
out.o.studio: 89
outostudio.com: 89
Ovezea, Diana: 114

Pagan, Juan Carlos: 115, 125, 235
Pagliardini, Davide: 236
Paige Smythe Studio: 160
Paizs, Flo: 86
Pancini, Cosimo Lorenzo: 236
Pane: 336
Pané-Farré, Pierre: 43
Panitz, Lisa: 70
Pankova, Olga: 237
Pantheon Drukkers: 130
Papanagiotou, Katerina: 103, 183
Papazoglou, Laios: 183
Paprika: 78, 144
Parachute Typefoundry: 105
parachutefonts.com: 105
PARADISE: 164, 181
paradise.work: 164, 181
Park, Ga Young: 158
Park, Hiromi: 172, 174
Park, Youngha:231
Parsons School of Design: 274
Patanè, Michele: 110
Paternoster, Francesco: 236
Pellerin, Patrick:178
Pentagram Design: 101
Pentagram New York: 55,
104, 122, 148, 163, 198
Perpetuini: Francesca: 236
PetChoy: 154, 176, 200
Peters-Collaer, Lauren: 60
Peterson, Ellen: 113
Petrova, Daria: 298, 299
Petrucci, Marco: 236
Pham, Anh: 154, 176, 200
Pham, Michelle:243
Philippin, Frank:239
phoebehsu.design/This-Book-
is-a-Time-Machine:268
Phoenix Fine Arts Publishing:76
Piedmont Art Walk: 151, 179
Pierassa, Riccardo:236
Platia: 321
Plau: 98

PLEA: 49
Poddar, Chandni: 115, 125, 235
Pöhler, Leon: 259
Porto, Leo: 186
PORTO ROCHA: 186
Powell, James: 168
Principal: 143, 178, 208
principal.studio: 143, 178, 208
Prodiseño School of Visual
Communication: 228
Providencia, Lourenco: 164, 181
Pulgar, Gabrielle: 277
Puraeva, Alyona: 268
PXL-MAD School of Arts: 257

Q-Create: 138
Qiao, Junqing: 87
Qing Mocai Lishu:330
Qualischefsk, Ash: 317i
Qiu, Yin: 314
qiushuoli.com/beam: 138

R

r-itual.studio: 228
R&M: 41, 46
Radziejewski, Robert: 72
Ragan, Jesse: 172, 174, 186
Rahim, Hassan: 40, 41
Rajan, Aadarsh: 301, 331
Rajkumar, Sulekha: 301
Ramírez, Gen: 336
Ramírez, Marcelo: 59, 93, 118
Rausch, Ulrike: 306, 307
READSEARCH (MAD-Research
& Hasselt University):97
Reber R41: 236
Reginiano, Dana: 198
Reiser, Lina: 243
Renata Moroni Design: 145
renatamoroni.com: 145
Research Center of Ancient
Chinese Characters Art: 81
Research Foundation -
Flanders (FWO): 97
Resonay: 307
Rickli, Hannes: 82
Rietbergen, Daan: 130
Ritual: 228
Riverhead Books: 60, 63
Rizzotti, Fabio Mario: 110
robclarke.com: 180
Robertson, Luke: 177
Robinson, Dana: 198
Robinson, Johanna: 67
Robitaille, Daniel: 78, 144
Rocha, Felipe: 186
Rocha, Jade: 275
Roche, Valentine: 59, 93, 118
Rochefort, Sarah: 178
Rodriguez, Marie-Hélène: 143
Roemer, Emily: 266
Rogatty, Zuzanna: 113
Rohrbach Gruppe: 165
robclarke.com: 165
Roizental, Jack: 122
Romano, Marco Goran: 236
Roque, Alexander: 93
Rosenoff, Julie: 59, 93, 118
rozi.fun/dream-bubble: 140
RT Creative Lab: 27, 215
Ruechel, Naila: 90
RVS Basic: 328
ryanbugden.com: 41, 45
Ryden, Mark: 109

S&Co: 202
Sabach, Jan: 209
Saeedi, Mehdi: 42, 43
Sagawa, Natsuki: 57, 211
Sahu, Mahesh: 301
Sakkal, Mamoun: 308, 309
sakkal.com: 308
Samarskaya, Ksenya: 294, 295
Sánchez, Carlos: 189
Sandoval, Carina: 172, 174
Santamaria, Raffaella: 236
sarahstendel.com: 25
Sauterleute, Elisabeth: 243
Sawaria, Sanchit: 33
sawariasanchit.com: 33
Sbarbati, Simone: 236
Scher, Paula: 122, 148, 163
Schiaparelli, Kathleen: 172, 174
Schmid, Sabine: 234
Schmid/Widmaier: 234
School of Visual Arts: 240, 252,
253, 255, 258, 260, 267, 269, 273
Schriftlabor: 323
Schröder, Nicholas: 186
Schule für Gestaltung Basel: 210
Scofield, Laura: 44, 45
SEARCH For Arts Leadership: 193
Sebek, Anezka: 140
Seidenberg, Ephrat: 172, 174
Sejong University: 158, 272
Seligman, Spencer: 175
Senna, Leandro: 129
Serrato, Stephen: 264
Sesia, Valentina: 236
Seven: 168
SF Arabic: 316
SF Symbols 3: 333
Shallcrass, Fred: 174
Shandong University: 338
Shanghai Institute of
Visual Arts: 276
Shanghai University of
Engineering Science: 29, 244, 247:
Shanghai Version
Design Group:,142
Sharma, Shantanu: 273
Shaw, Han-yi: 312, 330
Shao, Zhuohan: 132
Shen, Youyou: 281
Shi, Jincheng: 241,
248, 263, 270, 288
Shinbakusai Reisho: 312
Shingre, Maithili: 301
shinn.co.jp: 233
Shinnoske Design:233
Shiwan, Shabnam: 229
SHOEI Inc.: 57, 211
Short Waves: 146
Sibling Rivalry: 187
Siciliano, Carl: 59, 93, 118
Siegenthaler, Oliver: 202
Sikora, Justyna: 157
Sikov, Jonny: 55
Sio, Ivan: 194
Six Sense Studio: 81
Siyu Mao: 206
Slanted Publishers 66, 70, 77
Slavin, Leonid: 280
SM Studio:173
Smeijers, Fred: 328
Smith, Sarah 75
Social Species: 57, 65, 127
Socio: 114
socio-type.com: 114
Sociotype:114

Sociotype: 114
Sociotype Journal: 114
Sofar: 106
Song, Hyejin: 186
Sonos, Inc.: 203
Soria, Matt: 153
Southern Liviing Arts Festival: 91
Spanó, Cristina: 111
Sprouls, Elizabeth: 137
Squirrels: 180
St-Pierre, Marianne: 144
Stadt Tuttlingen: 124
Stadler, Maz: 82
Stanford d. school: 90
Stariha, Megan: 90
Steben, Eve: 58
Steen, Marie Louise: 156, 185
Stehle, Barbara: 71, 223
Steinbeck, Birthe: 108
Steinberg, Em: 243
Stel, Myrthe: 325
Stendel, Sarah: 25
Stenkhoff, Pit: 37, 86
Stewart, Michelle: 172, 174
Stiftung Buchkunst: 72
Stillittano, Giovanni: 236
Stiuso, Jack: 175
STONES DESIGN LAB.: 69
Strawberry Western: 41, 45
Studio Bang-Gu: 47, 65, 127
Studio Daniel Peter: 218
Studio Garbett: 184
Studio Saber:128
studiobanggu.com: 47, 65, 117
studiofrth.com:38
Süddeutsche Zeitung: 108
Sugisaki, Shinnoske: 233
Sunac Folk Art: 190
Sunday Afternoon: 115, 125, 235
sundayafternoon.us: 115, 125, 235
Sunday Buro: 135
Suomalainen, Jaakko: 116
Superness: 110
Supple Studio: 180
supplestudio.com: 180
Super Freak: 109
Surányi, Miriam: 323
swdesign.de: 234
Sweetnich, Dean: 153
Swiss Typefaces: 74
swisstypefaces.com: 74
Symann, Maik: 259
Syros International Film Festival (SIFF): 103
syrosfilmfestival.org: 103

Tai, Ming: 250
Taichung Blossom Pavilion, Taiwan: 131
Take It Easy Films: 197
Takebayashi, Kazushige: 57, 211
Tanrie Type Family: 335
Tao Graphic Design Studio: 226
Tartarelli, Andrea: 236
TEN BUTTONS 150, 201
Teng, Jiao: 182
Tehran Museum of Contemporary Art: 297
The, Richard: 140
The Epicene Collection: 322
The Founding Types: 149
The Lettering Artists Association of Macau: 196
The Mānuka Collection: 324
The New School: 140
The New York Times

for Kids: 109, 111
The New York Times Magazine: 51, 109, 111, 112
The Scientist Coffee: 232
The Wildest:186
Theater Aeternam: 222
Theater Erlangen: 37, 86
Théâtre Prospero: 208
THERE IS STUDIO: 58
Thompson, Henrietta: 114
Thonik: 149, 213
thonik.nl/work/: 149, 213
Thoughtput: 99
Tifrere, Melissa: 59, 93, 118
Tinnes, Andrea: 43
Togakushi Soba Festival Executive Committee: 207
Todot: 209
TOKYO TDC: 224
Tongji University Shanghai: 256, 278
Tool: 103
Torres, Jeth: 126
tosche.net: 315
Trabucco-Campos: 193
Trabucco-Campos, Andrea A: 108
Tre, Hector: 119
Trehan, Khyati: 128
Triboro: 79
Trigo, Carolina: 287
Troncone, Rudy: 59, 93, 118
Troxler, Niklaus: 221
troxlerart.ch: 221
Tshuma, Osmond: 46, 47
Tsinghua University: 81
Turner Classic Movies: 187
Twoo®: 98
Typaldos, Claire: 187
Type West at Letterform Archive: 335
Type@Cooper: 336
TypeMates: 299, 307
typemates.com: 299, 307
TypeType Foundry: 154, 176, 200
Typical Organization: 106
typophrenic.com/believe-lettering-blanket: 135
Typotheque: 331, 332, 334
Tyrol University College of Teacher Education: 157
Tyson, Sara: 109

Uebele, Andreas: 124, 157
Um, Tomi: 111
Uniforma s.c.: 146
University of Applied Sciences Northwestern Switzerland: 223
University of Reading: 337
Untitled: 166
Urruty, Amandine: 109
USA Pavilion at Expo Dubai 2020: 121
Uwabani: 311

Vainesman, Diego: 48, 49
Vainio, Ville: 116
Valentene, Chantel: 153
Valladares, Dev: 195
Vallin, Carl-Hampus: 203
Vamvounakis, Theo: 106
van Blokland, Erik: 303, 328
van der Laan, Paul: 303, 325, 328
van Gastel, Mikon: 187

van Rosmalen, Pieter: 325
Vanity Teen Magazine: 119
Varumo, Ville: 116
Vaskovic, Vedran: 144
Vasquez, Miguel: 228
Vassiliou, Panos: 106
Vereins Basis Kunst und Bau: 214
Verheul, Peter: 303, 328
Verleger, Hagen: 73
Verreault, Luc: 144
Veziko, Marina: 116
Vilaverde, Maria João: 107
Villagio, Sara: 172, 174
Vis, Mickael: 116
Vishnyakov, Svyat: 251, 267
VJ Type: 63
Vlachakis: Kostas: 106

Walden, Ariel: 67
Walker, Camille: 59, 93, 118
Walker, Claren: 186
Walser, Laura Marie: 242
Walters, Kelly: 50, 51
Wang, Chun-chi: 84
Wang, Cindy: 131
Ward, Olivia: 203
Warlies, Anke: 259
Watanabe, Kohki: 57, 211
Watanabe, Takayuki: 57, 211
Weigler, Stefanie: 79
Weinreich, Clara: 70
Wellnhofer, Florian: 119
What Unites Us: 209
Widmaer, Lutz: 234
Wiesmann, Daniel:72
Willey, Rachel: 51
Wilson Center:101
wilsoncenter.org/sciencestack:,101
Wiltshire, Frederick: 337
Winders, jp: 59, 93, 118
Wiraatmaja, Aditya Prasetya: 336
Witt Design: 166
Won, Myung Jin: 158
Wright, Joe: 187
Wu, Siguang: 232
Wufang Architectural Design Firm:192
W.W. Norton: 79

Xing, Chen:69
Xing, Zhiqiang: 314
XYZ Type: 172, 174, 186
Xu, Luomin:265
Xue, Tianmeng: 313
Xue, Xiaoyu: 115, 125, 235

Yamada, Kazuhiro: 310, 311
Yamashita, Shunichi: 57, 211
Yang, Ben: 67
Yendrys, Sean:117
Yentus, Helen: 60, 63
Yilmaz, Erman: 220
Yip, Amy: 317
Yoshida, Akihiro: 57, 211
yotamhadar.com: 117
You, Jungln:122
youfab.info/2021: 57, 211
YouTube Art Department: 317
YouTube Sans Arabic: 317

youtube.com/watch?v=p5f6VuYagF8: 131
Young, Seo: 109
yuchen-creative.com: 95
Yun, Lynne: 335

Zablit, Albert: 58
Zahr, Oussama: 59, 93, 118
Zalfia: 303
Zech, Johanna: 37
Zetafonts: 236
zetafonts.com/blog/coppa-stadio: 236
Zhang, Aiqi: 282
Zhang, Lingli: 314
Zhao, Qing: 76
Zhejiang Gongshang University: 133
Zheng, Cindy: 151, 179
Zheng, Songwen: 87
Zhong, Ranyi: 314
Zhou, Liang:314
Zhu, Rozi: 140
Zhu, Tao: 76
Zhu, Zipeng: 174
Zhuk, Zhenya: 271, 281
Zhuopeng: 205
Zook, Amanda: 172, 174
Zhou, Ruiqi: 283, 287
Zidić, Neva:303
zrq.cargo.site/ONE_VINYL_1: 283
zrq.cargo.site/provo: 287
Zukerman, Julio: 129
Zuni Icosahedron: 217
何宇轩: 88

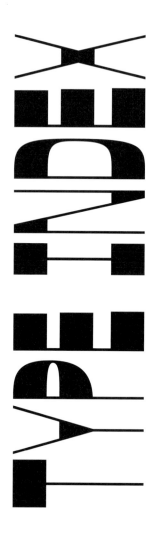

A

A2 Gothic: 151, 179
A2 Type

ABC Diatype: 110, 156, 185
Johannes Breyer and Fabian
Harb, with Elias Hanzer
ABC Dinamo

Action Condensed Bold: 163
Erik van Blokland
Commercial Type

Adelphi: 110
Simona Alina And one

Adobe Song: 69
Adobe

Aeonik: 194
Mark Bloom and Joe Leadbeater
CoType Foundry

glyphworld Airland: 281
Leah Maldonado
Glyphworld

Akkurat Mono: 286
Laurenz Brunner
Lineto

Aktiv Grotesk: 203
Dalton Maag

Aktiv Grotesk CNSG: 256
Dalton Maag

Albertus Nova: 166
Toshi Omagari
Monotype

Allgemein Grotesk: 43
Andrea Tinnes
Typecuts

GT Alpine: 100
Reto Moser
Grilli Type

Amaala: 318
Bahman Eslami and Ilya Naumoff
GlyphSets and IntervalType

Amateur: 43
Pierre Pané-Farré

GT America: 124, 240
Noël Leu with Seb McLauchlan
Grilli Type

American Typewriter: 265
ITC Fonts, Monotype

Ammo: 272
Miji Kim

Anek Multi-script Variable
Type Family: 301

glyphworld Animal Soul: 281
Leah Maldonado
Glyphworld

Anonymous Pro: 261
Mark Simonson
Mark Simonson Studio

Arial: 75
Robin Nicholas and
Patricia Saunders
Monotype

Arimo: 271
Steve Matteson
Google

Assemble: 175
Andrew Bellamy, Eddy
Lee, and Oliver Maltby
Interbrand In-House

Atak Regular:155
Philip Hermann
Out of the Dark

Atamira: 229
Lloyd Osborne and
Shabnam Shiwan
Osborne Shiwan

Authentic Sans: 272
Christina Janus and
Desmond Wong
Authentic

Avangarde by Bankov: 27
Peter Bankov
Bankov Posters Prague

B

Balloon: 160
Bahnschrift: 267
Aaron Bell
Microsoft

BAKUB 2: 214
Kornhaus Atelier (Céline
Beyeler and Stephan Nopper)

BallPill: 287
Benoît Bodhuin

Monotype Baskerville: 73
John Baskerville and
Monotype Design Studio
FontShop

FF Bau Pro: 43, 143
Christian Schwartz
FontFont

Bauer Bodoni: 73
Giambattista Bodoni
& Heinrich Jost
FontShop

Bayard: 198
Tré Seals
Vocal Type

BEAM: 138
Qiushuo Li
Q-Create

Beastly: 90
James Edmondson
OH no Type

Bebas Neue Pro Bold: 189
Carlos Sánchez
Creatias

Berthold Akzidenz
Grotesk: 36, 77, 162, 239
Günter Gerhard Lange
Berthold Type Group LLC

Bespoke: 180
Rob Clarke and Phil Skinner

JB Bingo: 75
Johannes Breyer

Bleeny: 59, 93
Spike Spondike
Dalton Maag

Bodoni Oldstyle: 188
Giambattista Bodini

Boogy Brut Poster: 283
Julien Priez
Bureau Brut

LL Bradford Mono: 242
Laurenz Brunner
Lineto

LL Bradford Regular: 155, 242
Laurenz Brunner
Lineto

Brwon (modified): 226
Aurèle Sack (chenzhangleyi)
Lineto (bytoby)

Bubble Type: 140
Rozi Zhu

C

Cactus: 202
Gareth Hague
Alias

Cádiz: 172, 174
Luzi Gantenbein
Luzi Type

Cako-Black: 166
Jérémy Schneider
VJ Type

Adobe Caslon: 87
Carol Twombly
Adobe

Caslon Doric: 159
Paul Barnes
Commercial Type

Casual Grotesque 288
Jincheng Shi

Century Gothic: 264
Monotype

Charisma: 319
Hirbod Lotfian

Clarendon (metal): 227
Hermann Eidenbenz (1950)
Haas'sche Schriftgiesserei,
Münchenstein, Switzerland

Cooper BT: 99
Oswald Cooper
Bitstream

Copperplate Gothic Std: 199
Fredric W. Goudy
Linotype

Corona: 43
Chauncey H. Griffith
FontFont

Cusongti: 56
Zhang shifeng

D

Das Grotesk Mono: 106
Panos Vassiliou
Parachute Typefoundry

glyphworld Desert: 281
Leah Maldonado
glyphworld

Di Grotesk: 70
Marian Misiak
Threedotstype

Dinamo Diatype: 152, 169
Johannes Breyer & Fabian
Harb, with Elias Hanzer
Dinamo Typefaces

Dida: 59, 93
Jérémy Schneider
VJ Type

Distorted Pixel: 230
Chen Zhang Le Yi
Bytoby

Dromon CF Regular: 183
P. Haratzopoulos
Cannibal, fonts.gr

Druk XX Condensed: 251
Berton Hasebe
Commercial Type

GT Eesti: 157
Grilli Type

Editorial New: 262
Mathieu Desjardins
Pangram Pangram

Englisch: 329
Interval

Enea: 110
Benedetta Bovani

Epilogue: 104
Tyler Finck
Etcetera Type Company

Euclid: 74
Swiss Typefaces

Euclid Circular A Medium: 223
Swiss Typefaces

Eulji Gil: 158
Seung Yeon Ji and Ga Young Park

Eva Maria: 198
Tré Seals
Vocal Type

Executive: 210
Gavillet & Rust
Optimo

Fabrik: 270
Fabian Fohrer
Tighttype

Fakt: 178
Thomas Thiemich

Fangzheng Baosong: 81
Hua Weicang
Founder Type

Fangzheng Song
Keben Xiukai
(方正宋刻本秀楷): 276
Ting Tang
Founder Type

Fangzheng Lanting Black Flat: 265
Li Qi
FangZheng

Fano: 110
Anna Damoli

Favorit: 252
Johannes Breyer & Fabian
Harb, with Erkin Karamemet
and Immo Schneider
Dinamo

Feixen Sans: 202
Studio Feixen

Fernhout:149
Wim Crouwel, The Foundry
Types, Thonik
The Foundry Types

FEW Display: 116
Jaakko Suomalainen

Flamenco F: 213
Thonik

GT Flexa: 269
Dominik Huber with
Marc Kappeler
Grilli Type

glyphworld Flower: 281
Leah Maldonado
glyphworld

glyphworld Forest: 281
Leah Maldonado
glyphworld

Forma: 251
David Jonathan Ross

FOT-UDKakugo Large Pr6N: 88
Fontworks

Founders Grotesk: 270
Kris Sowersby
Klim Type Foundry

Fournier: 172, 174
Monotype Studio and
Pierre Simon Fournier
Monotype

Fragen: 154, 176, 200
TypeType Foundry

Freight Display Pro: 274
Joshua Darden
Darden Studio

Frezeit: 238
Lewis MacDonald
Polytype

Frutiger: 233
Adrian Frutiger
Monotype

Futura: 49, 115, 125, 208, 235, 254
Paul Renner
Bauer Type Foundry

Futura PT: 88, 147
Vladimir Andrich, Isabella
Chaeva, Paul Renner, and
Vladimir Yefimov
Paratype

Futo Go B101: 207
Tatsuya Nishi

FZ QianLongXingShu: 305
Tong Lin
FounderType

ITC Garamond: 80
Tony Stan

Garamond Premier Pro: 272
Robert Slimbach
Adobe Originals

Generation Mono: 51
David Gobber and Hoang
Nguyen of Nguyen Gobber
Nguyen Gobber

Gesto:110
Ruggero Magri

Gestura: 114
Joe Leadbeater, Diana
Ovezea, Nigel Bates
Sociotype

Giger: 240
RASDESIGN

Gill Sans: 107
Eric Gill
Monotype

F37 Ginger Pro: 47, 65, 127
Rick Banks
F37® Foundry

glyphworld Glacier: 281
Leah Maldonado
Glyphworld

Goldich: 326
Jasper de Waard
Bold Monday

Gotham: 266
Tobias Frere-Jones
with Jesse Ragan
Hoefler & Co.

Gramatika Bold: 83
Roman Gornitsky
The Temporary State

GrandSlang Roman: 196
Nikolas Wrobel
Nikolas Type

ABC Gravity XX Condensed: 228
Johannes Breyer, Fabian
Harb, and Robert Janes
ABC Dinamo

Greta Sana Armenian: 334
Typotheque

Grot12 Extended: 68
Henrik Kubel and Scott Williams
A2/SW/HK+A2-TYPE

Guangminglu Condensed: 226
Tao Lin
Bold Matt Rough

FZ GuoMeiJinDao: 314
Huasha Chen, Lixiao Chen,
Bingquan Guo, Xu Han, Yanqing
Li, Huanbin Liang, Yanzhao Lin,
Jiayu Lu, Xiduo Luo, Yin Qiu,
Zhiqiang Xing, Lingli Zhang,
Ranyi Zhong, and Liang Zhou
FounderType

Halyard: 198
Joshua Darden with Eben
Sorkin and Lucas Sharp
Darden Studio

Hanyi Qihei
(汉仪旗黑): 86, 276
Li Qi
Hanyi

Hanyi Yi Hei Xian Jing: 327

Hanzi Sheji Shi: 81
Chen Nan
Chen Nan Studio

HarmonyOS Sans: 188
Hanyi font library

Hei Regular: 69
Kenneth Kwok and Robin Hui
Monotype

Helvetica: 36, 76, 81, 103, 217, 224
Max Miedinger
Haas'sche Schriftgiesserei,
Münchenstein

Helvetica Neue: 130, 188, 250, 254
Max Miedinger

Helvetica Now Variable: 69
Charles Nix
Monotype

Holland Regular: 226
Muhammad Sirojuddin

Huan Yuan Calligraphy: 338
Chang Liu
Lettersiro

HYQuanTangShiL 284
Ying Song
Hanyi Fonts

Ichigo: 41
Ryan Bugden

ICP Logo Generator: 55
Pentagram New York

Impressum: 110
Michelangelo Nigra

Intergrowth: 285
Di Gu

F37 Jan: 86
F37

JC Bacteria Mu (custom): 260
Jiin Choi

Johanna I: 37
Johanna Zech and Flo Paizs
Neue Gestaltung

Jinhua-Mincho: 313
Tianmeng Xue
Mallikātype

Juxta Sans: 139
Naumtype

Kawak Black and Light: 94
Javier Viramontes
Latinotype

Klaket: 315
Toshi Omargari
Omega Type

Klarheit Kurrent: 241, 263
Alex Dujet
Extraset

Knockout: 226, 266
Jonathan Hoefler
Hoefler & Co.

Kobe: 63
Jérémy Schneider
VJ-Type

Kristal: 325
Barbara Bigosińska, Eyal
Holtzman, Myrthe Stel,
Paul van der Laan, and
Peter van Rosmalen
Bold Monday

Lab Groteque: 282
Göran Söderström
Letters from Sweden

Ladybird: 277
Alli Cunanan
Type Department

Lanting Hei: 150, 201
Qi Li
FounderType

Latin American Artists
Alphabet: 145
Renata Lehr Moroni

Lausanne 4300:71, 255, 26, 277
Nizar Kazan
WELTKERN SÀRL

Lava Syllabics: 332
Typoteque

Letter Gothic: 182
Roger Roperson
Adobe Fonts

Letterform Variation 00, 66
Letterform Variation 01 IR, 66
Letterform Variation 02 DFO, 66
Nigel Cottier, Christian
Schwartz and Max Miedinger
Commercial Type

Libre Franklin: 101
Pablo Impallari
Impallari Type

Li Song Pro 宋体: 76

Lipa Varible: 169
Kurt Bullock

LL Mono: 276
Cornel Windlin
LLineto

Louche:267
Joona Louhi
Futurefonts

Louize Display:277
Matthieu Cortat
205TF

Lubeznik Display: 163
Will Miller and Dean Sweetnich
Firebelly Design

Lyon Text: 268
Kai Bernau
Commercial Type

Mabry:163
Will Miller and Dean Sweetnich
Firebelly Design

MAH Sans: 141
Scott Vander Zee and
Hubertus Design

Marfa: 218
Fabian Harb and Seb
McLauchlan, Mastering
by Robert Janes
Dinamo

Margit: 323
Miriam Surányi
Schriftlabor

Marlet: 106
Panos Vassiliou
Parachute Typefoundry

Martin: 60, 198
Tré Seals
Darden Studio

GT Maru: 222
Thierry Blancpain
Grilli Type

ABC Maxi Round Mono
Variable: 287
Johannes Breyer and Fabian
Harb with Andree Paat
Dinamo

glyphworld Meadow: 281
Leah Maldonado
glyphworld

Mithaq:309
Yara Khoury Nammour
AlMohtaraf Design House

Modular (customized): 47, 65, 127
Studio Bang-Gu

Mokoko Regular: 250
Dalton Maag

Molecular Round and
Molecular Square: 136
Kobi Franco
Kobi Franco Design

Monosten: 47, 65, 127
The Entente
Colophon Foundry

Monument Grotesk: 82,
116, 214, 228, 248, 267
Kasper-Florio (Larissa Kasper
& Rosario Florio) and Dinamo
(Robert Janes, Fabiola Mejía)
ABC Dinamo

Monument Grotesk Variable: 242
Kasper-Florio (Larissa Kasper
& Rosario Florio) and Dinamo
(Robert Janes, Fabiola Mejía)
ABC Dinamo

glyphworld Mountain: 281
Leah Maldonado
glyphworld

Nausea: 337
Frederick Wiltshire
Fredfonts

Neue Haas Grotesk:
66, 80, 119, 275
Christian Schwartz after
Max Miedinger
Linotype

Neue Haas Unica: 37,
55, 86, 90, 184, 209
Toshia Omargari
Monotype

Neue Montreal: 64, 246, 262, 279
Mat Desjardins
PangramPangram Foundry

Neue Plak Condensed: 43
Toshi Omargari
Monotype

Neurial Grotesk: 274
Deni Anggara
Indian Type Foundry

News Gothic: 249
Morris Fuller Benton
American Type Founders

Next:144
Ludovic Balland
Optimo

Non Natural Grotesk: 165
Jona Saucedo
NonFoundry

Norbert: 299
Philipp Neumeyer
TypeMates

Nostra: 196
Lucas Descroix

nothing (无) : 161
Cheliang (車良)
Liangxiang Design (良相设计)

Noto Mono: 257
Google Fonts

November Tamil: 331
Peter Bi'lak and AAdarsh Rajan
Typotheque

Nunito: 154, 176, 200
TypeType Foundry

NYT Mag Sans: 111
Henrik Kubel
A2-Type

NYT Mag Serif: 111, 112
Henrik Kubel
A2-Type

Objectivity: 285
PngramPangram

Obviously: 148
James Edmondson
Oh No Type Co.

Oceanic: 320
Ilya Naumoff
Interval

Octin Stencil Regular: 226
Ray Larabie
Typodermic

Omotesando: 123
Harley Johnston

AT Opale:110
Gabriele Fumero
Archivio Tipografico

Oracle and Oracle Triple: 72
Johannes Breyer with Andree
Paat & Robert Janes
ABC Dinamo

Pane: 336
Aditya Prasetya Wiraatmaja

Permanent: 110
Alberto Malossi

Plantin: 186
Robin Nicholas
Monotype

Platia: 321
Toshi Omagari
Omega Type

Pompilia: 110
Piero Beninato

Portrait: 181
Berton Hasebe
Commercial Type

Publico: 55
Paul Barnes and
Christian Schwartz
Commercial Type

Qing Mocai Lishu: 330
Quadrant Text Mono: 116
Matter of Sorts

Raleway: 219
Jun Cai, Bob Lei, and Libby lei

Reckless Neue: 279, 282
Martin Vácha
Displaay Type Foundry

Regal: 106
Panos Vassiliou
Parachute Typefoundry

Regola Pro, 177
Piero Di Biase, Think Work
Observe Type Dept.

NN Rekja: 106
Anton Studer
Nouvelle Noire

Relicario Type: 173
Silvia Filipe Ferreira Matias

Replica: 92
Dimitri Bruni and Manuel Krebs
Lineto

Resonay: 307
Andrej Dieneš
TypeMates

Rhode: 197
David Berlow, Font Bureau

Rhymes: 86
Jakub Samek

Rigby and Rigby Display: 79
Triboro with Omnibus

Roboto: 59, 93
Christian Robertson
Google

Roobert: 99
Martin Vácha
Displaay

Rosewood Std Fill: 207
Tatsuya Nishi

Roumald: 206, 253
Erkin Karamemet

RVS Basic: 328
3Type

Scto Grotesk: 204
Schick Toikka

Self Modern Italic and Self
Modern Regular: 84
Lucas Le Bihan
Bretagne Type Foundry

Sen: 59, 93
Kosal Sen

Serifbabe: 270
Charlotte Rohde
FEMME Type

SF Arabic: 316
Apple Design Team

SF Symbols: 333
Apple Design Team

Shinbakusai Reisho: 312
Han-yi Shaw
HYS Design

Shu Song: 91
Founder Type

Signifier: 90
Kris Sowersby
Klim Type Foundry

Simplified Chinese: 91
Founder Type

Sirba: 248
Nicolien van der Keur
TypeTogether

Siyuanhei: 162
Google

SK Modernist Bold: 146
Sean Kane
Sean Kane Design

Söhne Breit: 51, 177
Kris Sowersby, Klim Type Foundry

Source Han Sans: 29, 171
Ryoko Nishizuka
Adobe

SourceHanSerif: 29, 87,
199, 232, 256, 278
Frank Griesshammer, Ryoko
Nishizuka, Soohyun Park, Yejin
We, and Wenlong Zhang
Adobe

Space Grotesk: 264
Florian Karsten
Colophon Foundry

Space Mono: 101
Florian Karsten
Colophon Foundry

Stabel Grotesk: 25
Christian Jánský
Kometa Typefaces

Stadio Now: 236
Original Design by Aldo Novarese
Revival by Cosimo Lorenzo
Pancini and Andrea Tartarelli
Cyrillic Glyphs by Vika Usmanova
Zetafonts

Stempel Schneidler LT: 243
Ernst Schneidler
Linotype Design Studio

Stop Killing Black People: 96
Terresa Moses
Blackbird Revolt

Suisse Int'l: 97, 120
Ian Party
Swiss Typefaces

Suisse Int'l Mono: 143
Ian Party
Swiss Typefaces

Suisse Int'l Trial: 253
Swisstypefaces

Suisse Works: 97
Ian Party
Swiss Typefaces

FF Super Grotesk: 73
Arno Drescher and Svend Smital
FontShop

Superpose: 208
Julien Hébert

Tanrie: 305
Ryan Hutson

Terza Author: 117
Greg Gazdowicz
Commercial Type

Terza Reader: 117
Greg Gazdowicz
Commercial Type

The Epicene Collection: 322
Noe Blanco and Dave Foster
Klim Type Foundry

The Mānuka Collection: 324
Klim Type Foundry

Times Roman: 76
Victor Lardent and
Stanley Morison

Times New Roman, 256, 257
Stanley Morison
Monotype

Timmons NY: 266
Matt Wiley

TT Trailers PetChoy: 154, 176, 200
TypeType Foundry

TT Trailers: 176
TypeType Foundry

Trois Mille Bold-25: 166
Marc Rouault
Sharp Type

Typold: 145
Jonathan Hill
The Northern Block

Typotheque Lava: 67
Typotheque

Typotheque November: 67
Typotheque

Uipapuru: 61
Thiago Lacaz

Univers 55 Roman: 232
Adrian Frutiger
Linotype

Untitled: 168.249
Klim Type Foundry

Uwabami: 311
Hisashi Iwai

VESHCH logo typeface, 147
Irina Goryacheva
Design Studio Baklazanas

Vinila: 98
Flora de Carvalhom
and Rodrigo Saiani
Plau

Visuelt Pro: 286
The Entente
Colophon Type Foundry

VKHUTETYPE: 215
Peter Bankov, Revaz Todua,
and Vsevolod Vlasenko
Bankov Posters Prague

VT 323: 154, 176, 200
TypeType Foundry

glyphworld Wasteland: 281
Leah Maldonado
glyphworld

ABC Whyte Inktrap: 283
Fabian Harb and Johannes
Breyer, with Erkin Karamemet
and Fabiola Mejía
Dinamo

Willow: 164, 181
Joy Redick and Customized
by Lourenço Providência
Adobe Fonts
Berton Hasebe

Y

YouTube Sans Arabic: 317
Lara Captan and YouTube
Art Department

Zalfia: 303
Neva Zidić

Zeitungs-Grotesque (revivial): 108
Danzig-based Francke
type foundry 1874
方正兰亭黑
齐立
Founder Type

TEREZA BETTINARDI

This year's TDC Call for Entries branding campaign was designed by Tereza Bettinardi and her team, based in São Paulo, Brazil. "The design process started with one question: what if we expand the inner shapes of the letters to create new forms?." she said. "As these small shapes expand and are used to create entirely new forms, at some point we end up also setting new rules to this infinite game."

Tereza also brought warmth to the design system by using vibrant colours and gradients—a way to share a bit of her landscape—inspired by vernacular lettering and signs. "Living and working in Brazil, much of my practice was coined in dealing with restrictions, such as how to find drops of wonder even in the driest places," she explained. "In this sense, you need to pay a lot of attention because every minor gesture counts."

Since 2014, Tereza runs her own studio, which has since worked across different fields of design, including editorial, visual identity, packaging and environmental design. In 2020, she founded Clube do Livro do Design, a virtual book club turned into a publishing house devoted to expanding the range of design books available in Portuguese.

"LIVING AND WORKING IN BRAZIL, MUCH OF MY PRACTICE WAS COINED IN DEALING WITH RESTRICTIONS, SUCH AS HOW TO FIND DROPS OF WONDER EVEN IN THE DRIEST PLACES."

TEAM: Tereza Bettinardi (creative director), Lucas D'Ascenção and Gabriela Gennari (designers)

terezabettinardi.com
○ terezabettinardi

Bettinardi was a three-time winner in previous TDC competitions, receiving certificates for *As Mulheres Contam* on behalf of Carambaia in Books/Single, and *Cursos E Oficinas* for Sesc 24 de Maio in Miscellaneous/Campaigns (2020) and for Memórias Póstumas de Brás Cubas (2019).